SPITFIRE ACE

SPITFIRE ACE

SPITFIRE ACE
My Life as a Battle of Britain Fighter Pilot

GORDON OLIVE, DFC
Edited by Dennis Newton

AMBERLEY

*To the memory of Charles Gordon Chaloner Olive and those like
him, who served their country in war and peace*

*To Beryl Olive and family: Rick and Helen; Denys and Mandy;
Maria and Kent*

First published 2015
This edition published 2016

Amberley Publishing
The Hill, Stroud
Gloucestershire, GL5 4EP

www.amberley-books.com

British Library Cataloguing in Publication Data.
A catalogue record for this book is available from the British Library.

ISBN 978 1 4456 6020 2 (paperback)
ISBN 978 1 4456 4437 0 (ebook)

Typeset in 10.5pt on 14pt Sabon.
Typesetting and Origination by Amberley Publishing.
Printed in the UK.

Contents

Preface

13 September 2013
Battle of Britain Wreath-Laying Ceremony
Australian War Memorial, Canberra

An Address
by
Her Excellency the Honourable Quentin Bryce AC CVO
Governor-General of the Commonwealth of Australia

We gather here today to remember the sacrifices of the Second World War, and in particular the courage and determination of the RAF, the Commonwealth and other Allied forces in defending the shores of the United Kingdom, in what we know with pride as the Battle of Britain.

Winston Churchill, in his speech to the Commons, said, in what seemed to be the end of Hitler's planned Operation Sea Lion: 'Never before in the field of human conflict was so much owed by so many to so few.'

I want to talk to you about one of the 'Few'; in fact one of the very few Australians who flew with the RAF squadrons in that epic battle.

His name is Wing Commander Gordon Olive DFC, and I have a particular reason for singling out Gordon, because our lives became entwined for some years.

Charles Gordon Chaloner Olive was born in 1916, attended Brisbane Grammar and RAAF Point Cook, where he gained his pilot's wings in 1936.

He took a posting to 2 Flying Training School RAF, on a Short Service Commission.

In August 1939 he was promoted to flying officer and piloted a Spitfire as a flight commander between September 1939 and March 1941, completing 193 sorties, totalling 165 hours.

In the Battle of Britain he was credited with destroying five enemy aircraft, though his unconfirmed total tally was much higher. Promoted to flight lieutenant in August 1940, he was awarded the DFC in September, and in December shot down his sixth confirmed enemy, officially entering the list of 'aces'.

In 1941 Olive was appointed the first Commanding Officer of No. 456 Squadron RAAF, Australia's first and only night-fighter squadron, after which he rejoined the RAAF and served in several significant command posts including Morotai in the Pacific, and transferred to the Reserves in 1946 with the rank of wing commander.

One of the remarkable feats of Olive's service was a prodigious memory and artistic skill, which years later led to a series of graphic paintings of combat over the skies of Britain.

These paintings from his memory provide an unique record of multi-aircraft engagements from the pilot's cockpit.

Gordon Olive was appointed an Honorary ADC to the queen; in 1967 he was appointed MBE for organising the Empire Youth Movement, and in 1978 elevated to CBE.

Gordon Olive was an example of the daring, pluck and humour that gave the RAAF its deserved reputation in the service of the RAF.

Shortish, wiry, cocky, moustachioed and highly intelligent, he was the archetypical 'fighter pilot'. To me, he was the Battle of Britain.

In 1955 I was a cadet pilot officer in the Air Training Corps. I was seventeen. Wing Commander Olive was Commandant of the ATC in Queensland. He was then thirty-nine.

He was a legend and an inspiration to us all, and he was to define my life from then on.

Gordon died in 1987, and left a lasting legacy in his community work in Brisbane, tirelessly supporting veterans and his mates.

It is in men like Gordon Olive that a whole generation of younger men have found inspiration and a sense of an ideal – men with positivity, modesty, cheerfulness, loyalty to their mates and pride in their service.

While the legacy of the Battle of Britain held such people high, it will always remain an example of how courage and determination can overcome mighty odds.

It was also a tragedy of huge proportion that we honour here today, and we remember those who paid the ultimate sacrifice.

As Churchill most famously said: 'If the British Empire and its Commonwealth last for a thousand years, men will still say 'This was their finest hour'.

Lest we forget.

Published on the website of the Governor-General of the Commonwealth of Australia (https://www.gg.gov.au)

Introduction

Charles Gordon Chaloner Olive was born in Bardon, Queensland, on 3 July 1916, the son of New Zealand-born Mr Hugh Chaloner Olive and his Queensland-born wife, Lucinda Maud (*née* Exley). He was educated at Brisbane Grammar School and was a civil engineering cadet at Queensland University in Brisbane when he enlisted in the Royal Australian Air Force as a cadet in January 1936 at Point Cook in Victoria. He was awarded his Pilot's Flying Badge on 8 December 1936, but in January 1937 he sailed for England to take up a Short Service Commission with the RAF.

From 19 February 1937, with the rank of pilot officer, he was at an RAF depot but eight days later was posted to No. 2 Flying Training School (FTS), where he remained until 22 May, when he was sent to 65 Squadron. At the time the squadron was equipped with Gloster Gauntlet IIs but in June it converted to Gloster Gladiators.

In England, Gordon Olive was as active in service and inter-service athletics competitions as he had been at Point Cook. He was particularly successful with the javelin, in which discipline he was victorious in 1938, coming second in the following year despite breaking the existing record. He was promoted to Flying Officer on 19 August 1938, and less than a year later, on 24 July 1939, he was made acting flight lieutenant. By then 65 Squadron had converted to Spitfires, the first having arrived in the preceding March.

In September 1939, when war broke out, 65 Squadron formed part of the Hornchurch Wing and it flew its first scramble on 5 September without result. The squadron achieved its first kill in May 1940, towards the end of which month offensive patrols began to be flown over

France and the Low Countries to cover the evacuation of the British Expeditionary Force (BEF) from Dunkirk.

On 26 May, Gordon claimed a Messerschmitt Me 109,[1] probably destroyed when the squadron became mixed up with about thirty German fighters near Calais. The next day, in another action east of Dunkirk, he heavily damaged a Do 17, silencing the rear gunner and setting the port engine on fire. On the 28th it was his turn when he was listed missing 'as a result of air operations'. Three days later he was reported safe but slightly injured, having been shot up and wounded in the leg. Up to this time he had completed twenty-five operational sorties totalling thirty-five hours flying time.

After action over Dunkirk, 65 Squadron played its part in the Battle of Britain. It was heavily involved in the fighting of July and August so that by the time it transferred north to Turnhouse on 28 August it could claim the destruction of twenty-six German aircraft for the loss of eleven. Gordon scored his first confirmed victory, a Messerschmitt Me 109, on 20 July and on 12 August he probably destroyed another. The following day he shot down two and probably a third and on the 14th he scored another probable. Two days later he damaged an Me 109 and then attacked a lone Ju 88, which he left disappearing into cloud in an almost vertical dive with smoke pouring from both engines. On the 19th he was promoted from acting flight lieutenant to flight lieutenant. In an action on the 24th he probably shot down another Me 109, and he brought his score to five on 26 August by destroying an Me 110.

At Turnhouse the squadron rested and was brought up to strength, taking no part in the air battles of September and October. Meanwhile, Gordon received a DFC, which was gazetted on 24 September. Two officers, Gordon Olive and F/Lt 'Sammy' Saunders, were called upon to give their impressions of the air battle over the radio. They were interviewed anonymously for the BBC and the broadcast went to air on 4 October.

It was late November before 65 Squadron went south again, this time to Tangmere. On 9 December, Gordon shot down an Me 110 for what turned out to be his sixth and final official victory, although he claimed a probable Ju 88 on 15 February 1941. In March 1941, he was promoted to acting squadron leader and took up fighter controller duties at Tangmere for the next three months, during which time the aerodrome was bombed at night on at least ten occasions.

On 20 June 1941 he was appointed to command 456 Squadron,

which was being formed at RAF Station Valley on the Isle of Anglesey. This was Australia's first night-fighter squadron and initial equipment consisted of sixteen Boulton Paul Defiants. The squadron became operational in August, but towards the end of September it began to be re-equipped with Bristol Beaufighter Mk IIs, which necessitated retraining and conversion to twin-engine aircraft. The unit's first victory came on the night of 10/11 January 1942, when a Dornier Do 217 was shot down in flames. Gordon was promoted to squadron leader on 8 January 1942, and altogether he carried out seventeen sorties with 456 Squadron before ill health cut short his tour of duty. On 1 March, he was posted to Station Valley, Fighter Command.

Other postings during his career with the RAF included No. 9 Group (20 April 1942), No. 81 Group (9 July 1942), No. 55 OTU (15 July 1942), No. 58 OTU (28 October 1942) and No. 83 Group (25 May 1943). He was still with 83 Group when, on 3 June 1943, he rejoined the Royal Australian Air Force, thus relinquishing the rank of acting wing commander he had attained on 29 December 1942. He recorded another interview on the Battle of Britain for radio, which was broadcast over the BBC on 24 September.

Meanwhile, although he had joined the RAAF, he stayed with the RAF's No. 83 Group until 20 October 1943 when he was attached to Overseas Headquarters, RAAF. Ten days later he left England for Australia.

In December he was attached to No. 3 Embarkation Depot (ED) pending a posting. On 12 February 1944, he went to RAAF Command where he received the rank of acting wing commander on 1 April. He stayed there for the remainder of the year until he was posted to No. 101 Fighter Control Unit (FCU) as commanding officer on 29 December, but his stay was short because he was then sent to Air Defence HQ Sydney on 21 January 1945. His final wartime posting was to Air Defence HQ, Morotai, which he commanded from 16 July 1945.

Altogether, W/Cdr Gordon Olive DFC completed four tours of operational flying involving 219 sorties, many of them of short duration during the hectic days of the Battle of Britain, and 180 hours of operational flying. He was discharged from the RAAF on 7 March 1946.

Over the following years, when time permitted, Gordon began to write. He noted everything down, incident by incident, combining and refining things over and over, striving to form a continuous account. With brush and canvas, he created a series of eyewitness paintings and linked them to his narrative, portraying his own personal experiences within the overall drama of the war.

His work developed into something truly unique. Ever the perfectionist, he unfortunately still did not have his story ready to be published before he passed away after a long illness towards the end of 1987.

I met and corresponded with Gordon in 1986 while researching for my book, A Few of 'The Few', on Australians in the Battle of Britain. After this book was published by the Australian War Memorial in 1990, members of Gordon's family requested that I complete his work on his behalf and supplied me with all of his notes and incomplete manuscripts. For this privilege I thank them as it gave me the rare opportunity to come to know Gordon Olive personally, not only the air ace but also Gordon Olive the man.

There was much to examine as Gordon had compiled an extraordinary amount of notes on paper and in booklets. As I read through it became obvious that there was not just one manuscript but several, often quite different, reflecting his thoughts and changes of mood at various times, and some versions of others which were often just fragments. A great deal of the material was typed but much was still only handwritten. Some versions were detailed and some were little more than sketchy outlines. What should be included? What should be deleted? What to amalgamate?

The following work begins with Gordon's Point Cook days and covers his air force career to the end of the Second World War.

This is not a biography of his life, nor is it meant to be because that is not what Gordon set out to write. It is written, using his own words, in the way I believe he meant to create his book.

Gordon's memoir fully captures the dramatic time when Britain's very survival was at stake, particularly during the desperate days of fighting in 1940. It is meant to be a tribute to a man I have come to greatly respect, a man of courage whose achievements and service should not be allowed to be forgotten.

This work could not have reached completion without the generous help and support of many people and organisations. The people included Beryl Olive, Rick and Helen Olive, Maria and Kent Marchant, Denys and Mandy Olive, Bill Hughes, Neville Parkinson, Alex Gould, Grant Lindeman, Pete Bjelke-Petersen, Alf Pascoe, Betty King, Bob Geale, John Young, Bryan Philpott, Brenda Walch, John Wallen, Reg Moore, Tom Scott, Cec Graham and Mike Taylor.

The organisations included the RAAF Museum Point Cook, Military Aircraft Photographs (MAP), Imperial War Museum (IWM), Bundesarchiv-Militarchiv, Australian War Memorial (AWM) and the United Service Club of Brisbane. Of course, members of the staff of Amberley Publishing, particularly Jonathan Reeve, deserve special mention.

I especially acknowledge the unstinting help and patience of my wife, Helen, and thank her for her infinite support.

Many thanks to all involved, but if any have been overlooked, I apologise for the unintended omission.

Dennis Newton

1

Point Cook Cadet

Looking back at it now, a first-class book could be written about most of the forty-five boys who gathered at RAAF Point Cook in that January of 1936, but that is not my purpose. Some of them became close friends, others spent part of their careers in close proximity to me. It was inevitable that many new friendships would spring up as we were all basically lonely and motherless and seeking the company of kindred spirits.

The trip from Queensland to Victoria was made either by boat or train in those days, in our case train, and it took two full days. On the way down I met two of the lads who were to be fellow cadets at the college. One of them, Lew Johnston, I had known for some years, but was unaware of his interest in flying until we met on the train. We became very good friends.

Another lad, Ashton Shorter, was also travelling down. He had been at Point Cook for six months. He was embarking on the senior course and was friendly and informative about our new home.

It is hard to think of a better place to have been born than Queensland. A mild and pleasant climate most of the year, plenty of sunshine and a lazy pastoral atmosphere, unhurried and good humoured. We lived in an outer suburb of Brisbane and our home was surrounded by gum trees, hills and hundreds of birds. Whenever there was a holiday that made the half-day journey worthwhile, there was a stretch of golden sand with the endless deep-blue ocean casting its great white breakers up day and night, summer and winter. We went there three or four times a year.

My earliest memories include an aeroplane. I was probably no more than two years old, but I remember this very old black object making a terrific droning noise as it flew over my little world; but this was no bird. It had two wings and a propeller. I spent days thereafter running around with three sticks tied together so as to look like a biplane and was kept very busy making the noise.

I was not a strong child, suffering for most of my early years from asthma, which was diagnosed as chronic bronchitis in those days. As adolescence approached, we moved to the other side of the city and closer to the beach. The move did wonders for my asthma and I became a normal, active teenager. Indeed, having been precluded for years from most sport, I now hurled myself into all its forms with tremendous interest and enthusiasm.

The depression of the early thirties emptied me out of school into the workforce in order to help the strained family circumstances – my mother, however, sold me on the idea of continuing my education at evening classes. By this routine I would eventually make the portals of the local university, a goal which was dear to the hearts of both my parents, who had great hopes for their firstborn.

As I settled into this dreary pattern of toil by day and study by night, my whole drab life suddenly exploded into a fantasy of gold and glory – a girl! She was the sister of a lad I had become friendly with at the night school. He and I had an intense mutual interest in aeroplanes and flying. My new friend's uncle had been a famous fighter pilot in the First World War, having shot down one of the first Zeppelins over London. He had made himself a full-scale glider and I visited his home, which was only a mile or so from where I lived, to view this ambitious enterprise. I was most impressed with this but it was nothing to the impact his sister had on me when she looked at me with her wide blue eyes.

Both were brilliant academically and their family placed great importance on scholastic achievement. Their education went far beyond the bounds of the state school system. They both had passed with top honours in the state's mandatory formal examinations. In such company I felt inadequate. I had always been an uninspired student but now I hurled myself into a frenzy of study to make up the leeway and to impress.

My industry knew no bounds. I romped through my studies and passed my exams with ease. The boy had his sights set on the Air Force as a career. This met with his sister's full approval and my sights turned there too. His objective was to learn to fly and he had a definite taste for living dangerously. I aided and abetted him.

He announced that the Air Force was only interested in people who were very fit physically, so we joined a gymnasium and spent endless hours exercising muscles, lifting weights and otherwise submitting to all the exquisite tortures necessary for the acquisition of physical fitness. All the time at the back of my mind were those bewitching blue eyes.

All this took place over a period of three years, but now the aches of first romance were over and I was on my way to become a cadet in the Royal Australian Air Force.

When forty-five young men collect together from all points of the continent there has to be an inevitable sorting-out process. It was all quite an adventure. For most of us it was the first time we had been away from home for more than a few days and the break was in the nature of a major change in the pattern of our lives.

The system was either organised to mix us up thoroughly, or it just happened that way. There was the barrack-block community where groups of us shared a hut, two to a room. Four cadets were allocated to each instructor and this bore no relation to the barrack arrangement.

We were split up into two flights, which were arranged alphabetically, and this had no relationship to the previous split-ups. Then we had positions in the mess, which were fixed at first so we dined and supped with yet another group.

Add to this the mix-ups on the playing fields when each afternoon we had two hours of compulsory organised sport, which reshuffled us yet again. It was thus impossible not to get to know each other pretty quickly.

Three of the boys became early friends of mine: Lew Johnston, Carl Kelaher and Peter McDonough.

Lew and I had discovered mutual interests on the way to Melbourne in the train. We enjoyed the same sports, had some friends in common back in Queensland and had already started planning a return to Brisbane at the end of the first term of six months.

Carl Kelaher was of German extraction. His family had changed their name during the first war to avoid the difficulties associated with being German. Carl was a tall, dark-haired, handsome lad who had a magnetic effect on women – whenever we had a day off, which was most rare, we would go to Melbourne. Carl always tagged on to Lew and me, and girls tagged on to Carl.

Carl usually selected the pick of them and expected Lew and me to accommodate the discards, which were quite often unattractive, sometimes downright ugly. Thus, this arrangement was not very successful. It was even less acceptable when Lew or I met some delectable young lass. Carl had no difficulty at all in attracting her interest to the exclusion of all else.

For all this, Carl was a delightful soul. He was one of the kindest people I have ever met and he spent a great deal of his time doing little things for other people by stealth, then watching them flounder around trying to find out who was responsible.

Peter McDonough shared a room with me for the first few months. It was a small, uncomfortable stable in a shed which he called the Wind Tunnel. It was not strictly part of the officers' mess, and seemed to be one of the remaining First World War shacks.

Peter had a quick, dry sense of humour, which he matched to his lazy drawl. This too went with a slouching gait which should have belonged to a much taller man.

As it turned out, Peter was short, even if very slim, and had all the mannerisms of a tall, gangling, uncoordinated adolescent. This was deceptive because he was actually as quick as a cat physically, which he demonstrated admirably on the sporting field in almost any game. His rich wit was equally swift and entertaining.

We all became very good friends and settled down to our new life in short order.

Our next-door neighbours were two dissimilar types who also became great friends. Bob Cosgrove was the eldest son of the Premier of Tasmania. He was a nuggety, pleasant lad with reddish curly hair and somewhat pale skin, which was unusual in a young man.

Pat Hughes, who shared the room with Bob, was a big, well-built fellow with more boisterous life in him than anyone I have ever met. Pat just loved life and lived it at high pressure. Part of his tremendous *joie de vivre* expressed itself as a compulsion to sing, and Pat sang at all possible opportunities. He had one volume: flat out at the top of his lungs. He was at his best in the shower – he took one three times a day in summer, and on each occasion he really shook the 'Wind Tunnel' with the vigour of his delivery.

Unfortunately for the rest of the occupants of the tunnel, Pat was tone deaf and most of his strenuous efforts were supported by a rich obbligato of catcalls, groans and complaints which rose to a crescendo as the ablutions progressed. But Pat seemed oblivious to these protests

– no doubt he drowned most of them out for most of the time, and, when he drew breath, thought he had really got the whole camp singing. The fact that the chorus of groans and abuse was not in harmony with his own efforts would have had no significance to Pat.

Eventually we gave up trying to shut him up; we just accepted it as part of life, but it was my first introduction to someone who was virtually tone deaf and quite oblivious and uninhibited about it.

A singer of a different order was Ernie Yde. Ernie was easily the most popular and most delightful character on the camp. Unusually good-looking and of medium height, he played the ukulele like a professional and possessed a repertoire of humorous songs which took a couple of hours to work through. Some of them were known to most of us, some were quite new, but in no time Ernie had us all in, and his end of the barracks was usually crammed with the boys who enjoyed a bit of a singsong when time permitted. He could have made a fortune as a professional entertainer.

Another entertainer in a different vein was Cec Mace. He received the nickname of Grappler early because of his build. This was reminiscent of a medium-sized gorilla, except for the face, which was pleasant and humorous. Grap had an endless supply of funny stories, many of them a bit spicy. He had an improbably high-pitched voice and normally laughed furiously at his own jokes. Instead of ruining the effect it was a contagious gurgle and Grap usually reduced us to helpless laughter at some stage each day.

Yet another entertainer on the camp was one of the senior-term cadets, and his name was Watson. He answered to the name Mac, as he had a Scottish Christian name. Mac was a large, shapeless cadet whom no uniform would fit. His clothes seemed to be wrapped around him like a crumpled paper bag and he was the despair of his flight commander whenever a 'spit-and-polish' show was necessary.

Mac was a very accomplished pianist and had collected a large number of traditional Air Force songs. These were mostly of First World War origin and his favourites were 'The Young Aviator Lay Dying' and 'I Don't Want to Fly over Germany'. There were many more and all entertaining, most of them in the bawdy class. His services were in great demand on 'dining in' nights, which were compulsory formal evenings. Mac would set up his stool at the piano and most of the cadets joined in with considerable gusto. If they did not know the words they soon learnt them.

Altogether we found our new life most absorbing, and with so many unique and delightful characters around there was never a dull moment.

Then, out of the blue, we had our first death. Chaplin, a quiet, gentlemanly lad whom we all liked immensely, was killed one morning just before lunch. There seemed to be no explanation for it. He had been practising aerobatics and the plane dived into the ground from about three thousand feet. We were all stunned; we were having so much fun that it seemed quite impossible that anything could mar it in any way. Chappie's death did so without any doubt.

But there was little time to dwell on it because we found ourselves very highly organised indeed. The officer cadet course in those days was of one year's duration. During that time the RAAF endeavoured to teach us some twenty-odd subjects.

Many of these applied to the problems of flying, such as navigation, the theory of engines, the theory of flight and airmanship (the art of conducting oneself around an aerodrome and an aeroplane in an intelligent and safe fashion). We had to learn Morse code by buzzer and by light and had to be able to read semaphore, the system of sending messages by flags.

Then we had a range of subjects relating purely to the service, to study. These were general administration, the organisation of the Air Force and a comparable knowledge of the Army and Navy and of civil aviation. Air Force law had to be clearly understood.

A knowledge of armaments, guns of various sizes, bombs of various types, all had to be understood, their construction explained and remembered and the theory of ballistics studied, as did the application of these subjects to the aeroplane and the theory and practice of their use.

Tactics and strategy were just words when we entered on the course, but they soon emerged as the contents of lengthy and profound books which had to be studied most carefully. Meteorology was another obscure and inexact science but we had to do the best we could with it, as was the case with photography and photograph interpretation.

Then there were the practical subjects, of which one was flying – others were associated with the anatomy of machine guns, bombs and cameras, which we were required to be able to dismantle and reassemble without enough parts left over to go into the second-hand business. There were also the practical sides of engineering and rigging to be mastered, involving dismantling and reassembling aeroplane engines and repairing damaged parts of aeroplanes.

All in all it was a formidable range of subjects and we worked at it six days a week and fourteen hours a day – roughly an eighty-hour week.

The day began at 6.00 a.m. with a blast on a bugle. The pace was hot from then on; beds made, rooms tidied up, shower, shave and breakfast at 6.30 a.m. Out on the parade ground at 7.00 a.m. in immaculate order, boots polished, buttons and all leather likewise. Three-quarters of an hour tramping up and down the parade ground learning the finer points of ceremonial drill. Then back to the barracks – divest ourselves of the rifles, belts, etc., grab books, pencils and notepaper and off for a mile-and-a-half march around the perimeter of the aerodrome 'flights'. This was an area of old sheds, hangars and lecture rooms where we toiled away furiously until noon, when we marched the mile and a half back to the mess for lunch. Forty minutes later we were on our way back to the 'flights' on foot for the afternoon sessions.

The days were mostly divided into two basically different sessions – theory and practice. If the morning was all theory, the afternoon was practice, that is flying, learning to send and understand Morse code, practical work on engines or airframes or on guns or bombs. On alternate weeks the day was reversed, with flying and practical work in the morning and theory in the afternoons.

At 4.00 p.m. we marched back to the barracks, and after a ten-minute tea break we were sent out to partake of sport from 4.30 p.m. to 6.00 p.m. This had to be cricket, tennis, football or hockey. There was no let-up here, either. If the instructors found anybody shirking, they were sent for a run around the perimeter of the aerodrome or out to the 'trees' (a line of trees roughly a mile and a half away) on orders to be back in a given time or do it again each evening until he could.

From 6.00 p.m. to 6.30 p.m. we were permitted to clean up, clean boots, etc. and prepare for supper or dinner at 7.00 p.m. This was a formal meal and everyone had to be back in their rooms and hard at study by 8.00 p.m. At 9.45 p.m., a whistle was blown which allowed fifteen minutes to clean up and get to bed. Lights were turned out at 10.00 p.m. sharp and by 10.01 p.m. nearly every cadet was out like a light from pure exhaustion. Most of the boys adjusted to the long hours of work very quickly.

For four years before I joined the Air Force I had been obliged to work for a living by day and, as I had ambitions to attend at the local university, study every evening at night classes. In this way I obtained my matriculation and launched myself on a course for a degree in science. It had meant long and unremitting work, but the routine was excellent as a toughener for Point Cook.

The Australian is ever critical of the English, and the RAAF system aimed at producing officer pilots in one year up to the standard of Cranwell in England, where they spread the material for study over two years.

Only one Sunday each month was allowed as time off to go to the city and visit friends or relations, if any. These days were greatly relished and about the worst disciplinary restraint in the book of penalties for misbehaviour was to be confined to barracks for that Sunday.

For all the pressure, the first half-year went by very quickly and we had two glorious weeks of leave ahead of us. We planned it out to the last minute, and when the great day came Lew Johnston and I set course north and for the sun of Queensland. By this time winter was upon us and we began by driving to Sydney. From there we went by train and spent a few days down on the golden beaches, soaking up sunlight. It was a wonderful improvement on Melbourne, which in winter time is not far removed from London for climate and dreariness. The last week we spent in the Australian Alps on the way back, where we both sampled skiing for the first time.

Flying in the second or senior term took on a different aspect. It became a matter of applying our knowledge of flying and the theory of flight to the processes of war. We now transferred to the Wapiti, an old biplane of similar performance to the Bristol F.2 Fighter of the First World War.

To begin with there was considerable formation flying at close quarters, which we soon mastered. This was very necessary in order to take a number of our planes through thick and dense cloud and be in a position to fight without the tedious necessity of making a rendezvous over a featureless cloud mass.

There was much cloud flying and flying 'under the hood', a process whereby a canvas hood was pulled over the pupil's cockpit so that he could not see out and was forced to fly on instruments.

In those days there were no artificial horizons and no gyro compasses, so all our instrument flying had to be done in a most primitive manner – it was possible, but only just, and gave me a new appreciation of the powers of endurance of Kingsford Smith and his crew, who flew for hours across the Pacific in violent storms in the *Southern Cross* using identical instruments – half an hour was a very tiring session.

High-altitude flying was another revealing experience. Temperature in the atmosphere drops by 3 °F for every thousand feet of altitude – this does not mean much when flying at four or five thousand feet or less, but when the altitude is stretched to twenty thousand in an open cockpit with no heat the process is very bleak. At this height the temperature is 60 degrees below the temperature at sea level. In wintertime in Victoria this is seldom above 60 °F so the air temperature at twenty thousand feet is 0 °F or 32 degrees below freezing point. With a hundred-mile-an-hour draught whistling around the cockpits the crew freeze very quickly and conditions are truly subarctic.

In doing these exercises we had to climb up fully loaded as for wartime operations. The last few thousand feet were gained very slowly and painfully. Two-hour trips were not unusual, and by the time we landed we were very cold and miserable. Much more to our liking was the dive-bombing practices and air-to-ground gunnery practice.

Both were rather startling the first time. The target was approached very slowly at about two thousand feet and then the nose dropped down into a 45- to 50-degree angle of dive. This always felt as if it were a vertical 90-degree dive and to begin with the pupil's stomach was left behind at two thousand feet. The aeroplane gathered speed very rapidly at this altitude. All the flying wires in the rigging between the mainplanes howled and vibrated and altogether it was quite impressive.

The art was to fire the guns or release the bomb at the lower part of the straight dive, then pull out in time so as not to hit the target yourself. The lower you went before firing the better chance you had of hitting the target with the bullets or the bombs, but it also raised the chances of diving into it too, so a sensible compromise was clearly called for.

These two exercises soon showed differences in temperament between the various cadets. The more nervous tended to pull out quite high and the reckless to go too low. The stupid were the ones to really watch; they were unpredictable and potentially dangerous. Fortunately, we had only a few in this category.

My flying instructor for this part of the course was a flying officer named Sam Balmer. Sam was a strange mixture of a man. He had a permanently sour expression on his face as if he had just sucked a green lemon. He was hardly a communicative man and tended to instruct in monosyllables which was very disconcerting. His ability as a pilot was unsurpassed and most people at Point Cook conceded that Sam was easily the best pilot in the RAAF. It did not follow that he was the best instructor, although I thought so.

On my first trip with Sam he said nothing as he motioned me into the pilot's seat and climbed into the back or rear gunner's seat, which had been modified for dual instruction. He held the Wapiti down at grass height long after we had gained flying speed and suddenly hauled it up into a full-powered vertical climb until it stalled at about a thousand or fifteen hundred feet, executed a stall turn and dived vertically at full throttle at the hangars. It was a 'beat up'. Another Wapiti was going through the same gyrations synchronised with us.

Each time the pull-out was at rooftop level, and even though I already had great faith in Sam's ability it was very frightening. Each time it seemed Sam had gone mad and we would dive straight into the end hangar, but no.

At last he settled down and flew up to Laverton, five miles north, where two Bulldogs attacked us out of a clear blue sky. A Bulldog was a nimble little biplane fighter of the early thirties and a squadron was located at Laverton. Sam weaved, dived, rolled and pulled around in the most violent climbing turns, keeping one or another of the fighters in his gunsights most of the time.

Eventually we landed, and as we walked away from the Wapiti Sam had the longest conversation with me we were ever to have on the pupil/instructor basis. He said, 'Those bums at Laverton think they can fly those Bulldogs – I'll stitch them up again tomorrow.'

It turned out that earlier that day, Sam, who was duty pilot, had been forced to make a report on one of his mates for low flying in the vicinity of the hangars. This had resulted in the victim being made duty pilot for a week as punishment. Sam accordingly beat the aerodrome up so that his friend would have no alternative but to do the same to him. It all seemed a bit childish but it was Sam's way of saying he did not like having to do it.

Sam's bête noire was 'Kanga' de la Rue, one of the personalities of the RAAF. He was an aging, tub-shaped wing commander with a face like Genghis Khan and his eyes were made for lining up young Hun pilots in his sights. 'Kanga' had a look of infallibility about him. What worse fate for an aspiring young German aviator than to have 'Kanga' on his tail in a steep right-hand climbing turn? With those eyes of his he would never miss.

'Kanga's favourite tactic was a steep right-hand climbing turn, an evasive measure against the natural movement of a pilot holding the stick with his right hand to pull it instinctively to the left. It had never let him down.

He and his boon companion 'King' Cole would come into the cadets' anteroom after a guest-night dinner, well primed with the 'red infuriator' (the mess red wine) and port. With a little judicious prompting and some well-phrased questions, 'Kanga' could always be induced to regale us with some first-hand accounts of aerial combats at ten thousand feet over the enemy lines in the Kaiser's war. Spads and Camels, Fokkers, Albatroses and other legendary aeroplanes suddenly were conjured up, all whirling around in an awe-inspiring mass in monumental dogfights. Lewis guns chattering, the Vickers and Spandaus spitting tracers and sudden death, explosions, 'spin-ins' from two miles up in the clear blue sky – it all came to light with magic wizardry as old 'Kanga' described some of his classics. We could see the machine-gun bullets stitching their way across the black iron cross of Prussia on the side of the Fokker.

King Cole was harder to get to talk. He had more medals than 'Kanga', so he must have done his share, but King was much more reticent about it.

'Kanga' had everybody bluffed except Sam, who seemed to have some compulsion not only to show 'Kanga' he was not worried by him but also to keep on showing him. As a result, Sam was more or less permanent duty pilot or orderly officer, two unpopular jobs which were normally done by turn but which were handed out as punishment to officers who were being intractable or just plain bloody-minded, as in Sam's case.

Each instructor had four pupils and Sam's were the envy of the rest of the course, partly because of his reputation and partly because he was known to be a most exacting master. 'Good enough' had no place in Sam's vocabulary and before he would pass any exercise the pupil had to try and try again and again until he could do it as well as Sam.

He also indulged very frequently in pitched battles with his enemies, the Bulldogs, and once the rules were understood it was an education to follow his tactics. Mostly the 'Dogs' attacked from above and if possible out of the sun but Sam was never caught. He would whip around and under their angle of dive, forcing them into an outside loop if they would try to keep their sights on him. Then he would haul up and straight into a steep climbing turn which he could maintain inside the Bulldog's turning circle, thus forcing the fighters to break off by fastening onto their tails. Fortunately there were no bullets, but the manoeuvres were precisely those of the dogfights of the First World War. I got the feeling that Sam cursed that he had been born too late to fight in those dogfights of 1914–18.

One day, for no reason at all, he spent almost two hours teaching me to land on one wheel. This was done by landing across wind with one wing down then keeping it down by gradually turning away from the wheel on the ground. This was a good trick to know if you lost a wheel on take-off or if a tyre burst. You could land on the good tyre and avoid a somersault. We must have tried it a dozen times before he was happy that I had the technique to perfection, then every few trips he would make me do it again. I had never heard of anyone landing with a burst tyre, but Sam assured me it had killed many pilots in the first war – 'bullets, you know', he explained – and persisted with his lessons.

Of course there were other flying instructors besides Sam, most of them interesting characters. For the most part we only saw them from a distance and learnt of their idiosyncrasies second-hand from the other cadets. There was one exception and he was our chief tormentor.

He was the one officer in the cadet squadron who seemed to have it firmly in his mind that he had to impress us with his importance. Why was never quite clear, but it was probably because he had a mean and petty streak within. He was always on the alert for the slightest slip-up and pounced with ruthless and malicious glee when he found it. So much was he like the proverbial cat stalking the canary that we called him Pussy – but naturally not to his face.

Pussy was *the* original aggressive arm swinger of the air force. The good book on drill and ceremonial procedures laid down the guidelines as, 'The arm shall be swung straight out from the shoulder', meaning that the elbow should not be bent. This had to be read in conjunction with the following direction that 'the hand should be loosely clenched and rise to the height of the belt'. Pussy's mini-brain registered the first part, but succeeded in getting it all fouled up because he swung his arm horizontally from the shoulder, keeping the elbow bent. At the same time he marched with an exaggerated bending of the knees and this overall effect gave the impression that he was climbing an invisible ladder. He would have been great as a fireman on parade. The absurdity of his action was accentuated by the fact that he was unable to co-ordinate the timing of his arms with his legs and his arms were always half a beat at least ahead or behind everybody else. As Pussy often led the squadron on the formal march pasts, he stuck out like a sore thumb and was a cherished object of derision. Bob Cosgrove would give an imitation of him on demand, which always reduced us all to tears.

No one cared for Pussy and by the time the course was over, he had succeeded in making himself universally and profoundly disliked.

As the year drew to its close, Pussy was involved in a flying accident with another instructor, one of the sergeant pilots who, by contrast, was immensely popular with the boys. It was a case of two aeroplanes circling the aerodrome in opposite directions. One was obeying the circuit of the day; the other was disregarding it. Pussy was doing the wrong circuit, so he was presumably at fault. Both men were hurt in the crash and the sergeant pilot died the next day from his injuries. This had the effect of dropping Pussy's stocks even further, if that was possible.

By the end of the year we were beginning to know a bit about the pilot's trade. In fact, we thought we were pretty good. We certainly knew a great deal more than when we started, and we all had a sense of considerable achievement. Twenty-five of our number had to go to the United Kingdom, as there was some deal worked out between Australia and the UK for the provision of a group of trained pilots every six months. The RAF paid the RAAF something like £6,000 for each of us and with this loot the RAAF purchased new aeroplanes and equipment. Some deal! We were all ecstatic when we heard about it years later.

At the time we were given the opportunity to nominate if we wished to go to the United Kingdom and most of the course chose to do so. I was one of them as I felt there was a far better range of aeroplane types to be flown in England than in Australia. Also, I was anxious to see some of the world and I knew very well that my chances to do that were best in the RAF.

It meant a complete severance from the RAAF, and for this I was quite sad. In that short year I had formed a very great affection for the service and an admiration for the men in it. Also, I would be leaving many good friends behind. On the other hand, I had little doubt that when the five years of Short Service Commission with the RAF was over I would return to Australia and pick up the threads once again.

My close friends Lew Johnston, Carl Kelaher, Cec Mace, Pat Hughes and Bob Cosgrove all made the same move. The only members of our gang to stay in Australia were Pete McDonough and Ernie Yde the entertainer.

As we made our farewells that summer none of us had much doubt that we would all get together in a few years' time and reminisce on that rather remarkable and altogether enjoyable year we had just spent together.

Events would dictate otherwise.

2

Royal Air Force

P&O's elderly liner the *Narkunda* arrived in the English Channel after crossing the Bay of Biscay in a cyclonic storm. The seas were mountainous and the winds bitterly cold. It was mid-February 1937 and our first glimpse of our future home was a bleak one. Between squalls of rain we could see a flat, grey coastline which was just discernible from the cold, grey sea.

Next day we docked in the Thames – how it rained – and disembarked into an arctic morning. Everything was bitterly cold and soaking wet. We took a train up to London, which travelled via the eastern suburbs. We were even less impressed with the prospect. How unbelievably wet and cold and dreary! And the millions of little houses all looking the same.

We were met in London by some officials from Australia House, then packed off to RAF Uxbridge, west of London, where we were 'sworn in' then instructed to go up to London and purchase a complete set of RAF uniforms. These differed from those of the Australian Air Force in colour, being a light-greyish blue, whereas the Australian uniform at that time was a dark royal blue, almost as dark as the Navy uniform. The cost involved was monumental, representing about two years' pay. This too contrasted with the Australian uniform, which was free. We were instructed to pay off this debt by banker's order, which would deduct a suitable amount from our monthly pay to clear the debt in four years. This reduced our very modest salary to even smaller dimensions and ensured an eternity of penury ahead.

It seemed one of the ancient tenets of the Air Council, which it had inherited from the Navy, was that money and young officers added up to headaches. The young officers developed a taste for unspecified but expensive vices which spelt trouble for their commanders. Poverty, while it did not guarantee virtue, at least inhibited some of the expensive and sophisticated vices in which they might otherwise be tempted to indulge.

It continued to rain and we were all numb with cold. It rained for the next month, and showed no sign of letting up. At the end of the first week I had endured enough. The locals seemed to be completely adjusted to this sort of thing, but the Australians became very quarrelsome and touchy. It was a very good example of the basic difference in the way of life between the British and the Australians. We were so accustomed to fine weather that we had great difficulty in accepting the confined existence of an English winter. As I was to learn in the next seven years, the English winter, like the Arctic night, is six months long, but the English winter is much wetter!

Day followed day of freezing wet weather with nowhere to go and nothing to do; even the tailor came down to the camp for the fittings for the uniform. Then, without warning, half of our number were told to pack up and go to Lincolnshire. Our destination was a place called Digby, some twenty miles south of the city of Lincoln. The other half went to Grantham. It all looked the same, grey and wet; the most we could see on any day was about half a mile. By the end of the month we were ready to go back to Australia en masse!

Digby was a dreary and dismal prospect. It consisted of small, temporary igloo-type structures erected during the First World War. They should have fallen down after a few months, but by some ill chance had survived some twenty years. If we thought the wind tunnels at Point Cook were rough, they were luxurious compared to the igloos. As Lew Johnston put it, 'There were two types of igloos, small and bloody small.' The larger ones had eight cells for the inmates, the smaller four. There was an additional cubby hole for the batman. The cells were minimal and presumably designed by an architect's clerk who took the quarters of a modern gaol as his model. There was just room for a bed, a chair, a cupboard for clothes and a mini-fireplace cringed away in the only unoccupied corner.

The fireplace was there for the simple reason that the igloos were so cold. Unless they had some heating each night, the occupant was likely to freeze to death during his sleep.

Between each pair of igloos was a toilet-cum-ablutions igloo. This worked on the principle that good fresh air was very healthful and that young officers should not luxuriate in hot baths under any circumstances. These were truly efficient wind tunnels and only the most determined of the Australians maintained their two-baths-a-day routine. One thing the wind tunnel did achieve was to stop Pat Hughes' daily bath song. Pat claimed that it was just not possible to sing and shiver to death at the same time.

The batmen were a corps of time-expired rogues from the Army or the Air Force. They were all past masters at the art of dodging work. I had a quarter share in one, and for this privilege had to hand over the remnants of the monthly pittance the Air Force paid me. The rest went on the crippling mess bills.

As explained, the Air Council seemed to have the philosophy that all young officers were virtually inseparable from trouble, and that the best way to combat this was to reduce them to abject poverty. In this they were most efficient, but the application was only partially effective.

Thus on one notable night the citizens of Lincoln were amazed to see three young men busily erecting a toilet pedestal, seat, cistern, chain and all on the footpath outside a pub called the 'Saracens Head'. Pat Hughes was the ringleader, and proved very efficient with a Stillson wrench which he had acquired from somewhere. Pat claimed the pub was run by a pack of bums and that the toilet seat combination was a more appropriate sign outside the establishment than that depicting the decapitated Saracen of ancient vintage.

The local constabulary arrived and took the matter up with Pat, and those of us who were sober enough took the matter of Pat up with the local constabulary. As a result, the toilet set-up was eventually replaced in its original location and we avoided the embarrassment of having to bail Pat out of the local jail. Pat, for his part, stoutly demanded to go to jail because he said it would just have to be warmer than the igloos at Digby.

The only change after the month of rain was a week of snow. At least it changed the colour from grey to white. Then the sun shone for a few hours, the snow turned to slush and it rained for another month.

I did not believe I could have been so heartily sick of anything, and cursed my stupidity for electing to go to the RAF – I thought I was going to fly interesting aeroplanes, but after eight weeks we were still trying to adjust to the hibernation.

To add to our torment, all the avidly awaited mail from home gave happy descriptions of our friends surfing and sun-baking in the sub-tropic summer. As Lew Johnston put it, 'even the birds walk in this bloody climate'. It was true; the aerodrome was dotted with groups of crows and seagulls pulling up earthworms which had come to the surface of the waterlogged aerodrome to avoid being drowned.

We filled in some of our endless waiting time by studying maps of the area for a hundred miles or so radius from the aerodrome. There were prohibited areas (to be avoided) such as Cranwell, which was an RAF training school. There were some civil aerodromes (also to be avoided), gunnery ranges on the coast, other service aerodromes where we could land if we were lost or in other trouble that made a landing back at our home base difficult or impossible.

Very important were the forests in the vicinity. These were isolated and not very large but they had very distinctive shapes and these were easy to pick out from the surrounding countryside. They were very valuable landmarks for bad weather.

Back in Australia roads and railways were always good landmarks because they were very few and far between. This, however, was not the case in England where there were literally dozens of roads and railways and it was a major problem identifying one from another. The occasional old Roman road was the exception; these ran for miles, sometimes forty or fifty miles in a straight line. This was most unusual in England as most country roads wandered drunkenly all over the countryside as if they could not decide where they wanted to go.

There were a couple of old Roman roads in Lincolnshire which ran up past one of the RAF aerodromes. They were the most useful of all the landmarks in that part of the world. Many a pilot saved his life in bad weather by finding an old road and flying it until an aerodrome appeared, then making an emergency landing.

We played a few games of rugby with the local boys and learnt that it was not as tough on the knees and other exposed parts as the same game is in Australia. In fact, the playing fields were as soft as sponges, and apart from churning up the mud and getting a liberal coating of it over everything, it was a much less violent sport than on the hard grounds back home.

The weather eventually eased up. The English boys claimed it was spring. It was April, anyway, but there was precious little sign of life, but first one clear day, followed by two or three of rain, then two clear days and, hey presto, it was almost fine. There were violent showers every hour or so, but more and more sunshine. The wind was still bitterly cold.

We started to do some flying as the weather cleared. A little more each day and soon we were hard at it. After some familiarisation with the local countryside we concentrated on camera-gun exercises. These were of two types – against ground targets and against air targets. I enjoyed this type of work from the start, and turned in some results well above average. We then took off for Yorkshire and did the same work from an aerodrome called Catfoss, which was near the east coast. Here we fired live ammunition against ground targets and at large flags towed by other aircraft over the North Sea. In all these exercises I was delighted to find that my results were right at the top, and it all seemed so easy.

We returned to Digby and two days later were packed off to our squadrons. I was amazed to find that I had been categorised for fighters. I should have anticipated this from the gunnery results, but eventual categorisation as a result had not entered my head, I just enjoyed doing it and found the work so easy and pleasant. This was quite a blow to me as I had hoped to go on to bombers or seaplanes. My objective still was civil flying after my commitment to the service had been met, and fighters were no help at all for this purpose. With bombers I would gain the experience in long-distance navigation and on handling multiengined large planes, which were taking over the airlines of the world. Fighter experience was quite useless for this purpose. Accordingly, I appealed to the chief instructor for a posting to bombers.

'What? With your results in air gunnery, Olive? Rubbish! You're a natural for the fighter world my boy! Good heavens man, most of the chaps going on bombers would give their eye teeth to get onto fighters. You've got no chance, so resign yourself to your fate. You know, you'll enjoy it,' he added as I left the room thoroughly deflated.

In fact most of the bomber boys were far from envious. The latest bomber, the Bristol Blenheim, was fifty miles an hour faster than the fastest fighter in service and popular opinion among the young pilot fraternity was that the bomber was now faster than the fighter and that this was the way it would stay. The fighter was a machine of the past! Even if the fighter could make up the speed gap, the new hydraulic four-gun turrets would shoot the fighter down long before it got into range.

I felt very unhappy. Up until this turning point I had taken very little interest in the fighter-*versus*-bomber debate. To be assigned to fighters was by no means accepted as a status category, and most of the boys so assigned were far from happy.

When I learned that the squadron to which I was posted was based on the Thames Estuary at a place called Hornchurch, my cup of disillusionment was full. Hornchurch was notorious for the worst weather in England, as it was always fogged in winter by the industrial murk from London. This was carried on the prevailing westerly drift of the air masses in those latitudes. If ever there was a reluctant fighter pilot, I was it. Besides, all my friends had been posted to bombers at aerodromes with famous names like Andover and Worthy Down and Abingdon, all in the beautiful western counties. I had to get Hornchurch!

There was one redeeming thought: Pat Hughes, who had been selected for bombers, appealed and was re-categorised to fighters. He was the only one who was keen on them.

With what philosophical resignation I could muster I accepted the inevitable, packed my bags and set forth for Hornchurch.

In summertime the English countryside becomes uniquely beautiful. The trees, so gaunt and black in winter, are laden down to the ground with cascading masses of leaves. Colours riot everywhere. The deep richness of the greens are unreal to Australian eyes where the countryside colours are all mostly drab olive or brown for most of the year. The temperatures can soar to unexpected heights, if only for brief periods, but as this invariably follows on a prolonged wet spell, the humidity also rockets up and a stifling form of jungle heat can follow.

This form of instant tropic summer struck as I made my way to Hornchurch aerodrome from the railway station of that name. There were no taxis so I walked, carrying my worldly possessions in two huge suitcases. The distance was almost two miles and by the time I reached the officer's mess I was very weary and very thirsty, and it was close to lunchtime.

On arriving at the cool portals of the Hornchurch mess, and observing a middle-aged portly character in civvies coming to meet me, I dumped my suitcase down and made some curt comments about the climate. At Digby, on working days, the only people who normally wore civilian clothes in the mess were the batmen and mess stewards and waiters. I took him to be the head steward.

'You look as if you've just walked across a desert,' he said. I detected a trace of Scottish accent.

'I feel like it too,' I grumbled. 'I just walked in from Hornchurch station.'

'Why didn't you go to Elm Park?' he asked. Nobody had explained to me that a railway stop called Elm Park was a hundred yards from the mess, while the Hornchurch stop was a mile and a half further on out in the countryside!

'Nobody told me so I did the obvious and went to the station of the same name as the camp. My God, I could do with a cold beer,' I added as I opened the suitcase with my coat in it and began putting it on.

The portly one smiled at my discomfort and vanished down a passageway. I went through a nearby open door into a room which was clearly the anteroom of the mess. Some twenty or more young men all about my own age were standing around chatting, mostly holding a tankard of beer in one hand. The other either had a cigarette in it or was used to add some fine shade of meaning to the description of a flying manoeuvre which was usually the main topic at such gatherings.

I asked the most intelligent-looking of a group of young pilot officers if any of them were 65 Squadron, and if so, I would like to pay my respects to the commanding officer. It turned out that they were all 65 Squadron boys and they were in the process of pointing out the CO when they all sprang smartly to attention, clicking their heels and so on, and I turned to see my 'steward' handing me a pint of beer with a broad smile.

I took the beer with the sudden realisation that the 'steward' was none other than the station commander. He handed me the tankard and announced, 'My name's Frew,' offered his hand, shook mine, then moved over to another group where three squadron leaders jumped up and stood to attention.

One of my new acquaintants asked, 'How come the wing commander welcomed you with a beer?'

'Oh! That's easy,' I said. 'I thought he was a steward and just ordered it as I came in the door.'

They looked at me in horror. I felt I had not made a very good start.

One of the squadron leaders noticed my discomfort and broke away, coming towards me. I took the hint and went across towards him. 'My name's Grace,' he said. 'I guess you are Boyd, or are you Olive?'

'Olive,' I replied. 'I don't know where Boyd is. We came separately. I guess I made a blue asking the CO for a beer,' I added.

'Forget it,' he said. 'Come and meet him officially.'

Thus I met the top serving fighter ace of the First World War still serving in the Royal Air Force, Wing Commander 'Bunty' Frew. Later I got to know 'Bunty' Frew as one of the finest and kindest people I have ever met. He was the most famous of the surviving fighter aces of the First World War still serving in the RAF and had some forty-five victories to his credit. A more unassuming man never lived, and it was entirely in character for him to personally get a beer for me in such circumstances. A lesser man would have smartly slapped me down. His gesture to welcome me was completely in character and in no way intended to embarrass. He was the idol of the camp and one of the legends of the RAF, one they claimed had every decoration for gallantry the Air Force had to bestow except the Victoria Cross, and there were many who said he should have had that too.

A flying officer was summoned to the presence of the squadron leader. His name was Jones. He was a New Zealander, and I guess he was about ten years older than I. Jones was acting temporarily as flight commander of 'A' Flight, so I was handed over to him by Grace, who told him to look after me and introduce me to the other members of 65 Squadron.

We went back to the original group. Their names were Saunders, Bicknell, Stanford-Tuck and Putt. Tuck was the spokesman; a lean, dark-haired, tall young man, he possessed a mild, laughing arrogance which I was to get to know quite well.

'Where do you come from?' he asked after I had exchanged a few words with the group. 'Australia?'

'Yes,' I replied. 'Queensland, to be more specific.'

'Oh! Do you have bisons in that part of Australia?'

'No, sorry, no bisons in Australia, you're thinking of America.'

'Oh! You must be a dirty specimen – I understood all Australians washed their faces in bisons!'

This produced hoots of mirth from all four and a rumble of approval from Jones.

My rejoinder was monosyllabic and vulgar, producing more hoots of mirth, and we settled down to more civilised chatter.

The settling-in period was a bit like Point Cook all over again, except that there was no high-pressure study and no super organisation of every minute of the day. But there were a lot of new faces to know and not one familiar one among them. By contrast to Point Cook, everything was very relaxed – too relaxed, almost, as there seemed to be little else to do but fly, and not so very much of that. At least not at first, for the squadron had about ten days to go to the big Empire Air Display, which was one of the focal points of the year's flying.

On Empire Day, which was always a Saturday late in May, the station was thrown open to the public for the afternoon and a concentrated programme of display flying astonished the assembled populace. This event was nationwide and every RAF aerodrome and most civil aerodromes took part in the 'air day'. The programmes were exciting and several pilots were killed each year on this day. This, of course, really drew the crowds – shades of Roman carnivals.

As our aerodrome was one of the most accessible to London, we always attracted a crowd of around a hundred thousand people, which was about a thousand times as many people in one spot as I had ever seen in my life before. Needless to say, with such a huge audience, the boys were anxious to put on as impressive a display as possible and thus the rehearsing of the various events took almost every spare minute and every available aeroplane for some weeks before. Thus I had much difficulty in even getting my hands on a plane, let alone flying it.

Some days were taken up by obtaining a parachute, maps and flying clothing, including heavily fur-lined jackets, boots, triple gauntlets, etc., in case my chance came. The gauntlets consisted of a silk inner glove, a knitted woollen intermediate and soft leather over gauntlets that came up to the elbow. It was a lot of hand covering, but in reality never enough at the altitudes we were expected to work at in open cockpits.

There were radio procedures and codes to learn by heart and an impressive number of prohibited areas such as petrol and oil installations, bomb and ammunition dumps, large electric power pylons and cables over the Thames and last, but by no means least, Whipsnade Park, where numerous lions and tigers roamed at large in a vast zoo. All these had to be memorised, their locations studied and avoided at all times, especially in the event of engine failure and forced landings. I, for one, took the zoo one seriously, as I could think of little less attractive than surviving a forced landing only to be eaten by a lion or a tiger.

No. 65 Squadron had been formed in the First World War and had some fame as the nursery of several of the greatest aces – however, the aces had reached their peaks in their units. It had been disbanded after the war, but when Mussolini began his African adventures in 1935 it was resurrected and had been in existence for its second round for about a year when I joined it.

For the most part the pilots were all in their early twenties and had little more time in the service than I had; the exceptions were the flight commanders and Squadron Leader Grace. The two flight commanders were Cooke and Bicknell – both flight lieutenants.

As I waited around by the offices and the crew rooms in the hangars, watching the flying and waiting for a chance to fly myself, I had an opportunity to see some of the formation flying which was to be part of the big display so much effort was going into.

I was astonished. Twelve aeroplanes rolled over the aerodrome as one; all packed tightly together they rose as one and then flew back and forth changing their pattern each time until on the last run, which was about the eighth, they came over in a long echelon to the right, each aeroplane out from and slightly behind its leading neighbour. It was all rock steady and precision flying at its best, then on an order from the leader they all half-rolled and dived down to the surface of the aerodrome, shooting past the tower at what seemed very great speed. I was immensely impressed and even more so when they quickly reformed and landed, all twelve of them as if tied together, with only three or four feet separating each aeroplane from its neighbour. It was all a bit unnerving and I found it impossible to believe that I could ever come up to this standard of flying.

At last I was allowed to fly one of the squadron's fighters. It was a Gloster Gauntlet and was one of the last of the biplane fighters. It was hardly a pretty aeroplane, having a short, stubby nose with a big round radial engine which churned out about 600 horsepower. It was a biplane and the wings had four sets of struts – two sets on each side with an intricate array of flying wires that braced the whole structure together. From the pilot's cockpit the wings looked somewhat like birdcages, and indeed the bomber pilots' taunt to the fighters in these days was that if one of the wires was broken you would never know – there were so many. The only way to find out was to always take a chook up with you; if it got out, a wire had broken! It was quite a strong little aeroplane for all that and the pilots who were training to put on the aerobatic displays threw them around with reckless abandon.

I soon got to know most of the pilots in 'A' Flight, to which I was attached. There was only one other officer besides Des Cooke, the flight commander, and that was the New Zealander Norman Jones. He was usually referred to as 'J. J.' Jones, as he had a trace of a stammer which the others unmercifully aped when addressing him.

There were also three sergeant pilots, MacPherson, Boxall and Edwards, who were a latter-day three Musketeers, full of fun and very skilful pilots – they were all British and an exceptionally likeable team. In the air, their flying, especially their formation work, was easily the best of the three squadrons at Hornchurch, and Boxall was the aerobatic star of the team. He and Saunders were to do synchronised aerobatics on the big day and each practised for a couple of hours daily to get their routine to perfection.

Boxall was a most likeable lad with a happy, laughing nature – he was universally popular with the officers and men alike. On my first flight he ran over all the 'taps' with me before I went off, and had several tips to offer about the problems of landing the little fighter.

The Gauntlet was certainly a delight to fly, even if its outward appearance left something to be desired. It had a top speed of about 210 mph, about 50 mph less than the Blenheims and Battles which were the bombers in service at that time. However, it could climb very well and was incredibly manoeuvrable. It was also a very 'clean' aeroplane and tended to 'float' a long way after the engine was cut back on the landing. As it had no flaps or air brakes, its landing attitude was very 'nose up' and with such a large, bulbous engine it was hard to see what was in front and the pilot landed almost blind. A few days before I joined the squadron, Jones had collided with a tractor mowing the aerodrome and the tractor driver had been killed as a result. Jones had not even seen him.

I pulled out the map and flew around the Hornchurch sector just to get an idea of what our territory was. It was roughly a wedge-shaped sector of the map with the Thames Estuary running through the long axis of the wedge. To our north was the North Weald sector and to the south was Biggin Hill. I spent an hour at ten thousand feet and then returned to the 'drome. To the west was the vast, sprawling mass of London, a smear of reddish-grey tiles and bricks with an unbelievable maze of roads.

There was a dirty smoke haze towards the west as the wind that day was a gentle drift from the east and the murk and industrial haze was being blown towards the western counties. This was rare for by far the greatest numbers of days of the year produced westerly winds or westerly drifts, which deposited the haze over Hornchurch.

I landed and felt very pleased with myself. The squadron warmed up and, with Grace leading, went off on another formation practice.

The next day was glorious too. The English summer had set in and it was as warm and as lovely as our best Australian days – perhaps not quite as hot as the peak of our summer, but it was good to be alive.

I talked to Jones and Boxall about aerobatics and they gave me a rundown on what to do. It seemed the Gauntlet had no vices, so I took off and spent the best part of an hour doing loops, rolls, stall turns, spins, the whole repertoire of my tricks, and the Gauntlet behaved to perfection. It was incredibly light on the controls and responded to the slightest pressure like a well-trained horse. Indeed, to do most manoeuvres it seemed almost enough to just think of them and they occurred with almost no effort.

After an hour I returned to the vicinity of the aerodrome, found the bend in the Thames which was our basic landmark for bad-weather flying – sure enough, there was the aerodrome about three miles to the north. I throttled back, spiralled down and landed. It was a good landing and I was very pleased with life. Fighters may have had no future, but they were a lot of fun. Those bomber pilots could not do aerobatics for an hour and pull off slide-slipping landings. How glad I was, after all, to be on fighters, even if there was no future for them. I was in a good mood to enjoy life and the world was a beautiful and exquisite sight from the cockpit of a fighter at ten thousand feet.

Boxall took the fighter over from me. He had it refuelled and we chatted about the beautiful weather and the delightful little Gauntlets, and he told me he was going over to a neighbouring civil aerodrome to practise aerobatics as he had to perform there on Saturday, having only two days off. He was such an infectious person and so full of life. He took off and I watched him circle away to the north, then I went into the office and sat down to tell Jones how I had got on with my first attempt at aerobatics in the Gauntlet.

As we nattered and I enthused over the feather-light controls of the machine, the phone rang and Jones gave a series of grunts to whoever was on the other end, then put the phone down and said, 'You flew the plane Boxall just took off in, didn't you?'

I said, 'Yes, you know I did. Why?'

'Well, he's just been killed. The wings came off in the second loop and the fuselage speared into the centre of the aerodrome.'

He grabbed his cap and stormed out of the room, jumped in a car and raced off to see the wreckage.

I was left in a half-stunned state. Boxall! Killed! It seemed quite impossible. Only five minutes ago we were laughing and joking together and I had been thinking what a pleasure it was going to be to get to really know this bloke. Dead! Had I through my ignorance or lack of experience strained the machine's structure, or had he flown a little too low in his practice and strained it himself? Was it my fault, or had I escaped the Gauntlet breaking up in mid-air by two loops? I would never know.

Squadron life went on. The three musketeers were now two, and a very subdued and unhappy pair. I shared their grief, but as I had only known Boxall for a few days I could only sympathise in their loss. They had lost their dearest friend.

I was given some formation flying practice on my next trip. It was much more demanding than my previous experience of that particular skill. At the training schools pupils were penalised if their aeroplanes flew within two wingspans of each other. This was to try to reduce the collision rate from inexperienced pilots trying to fly close before they were ready for it. Now I was expected to fly within four or five feet of the next aeroplane and never move regardless of what the leader did! In some ways it was easier to fly so close. Thirty or forty feet can double or halve without you being aware of it, but five or six feet was a distance easy to judge.

Actually we allowed a gap of about four feet out from the tip of each aeroplane so that if the leader suddenly stopped there would always be four feet or more between wing tips as the following machine slipped past.

It did not take very long before I felt very much at home, but close-formation flying was a very exacting exercise. While the leader flew with his throttle sitting on his engine, those following were constantly tending to overshoot or drag behind, necessitating endless use of the throttle. At the same time, the follower had to remain in the same relative position to his leader whether he was flying level, climbing, diving or turning.

Usually we did our formation flying practice at about six thousand feet. The air was close to freezing at that height, but I seldom returned from formation flying without my clothes being saturated with sweat. That was one of the reasons we always flew in overalls. We removed our uniforms and put on the overalls. We had two sets each and when one set became so smelly as to be intolerable, we would wash them and use the others. While I was learning to fly formation to the squadron standard I had to wash out my overalls every day!

The Empire Air Day came and went and the display was very spectacular. We were visited by two new bombers, a Fairey Battle and a Bristol Blenheim. These new low-wing machines looked very sleek and ultra-modern to eyes accustomed to two-wing struts and innumerable bracing wires. Still, the enthusiasts claimed the fighter's day would come soon and we would have a fighter which would leave the bombers for dead. Some said it would be capable of almost 400 mph, but that seemed a long way off in 1937. To a young man of twenty, a couple of years is an eternity of time – we had to live in the present.

The wing fly-past was the *pièce de résistance* of the air display, with thirty-six Gauntlets all in tight formations of twelve, and the best of the three was 65 Squadron – I had a feeling that this would be a very fine unit to cut my teeth on.

The dust blown up by the aeroplanes of the Empire Air Day display had hardly settled when we packed up and flew north to Catfoss in Yorkshire. This was the same spot I had visited from Digby to practice our air gunnery. Now the squadron would do its annual gunnery exercises against towed-flag targets and against ground targets. How lucky for me, I thought. I had just done this exercise very successfully on Hawker Furies, now I had to do it on Gauntlets.

We flew up and our clothes, etc. were flown up in an old bomber converted to a transport. It was quite a thrill for me to be part of a formation of fifteen aeroplanes which pressed on for over two hours to cover the three hundred miles. Although the Gauntlet could do 210 mph flat out, in formation the speed was reduced to about 149 mph and during the climbing period was reduced to 90 mph, so it was a laborious business.

My gunning results went to the top right from the start, with strong competition coming from Bob Stanford-Tuck, 'J. J.' Jones and Cooke. For three weeks we laboured daily and our figures improved all the time. Tuck took an aeroplane down to Hornchurch and for some reason beat up the mess with a series of exuberant dives and was promptly put under arrest, so that removed him from the contest.

On the third day, Cookie and I fired on the same flag and I came back to find that my score had suddenly rocketed well ahead of Cookie's. However, on all these exercises one of the two planes fired bullets tipped with red pigment and on this occasion Cookie had the red bullets and I had the plain. Because my score was almost double Cookie's, nobody would believe that the red pigment was working and all thought that most of my plain bullet holes on the flag were really Cookie's. I offered to do it with the red-tipped bullets, but got a blast of abuse for my suggestion and was banished out to do 'range officer', which effectively put me out of all further competition.

In my absence they all tried to equal my score, but could not get near it. As a result the verdict was final – Cookie's shooting had not all registered and I was on the outer because I was the new boy and I had the infernal cheek to think I could equal the old hands at air gunnery! I even began to doubt myself!

Back from the Gunnery Camp the squadron packed up for annual leave – a whole month and no work to do – also money in my pockets. My problem was to find something to do or somewhere to go. This, fortunately, was solved by 'J. J.' Jones, who had an identical problem, being a New Zealander. He knew some people in London, operating from Sloane Square, who specialised in finding hosts for overseas visitors and students. Run by Lady Frances Ryder, they were a voluntary hospitality group who kept themselves busy making visiting students, etc. welcome in the UK. Mostly their contacts were people of considerable wealth, who had previously lived in or visited places like Australia, New Zealand and South Africa and had enjoyed the hospitality of people in those lands.

In due course, I enjoyed ten days each with a great-aunt who had a small holiday cottage at a place called Westleton, in Suffolk; in the stately Tudor mansion in Cambridge belonging to a wealthy gentleman who was also a Member of Parliament; and on the estate of another in Oxfordshire.

3

Awakening to Danger

On return to the squadron, I found that we had been reequipped with new aeroplanes. These were Gloster Gladiators, an improvement on the Gauntlet. It was a faster machine. It reached nearly 250 mph at 12,000 feet. This seemed fairly good in those days but they still could not catch the bombers and there were some unpleasant things about them. We all had done a couple of trips in them, although we had not yet started throwing them about in aerobatics, when several pilots in widely separated squadrons were killed within a day or two. It seemed that the wings had folded up on them when they were flying upside down. At first nobody could discover what the trouble was. The aeroplanes were made at the new shadow factories which rumour had it were previously making curtain rods. The ground staff said that the workmen apparently did not know the difference between curtain rods and high-tensile steel as many parts had been made of the wrong materials.

The accidents always resulted in burned wrecks that told almost nothing. However, one day an intelligent individual, on his own initiative, pulled out the main centre struts which took most of the flying strain. By doing so he risked a court martial for damaging His Majesty's aircraft. He discovered that there was no strut there! The main fairing, which appeared to streamline a piece of steel tubing, turned out to be only a light aluminium fairing with no tubing at all. The centre six inches had been cut away, throwing the entire weight of a three-ton aeroplane on to strips of aluminium which would not stand the weight of a man on them. Sabotage?

On inspection, the majority of our new Gladiators were found to be similarly faulty so we were grounded for about a month until proper parts were made and the machines were safe. Even so, we took a long time to feel secure in those aeroplanes. My first taste of possible sabotage scared me a bit and I think it scared others too.

Winter set in with October, and with it nostalgia for Queensland's golden surfing beaches. I tried desperately to adjust myself to the English methods of hibernation, and by Christmastime had read more books than I had ever read before in my whole life.

To escape the claustrophobia, Bob Blake, the South African, and I applied for leave to go to Austria, where we were told there was plenty of sun and skiing. Blake knew of an organisation in London run for the benefit of university students and ex-students. It had reciprocal arrangements with similar organisations in every other country in Europe except Russia. Behind this organisation was the idea of encouraging young people to travel around the Continent and thus to know the people of other nations.

It was all accomplished on a shoestring, and as we were both hard up, and both qualified as exstudents, we decided to avail ourselves of the facilities offered. A trip was organised for Austria, so we joined it and eventually found ourselves in a raging blizzard in the Tyrol.

Our guides met us as we detrained in a town called Bludenz. They were men mostly of our own age group, the arrangement being that the Austrians acted as guides and ski instructors, while we spoke English and taught them to do likewise. They had free English lessons – we had free skiing lessons. This cut the cost considerably.

Furthermore, they arranged the cheapest accommodation possible, which we learnt with some misgivings were peasants' huts! This further cut the costs, and made the whole trip possible at about one pound a day, including some two thousand miles of travel.

Our particular guide's name was Helmuth Fally. He was short, stocky and endowed by nature with a happy disposition. Older than most of us, he was a doctor of law, a magistrate in Innsbruck and a captain in the Austrian army. He was assigned to us as we were assumed to have something in common. This turned out to be the case.

After a period of sorting ourselves out, during which the blizzard stopped, we set out to walk to our village named Lech. This involved a ten-mile hike through snow over a mountain pass at night so as to avoid the danger of avalanches, which became a menace by day. Eventually we were settled in our peasant's cot, and I was so weary it felt as good as the best bed in the world.

The following morning I awoke to the strong smell of something burning and discovered a small, round stove in the centre of the room glowing a bright cherry red, with two smoking socks on the top. The peasant wench had kindly lit the fire to warm the room for us when we awoke, and had carefully put our socks on the stove to dry out!

I threw the two foul smelling objects out of the window into the snow. The view from the window was breathtaking in its beauty. The orange light of the rising sun was already tinting the crests of the Alps. Down in the valley lay the village under its blanket of snow. The village church stood out with its tall, square tower capped with an onion-shaped minaret. The smell of woodsmoke from cottage fires was strong in the air and lay around in little layers above the village, too lazy to rise.

The peasant's cot was a simple iron bedstead with a crude spring mattress. On the spring mattress was a mattress of eiderdown about one foot thick, and over this was a sheet – then another sheet and another down mattress about a foot thick. Once inside this it was virtually impossible to feel cold unless you fell out of bed.

The walls of the room were of pine. The same V-jointed timber was common in the older Queensland homes I knew so well, but never have I seen so many knots in a length of timber. I started counting the knots for fun and went back to sleep.

Bob began moving around and enthusing over the view from our hut. Practising much willpower, I forced myself out of my cot and took another look around. The sun was now up, but the valley was still in the shadow of one of the peaks. It was an Alpine classic. About thirty picturesque gable-roofed cottages made up the village, with five or six larger buildings which were the 'pensions' or the hotels. The hotel which was to be our headquarters, the *Tannberghof*, was a brown timber building looking exactly as a Tyrolean guesthouse should look, with two feet of new snow all over the roof. Fringing the village were many groups of pine trees, which were so covered with snow that they looked as if they had been made by some giant confectioner.

We dressed and made for the headquarters where we had the usual Continental breakfast of a roll and a cup of coffee. I always felt ravenous after such a meal. So did Blake, so we bought blocks of chocolate to fill up the empty void.

In brilliant sunshine we collected our skis, ski stocks and any other impedimenta required for the sport, and set off up the slope in one squad of about thirty bodies, in Indian file. We arrived at the nursery slopes and

I decided to try my hand – or rather my balance – out and see if I could remember what I had learned at Mount Buffalo in Australia. I surprised myself by running quite well for a few hundred yards. Unfortunately I had no directional control whatsoever and could not stop. Just as I was confident that I was making quite a favourable impression on some of the fair members of our party, I caught a glimpse of a figure on skis making towards me at lightning speed. It was executing the most impressive turns, simultaneously shouting 'Achtung!' obviously addressed at me. Unfortunately my repertoire of tricks did not include an 'Achtung', and the next thing I knew I was buried under a pile of snow.

After a long struggle I emerged and found myself looking into a pair of blue Nordic eyes. They were feminine eyes, and they were viewing me in a distinctly unfavourable light. For once in my life I was very glad that I could not understand German, as the things she said were quite unprintable in any language. However, no one was hurt, and I returned to the fold.

Helmuth politely told me that I had skied through a flagged racing area where the locals were holding downhill races; he seemed mildly surprised that I was still alive.

After a day's skiing, the guides divided us into new groups according to our ability. It was with some gratification that I realised that I was not in the complete novice class, but I know I only escaped by a small margin. We were then re-allotted to guides. Helmuth stayed with us.

Helmuth's English was quite unrecognisable at first, and most of his attempts sounded as if he were trying to say the alphabet backwards with his mouth full of rusty razorblades. Slowly and painfully we sorted out the early stages. Then we discovered that he had quite a wide English vocabulary, and as he improved he told us that he had read over a hundred Penguin novels in English, but had never actually spoken to anybody in the language. The latter we had no difficulty in believing, and as time went on we were equally convinced of the former.

The next few days were spent in mastering the more elementary ways of stopping and turning. Very essential points as I had already discovered. Our skiing improved and so did Helmuth's English.

In the evenings after the strenuous efforts at skiing, we wolfed all the food we could find, and repaired to the dancefloor, where, following the local custom, we each bought a jug of wine for one shilling. This was enough to last for the whole night, as I estimate that it held at least half a gallon. The evening was then spent in dancing and singing to the Tyrolese music of the local orchestra. This consisted of a zither, an accordion, a clarinet and a drum. We danced in our ski boots, and in our ski clothes. Only the local girls and a few visiting lasses changed. They decked themselves out in their dirndls, the national folk dress. It all added up to a lot of fun for all.

After the basic principles of skiing had been mastered, our small team and Helmuth began daily excursions up to the higher grounds where we experimented with some cross-country skiing. The day was energetic and began before sunrise as we left after an early roll and coffee. We would climb for about an hour, then we would rest for a short spell and spend half an hour practising turns and stops. After this we would climb for another two hours, followed by a rest, an orange and some chocolate.

After some more practice we would have our lunch, which Helmuth would produce out of his knapsack. Lunch over, we would press on for another spell of climbing, until about 3.30 p.m. when we would stop for our final rest before the descent. At this stage the knapsack was turned inside out and we ate everything left in it or in our pockets. We were usually well up near the top of some alp by this point, from which we enjoyed views of snow-covered mountains. The sight never failed to thrill me and I guess it never would.

I imagine that the true mountaineer is like the true pilot, he never tires of the view no matter how often he sees it. It is something that always gives him a thrill inside and makes him marvel at the works of God.

After our brief spiritual uplift we would point our skis downhill and, with Helmuth leading to make sure that we avoided precipices, streak off towards the purple mists below. This last half-hour of the day was the payoff for all the hard work involved in gaining height. I never had the slightest doubt as to whether it was worth it; it was worth double the work and effort.

It was towards the last couple of days that, coming down very fast, I ran from soft, deep, powdered snow into ice-crusted snow, where the sun had melted the top of the snow during the middle of the day. It was like running into a wire and resulted in a terrific crash. That evening Heine Smidt, our chief guide and a newly qualified surgeon, inserted eight stitches in my leg under somewhat primitive conditions. I spent the remainder of the trip with the other unfortunates who had succeeded in breaking or damaging various parts of their anatomy.

There was one aspect of the trip about which I was to think for many a day in the future. On this first visit, Austria was still a free country.

That is, it had not been 'liberated' by Hitler. Life in Austria was just about as free and uninhibited as it was possible to be. The people were happy and friendly and our Austrian guides spoke to us quite openly on any subject we liked to bring up.

Being an Australian, and somewhat uninhibited on politics, it was not long before I tried sounding them out on their views. They were quite prepared to talk although they were a little shy of saying much about the Nazi movement when there were many present. Helmuth explained to me one day when we were alone that most of the guides were Nazi sympathisers. This was because most of them were ardent socialists. They believed that the Nazi Party led by Hitler was the only practical socialist party in Europe. They were the only ones who could be relied upon not to sell out to the communists.

Helmuth confided that he was a Nazi and went on to paint a glowing picture of life in Germany under the Führer. There was so much prosperity that all the young men were leaving Austria and going there. The result was that Austria was faced with the choice of joining the Reich or becoming a nation of old people.

To my queries about the likelihood of war, he was very reassuring. He felt that Hitler would never involve Germany in war even though he might threaten. Hitler had personally felt the horrors of war. They were all sure there was not the slightest risk.

The return to Hornchurch from Austria was made doubly depressing by the news imparted by John Welford as I walked into the mess.

'I suppose you heard about Ned?'

'No?'

'Killed last Friday. He and two others flew over to North Weald. Collided with another kite in the circuit. Funeral tomorrow afternoon.'

Poor Ned Austin-Sparkes, so full of life and fun. It seemed that those who loved life most were the ones to go. Boxall was the same type, and I had recently heard from Australia that Ernie Yde, one of my best friends, who had stayed behind in Australia, had been killed. He had crashed into Port Phillip Bay. Ernie had been the life of many a party with his ukulele, which he strummed to accompany innumerable entertaining little songs we all loved.

We buried Ned the following day, and it was a very silent trio who returned in Jones's car, each with his own thoughts.

Shortly after my return to England, I was shocked one morning to learn with the rest of the world that Hitler had marched into Austria. I was not surprised, however, that there had been literally no opposition to this big political move. If all the youth of Austria were as completely in favour of German methods as were my Austrian friends, it would probably be acclaimed as a stroke of national good fortune by most of the citizens.

Another Empire Air Display took place and I was very gratified to be a performer this time. There were two outstanding incidents for me in that pageant. With another officer I was detailed to entertain our guest of honour, Miss Jean Batten, the famous girl pilot, and the other was the appearance of the Hawker Hurricane fighter, the latest thing, which was parked in an obvious position where all could see it.

Only a few were allowed to look at it closely. At the right moment this aeroplane took off and flew past at what seemed to us, then, terrific speed.

An event of great interest occurred about a month later when a party of German generals and their ADCs came to visit our aerodrome. It was strongly rumoured that these officers were on a spying mission and that although it was apparently a friendly tour we were to be guarded in our comments.

Our CO was one of the fighter aces of the last war, and the same reputation followed the German General Udet, who was reputed to have several times engaged our CO in deadly duel during the last war. The pilot boys, myself included, were all agog to see these two rivals of the air meet on friendly terms. The event was very formal and we were all very impressed with the highly decorative uniforms of the German officers. Their uniforms, by comparison with our modest grey-blue ones, made a sparkling and dramatic display with much gold and red trimmings on a blue background. I could not help thinking how self-conscious I would feel if I had to wear such a uniform in public.

The young officers all spoke excellent English and by the way the generals were conversing with our CO they were all well versed in our language. The meeting was very fleeting and it was all over, so it seemed, in a few minutes. The CO personally conducted the party around the aerodrome and it was reported that the Germans did not believe, when they saw our old Gladiators, that they were seeing our first-line defence fighters.

August was the month for the annual 'war games'. During these, bombers from the RAF bomber groups flew out into the North Sea and 'raided' various points of strategic or tactical importance on the British mainland.

The exercises lasted a week and during that time all leave was cancelled for the permanent Air Force. The reserve squadrons and auxiliary squadrons were called up and became part of the air defence machinery of Great Britain. In previous years these operations had involved efforts to intercept the bombing raids with the help of the Observer Corps. The Observer Corps was a voluntary organisation, mostly of ex-servicemen from the Kaiser's war, who kept themselves familiar with the various types of military aircraft as well as civilian types. They reported all aeroplane movements to a central operations room, where the information was fed into Fighter Command's control room.

The system suffered many drawbacks. When there was much haze or mist they were unable to survey any significant area. On cloudy days if the aeroplanes were above the clouds they could only report hearing them – no accurate directions or heights were possible – and as the weather was notoriously indifferent in Britain even in summer, their efforts were only marginally valuable.

This time we had the help of a new electronic detector called 'Radio Direction Finder'. This was so hush-hush that even the words were secret, but for the first time we found ourselves being directed by ground-control radio on to one raider after another. Some interceptions were even managed out over the North Sea.

This was something very new. We still had our Gladiators and the frustrating aspect of it all was that most of the new bombers, the Bristol Blenheims and Handley Page Hampdens, could leave us miles behind. Sometimes we were fortunate in having five or even ten thousand feet extra height over the bombers. When that happened we could dive at full throttle, level out and possibly catch our quarry, but usually by the time we turned about and headed for the bombers they were too far away to catch.

We all felt rather helpless and useless – interceptor fighters unable to catch the bombers even when we started with a height advantage of five thousand feet. I had been in the RAF almost two years and still the bombers were faster than the fighters. Sure, there was talk about the new generation of monoplane fighters, the Hurricane and the Spitfire, but so far only one squadron had been equipped with a few Hurricanes and they were only slightly faster than the new bombers.

It seemed that those who believed that the bomber would always be faster than the interceptor were right. There were strong rumours of even faster bombers.

During these exercises our squadron was given the role of night fighters. For the last few days of the experiments we tried to intercept at night. The bombers attacking by night were older and slower than those used in the daylight raids. Even so the searchlights were unable to pick up those bombers even on clear nights so our efforts were wasted. On the last night the bombers turned on their navigation lights so that the searchlights could find them. So could we, but it was little consolation. The old, slow bombers used for night work could go through our defences, including our radio location, and we could never find them unless they turned on their lights. It seemed the night bombers were even safer than the day bombers.

The war games over, the squadron packed up and went on leave. The September weather was delightful. John Nicholas invited me to stay with him down at Portsmouth. From there we went over to the Isle of Wight and spent a few pleasant days with some of his friends. The sun shone brightly and the light breezes were warm and we were all set for a most enjoyable month, but a cloud hung over us.

Our enjoyment was marred by the newspaper reports of Adolf Hitler's increasingly strident demands for a piece of Czechoslovakia. For the first time we had to be on twenty-four-hour recall and had to stay in one place. All through the leave, the news became blacker and all my enjoyment was flavoured with a slight anxiety. The war of nerves had begun. As day followed day, the Führer's demands became more arrogant, until one morning a telegram arrived summoning us to return to Hornchurch at once. We both knew that war was a distinct possibility.

Just after this, a couple of us were sent to Uxbridge to do a course. It was while I was there that the crisis, which later became known as Munich, developed. It all seemed to happen very suddenly. The rumblings of war grew into a loud and unpleasant challenge. I think everybody was a little confused as to what really was at stake. Germany was insisting on having a slice of Czechoslovakia and Czechoslovakia was not prepared to hand it over. This seemed very unfair to the Czechs, but the lands which the Germans claimed were almost completely populated by Germans. It seemed a denial of the rights of the German majority to force them to remain under Czech rule if they were so insistent on joining the German Reich.

Of course, it is easy to be wise after the event and it is now apparent that this was Hitler's first move towards war. However, it was not clear at the time just what the real issue actually was as both the Sudetenlanders and the Czechs had almost equally strong cases. To us it seemed unjustifiable to go to war in support of a strategic frontier against the claims of self-determination of the German minorities. It was a denial of the first principles of democracy.

There was one angle which antagonised the civilised world and that was the truculent attitude of the Germans. It touched a familiar chord in the memories of men who remembered the events which led up to the last war. Hitler was threatening war against anyone who stood in the way of the rights of the Germans. This seemed the one inconsistent aspect of the German case for recognition for democratic rights. To many people this threat of force was proof that the Germans were returning to their old doctrine of 'might is right'.

In any case, whichever way the incident developed it would be a moral victory for the Germans, for if the interested parties recognised the moral justification of the Germans' claim it could also be construed as submission to the German threat of force. On the other hand, should the threat of force itself be accepted as a challenge and become the cause of a war, the Germans could still claim that the war was in the cause of international justice.

The political parties of the left and their press were against a war, and although they were becoming progressively antiGerman in their outlook (a result of German interference in the Spanish Civil War) they did not want war at any price over this affair. I agreed with them. In fact, it is true to say that the vast majority of Englishmen would have given little support to a war over the strategic frontiers of Czechoslovakia though they had no great love for the Germans.

The only case of enthusiasm for a fight in these days was a tirade delivered by an enormous padre at breakfast one morning. He was obviously in a preaching mood and thundered at length about his disgust with his fellow countrymen for not being able to see that this was a case of the Germans reverting to their policy of 'might is right'. The padre's war ribbons made us suspicious that he harboured an old-fashioned hatred of the Germans and I have no hesitation in saying that few of his audience took him seriously.

Mr Neville Chamberlain, Britain's Prime Minister, flew to Germany twice and the atmosphere was very tense. Nobody seemed to be very clear what was at stake but all were very clear that they did not want a war.

My companions and I were quickly recalled from Uxbridge. When we arrived at the aerodrome, we found that we had a new station commander. His name need not concern the reader but we soon learnt that he was a very different person from our popular Bunty Frew. He was clearly in a state of considerable excitement and already the station's morale was changing for the worse. First of all, we were issued with some old overalls and paintbrushes and were directed to paint our lovely silver Gladiators brown and green. This was a messy business but all hands had to get at the job. Urgency was extreme. In the evenings we had to load ammunition belts by hand as there was no machinery on the camp to do the job. Cartridges had to be fed carefully into the steel clips and the combination of cartridges and clips became a belt. We worked at this for days until we ran out of bullets. Even so, each aeroplane had only enough ammunition for half a dozen trips. After that all we would be able to do would be to shake our wings at the opposition. That was if we could catch them!

How depressed we were! To add to the gloom our hangars were blacked out by copious use of black paint over the glass so that every room was dismal and lightless. Night and day we laboured and at the same time we stood by on shifts to be prepared for instant action.

We had a visit from, and a most revealing talk by, an intelligence officer from Fighter Command. He brought down with him a number of beautiful models of sleek monoplanes with black crosses and red swastikas on them. He explained each type to us and told us how fast they could travel, at what heights they usually operated and where their defensive guns were located – their calibre, range and arcs of fire. They had all been successfully used by the German forces in the Spanish Civil War. It was the worst news I'd ever heard. All except one of the bombers were faster than our Gladiators by up to fifty miles per hour. The exception was the Junkers Ju 87 Stuka dive-bomber, which was just as fast as the others after it had dropped its bombs, so we would have little chance of catching one even if we saw it.

Even more disturbing was the fact that their Messerschmitt Me 109 fighter was a hundred miles an hour faster, had five guns – one a 20 mm cannon – and it could out-climb us with ease. Collectively the Luftwaffe was at least three times as large as Fighter Command and everything in it was better and carried a bigger punch. The intelligence officer did not have to tell us – we knew we were outclassed and outgunned. All we could do was hope and pray no war would begin until at least we had a few aeroplanes which were a match for the German models.

We were dumbfounded that such a force could exist or that we could be so pitifully unprepared. Their aircraft outnumbered ours by about ten to one and the performance figures (obtained during the Spanish Civil

War) were incomparably higher than ours. After the lecture there were many despondent faces and I heard such defeatist remarks as 'we haven't a hope in hell', or, 'we're not in the race' from men whose judgement and courage were later to win world renown in the Battle of Britain.

The old hands among the men, old veterans with First World War ribbons up, were no more encouraging. They often delighted in shaking the new pilot boys (and some of the older pilots too) with reminiscences of the last war. 'Yeah,' said our old flight sergeant, 'I remember when I was with 74 Squadron in the last war, we had nearly equal numbers with old Jerry then but the pilot's average life was about six days from the time he started fighting and the kites was pretty equal too!'

Equal numbers! And an average life of a week!

What were our chances with inferior aeroplanes and outnumbered by probably ten to one?

I thought back to Uxbridge and the RAF padre in the officer's mess sounding off about Hitler and what a monster he was. He had wanted war declared at once to stop all the nonsense. There was no sense of honour in Britain any more or we would all be battering Hitler into the ground, so preached the padre. I wondered if he had heard just how much better prepared for a fight the Germans were and, if so, would he have still used such brave words? It was one thing to talk fight and another to rush into a fight when it was heavily loaded against you. I just hoped that Mr Chamberlain was not as keen on war as the worthy padre.

Two days later we knew the answer. 'Peace in our time!' An agreement had been signed which mollified the Czech government and persuaded it to accept Hitler's terms. I admit to a tremendous surge of relief at the news for there would have been no future for any of us if we had gone to war at that time. We were hopelessly outclassed thanks to twenty years of pacifist politics. Gutless or not, Chamberlain had no choice if he knew the facts, and surely the Prime Minister would have known how disastrous was our plight.

The crisis might have been over for the newspapers but it was not over for the fighter pilots. Each day one of our three squadrons was 'on duty', which meant we flew with live ammunition by day and were prepared to intercept any surprise raids. By night we still filled ammunition belts when there were any available bullets. Each night, including weekends, a full crew of one of the squadrons stayed on the camp and slept in bunks in the locker rooms in the hangars. These were cold and poorly lit and it achieved little other than reminding us that war was possible at any time.

4

War Clouds Gathering

With the anxious days of Munich over, we settled down to training for battle. Exercises were now taken more seriously and tactics studied more closely. The ground crew and air crew had been badly scared, though the ground crews were not enlightened as to the full extent of our weakness. For the next year, until the outbreak of war, we had to retain one squadron ready at ten minutes' notice every day, both day and night, to give battle should the Hun try one of his surprise blitzes.

A month after Munich, a squadron at Duxford was equipped with Spitfires, the first in the RAF. There was great excitement as we had been told that they would do a comfortable 360 mph. Our Gladiators were supposed to do about 260 mph but we were lucky if they came within 10 mph of it. Some of our pilots were selected to go up to Duxford to learn to fly these new fighters. They were away about a fortnight. We heard nothing during that fortnight until one day through a thick haze we saw a tiny, pretty aeroplane flying at least twice as fast as anything we had ever seen before. It vanished almost as soon as it appeared and left us astonished, and a little apprehensive about our ability to fly it.

The boys returned and told us all they knew about the Spitfire. Yes! It did more than 360 mph. It handled like a dream. It could be looped and rolled and was the perfect aeroplane. It all seemed incredible.

Autumn gave way to winter and once again in the cold London mist I thought of the sunshine on the brilliant snow of the Tyrol. Bob Blake and my old Australian friend Lew Johnston applied for permission to make a trip once more to Austria. To my surprise, the request was granted and we all found ourselves bound for the sunny south.

As we sped to Folkestone the three of us debated the changes which would have taken place in Austria since the seizure by Germany. We had discovered that three of our guides were to be the same as previously. This was of the greatest interest to me because these men were all of Nazi sympathies before the last visit and we would now see the situation in the clearer light of first-hand experience.

My interest in international politics, however, suffered a partial setback at Ostend as our party of three was joined by three girls. The conversation naturally took a personal turn and before we reached our destination I found that one of our fair friends, Helen, had lived in Germany for nearly a year. She was meeting her Austrian boyfriend on this trip who happened to be one of our guides. He was a Nazi and a company leader in the SS, which I was told was Hitler's elite corps. I think it was then that I became strongly prejudiced against Nazis in general and SS troops in particular!

Our entrance into Austria was very different from that of twelve months earlier. The Nazi customs officials, looking distinctly like army troops, with large jackboots and peaked caps, moved everywhere. One coarse-looking brute spat some remark to me in German which I did not understand but fortunately my female friend, who spoke fluent German, sorted out the trouble. I never did find out what it was about but we were permitted to enter the country.

It was obviously a very different Austria. All along the railway route were signs of war, camouflaged military trucks, soldiers everywhere, while here and there were squads drilling or receiving instruction in the use of various pieces of equipment. Everywhere floated the Nazi swastika.

Eventually we arrived at our destination, which was St Anton. We were to have been accommodated in one of the local hotels but when our guides met us they were very disturbed and apologetic and explained that at the last minute the Nazis had commandeered all accommodation for troop manoeuvres. However, they had managed to find a small hotel in the nearby village and they had arranged for all of us to be billeted around at various village houses and have our meals and headquarters at the hotel. There was much excitement on meeting our guides and searching for familiar faces. I got one of my friends to one side and asked him how he liked being a real Nazi. He looked slightly anxious and put his finger to his lips. 'Later,' he said, 'when we are alone. Sometime I will tell you but do not mention it until I do.'

We picked up our baggage and moved off. At a street corner was a bunch of rough-looking louts in uniform. The leader of our party was aggressively challenged with 'Heil Hitler'. He immediately answered, 'Heil Hitler.' My friend said to me in a whisper, 'You see!' Later, as we were spread out climbing up a steep slope, he said, 'Always answer "Heil Hitler" if you value your life. It is very dangerous not to do so.'

In a couple of days I felt as if I had never left Austria. It seemed impossible for a year to have slipped past since I had been there before.

My friend Helmuth Fally came up from Innsbruck to see me. He was unable to be with us for the whole trip as he could not get leave. However, he came up on Saturday morning and stayed until the following evening. We had two very pleasant days together.

On my previous visit he had confided to me that he was an undercover National Socialist. He had firmly believed that Hitler had something to offer Austria. I was anxious to know how he felt now as I had a very high regard for Helmuth's sincerity and judgement. The first time I asked him he evaded the question. There were very few people with us but it was clear that he did not want to talk.

The following morning it was arranged that Helmuth and I would go off for a short excursion on our own up one of the local alps, where he would give me some special tuition. We climbed for a couple of hours. It was a typically beautiful midwinter's day and up near the top of one of the lesser peaks Helmuth stopped. He stamped his skis around in the waist-deep snow and made a firmer platform in it about three feet below the level of the surrounding snow, then he took his skis off and sat down. I did likewise. We were out of sight, even if there had been any skiers in the near vicinity. We had seen no other humans for the past hour. Helmuth was being ultra-cautious.

'Now we can talk,' he said, reassuring himself by carefully surveying the scenery for a complete circle. 'You think I'm being too cautious, Gordon? You cannot be too cautious in Austria today. I know I am still a magistrate but it is intolerable. I am not allowed to dispense justice. I must do exactly as the party leader tells me to do. It is hopeless. I want to escape from it. Can you help?'

'Me help? How can I help?' I said.

'Maybe you know somebody who could provide employment for me or a room to live in until I can find some employment.'

I explained to Helmuth that I had no relatives in England who could help. I could not smuggle him into an Air Force camp and I was at a loss to know what to do.

'You must come down to Innsbruck and see what happens now in Austria,' he said. 'It is terrible. We have been completely fooled by the Nazis. They have tricked us into submission without a fight.

'Lies! Lies! And still more lies! It is unbelievable! I cannot live with my conscience and remain a magistrate. If I do not send people to the concentration camps when I am told to even though they are innocent – some of them are my friends – I will be sent there myself. You never come back from those camps.' He gave a shudder.

For the next half hour Helmuth talked. He obviously wanted to get it off his chest.

'There is going to be a war,' he said finally. 'Hitler is going to try to conquer the world. All party members know this. You must win it. It is too late for us. We are already conquered. The national socialists are incredibly evil. If they conquer the world, civilisation will go back to another Dark Age. It will be made worse by the tyrants having all the aids of modern science to help keep the world in slavery.'

I was astonished and dismayed by his outburst and at the sense of horror with which the Nazis had filled my friend. Helmuth was no fantasising youth. He was a mature man, perhaps prematurely aged by the horrors he was witnessing. I tried to soften his mood but he only tried the harder to convince me.

'Tomorrow you and Lew come down to Innsbruck and spend the evening with me. You can stay the night and go back on Tuesday morning. I will show you some of the things that go on in that place. I will show you what hundreds and thousands of national socialist thugs and terrorists are doing to this nation all over Germany and Austria. I will show you what will happen to you if you cannot win the war that is coming. You will not like it, but you must see to believe it.'

I did not believe that a country like Austria could be conquered without a blow.

'It is not only Austria, it is the whole of Germany and in a few years, the whole of Europe, and, if you lose, the world.'

I felt Helmuth was being too theatrical, something I had not suspected in him before, but I agreed to go to Innsbruck.

On Monday afternoon, Lew and I caught the train for Vienna at St Anton Station. Helmuth would meet us at Innsbruck. The trip down was fascinating. Groups of the local peasantry joined the train at each stop. Equally large or larger groups were on the stations to bid farewell to the travellers. Almost without exception the groups each had a harp and others in the group had accordions, zithers or clarinets. They would take over a third or more of a carriage, and then as we rumbled on our way they'd start to sing. I'd always believed that the European peasants were a miserable, poverty-stricken and oppressed lot but these showed no signs of poverty or misery. Their singing was happy and contagious and I only wished that I knew more German so that I could appreciate the finer points of their songs.

Outside the train the spectacular alps that run down either side of the Inn Valley reached up into the deep-blue sky. Snow covered everything and every half-hour or so we would pass one of the 'schlosses', castles on little mini-alps which seemed to pop up along the valley every few miles. In past ages these had been avidly acquired by the feudal leaders who had built what in those days were impregnable fortresses. Now they looked like some half-forgotten memory of a fairy tale become real. I almost expected a giant in seven-league boots to materialise, or a fire-breathing dragon.

But if a counter influence was natural in such beautiful surroundings, it was there all right. At every railway stop groups of a hundred or more grey-uniformed infantry soldiers were parading with machine guns and tommy guns. They carried out their parade-ground routines with grim, severe faces. War and death were not to be forgotten.

As on the trip from the border to St Anton, at every village and township along the railway line we saw troops, mostly wearing German grey uniform but some in white and wearing or carrying skis – alpine troops. Others, just a few, wore the black of the SS regiments, the military wing of the Nazi Party, the executioners of the Third Reich. They sent a shiver down my spine in spite of the warm Austrian midday sun. We duly arrived in Innsbruck and Helmuth was there to meet us. As we walked to his flat, he also warned us about the Nazi Brownshirts. He said that, while they had no authority as such, if you tried to oppose them they would turn nasty and could well beat you up. There was no redress against them from the law, so it was best to give them a wide berth.

We arrived at his apartment after half an hour's walk and he welcomed us with a glass of beer. Later, he said, we would go to one or two of the beer gardens and join in the usual evening's activities. We talked for a while about the snow, the weather, the scenery down the Inn Valley, the peasants and their addiction to folk music, and the history of the Tyrol, which had given Napoleon his only defeat except Waterloo and the Russian winter. After a light supper we went out to the first of the beer gardens.

It was a much larger room than those beer gardens at St Anton and Bludenz. There were probably two hundred people sitting in groups at tables. We sat at a table for four and the other chair was removed so that we could have the table to ourselves. As was the custom, there was a band up on a small stage. It comprised a harp, a zither, a couple of clarinets, an accordion and a set of drums. They played all the well-known local tunes and everyone sang along. There was not much chance for conversation as the music was continuous, and as the evening progressed the volume of the sound rose.

Then it happened! I was enjoying it all so much that I had completely forgotten the purpose of our visit. Instead of the next item by the band, there was a sudden hush. Helmuth warned, 'No matter what happens say nothing. They are coming in the door now.'

I looked across at the entrance. Four men came into the room. Two wore raincoats and felt hats – the Gestapo. The other two were in the black uniform of the SS. They moved to the first table. The two in raincoats appeared to have photographs in their hands. With agonising slowness they scrutinised each face in turn at that table. The whole room held its breath. Then they moved on to the next table. After an age they moved to the next – then the next. No one moved. For the next half-hour there was no sound except for the jackboots of the SS men and the sinister shuffling of the Gestapo men as they moved from face to face. Finally they reached the table next to ours. The tension was unbelievable. Sweat was already on my hands and I felt it also on my face but dared not wipe it off. Yet I had nothing to fear unless I resembled one of those photographs. Fear is contagious and I discovered that I had little resistance to that type of fear.

It was our turn. Each Gestapo man took his time. I looked back at the first one. Sweat on my face must have told him how I felt. He was a nasty-looking customer with a very mean look in his eyes. He moved on. Then it was the other Gestapo man's turn. He looked even meaner. He was short and strongly built. The SS men stood at attention next to our table. They were armed with Luger pistols and there were short bayonet type weapons on their belts, presumably for use if they ran out of ammunition.

After what seemed an eternity they moved on to the next table. I waited until they were several tables away before I pulled out a handkerchief to wipe my face and hands. I looked at the others. Our reactions had all been the same.

Eventually the visitors left and a low buzz of conversation built up. They had not arrested anybody but they had effectively terrified everyone in the hall. The band struck up again but the spirit was gone. One by one the patrons rose to go home. I looked at Helmuth, who said in a low voice, 'They didn't arrest anybody here tonight so would you like to go onto another beer garden to see what the effect is like?'

Lew and I agreed that we had seen all that we wanted to see. We finished our wine but somehow it didn't taste so good. Then we got up and walked back to Helmuth's flat.

It was a long time before I got to sleep. The effect of this technique on the millions of beer-garden-loving Germans and Austrians was obviously devastating. That, plus the ever-present fear of the knock on the door in the middle of the night by the Gestapo and the SS had totally changed a pleasant and civilised way of life to one of permanent anxiety and fear.

What a different Austria to the one I had grown to love so much on my first visit. The people were the same – at least the ones I mixed with were the same – but a brutal element had been mobilised to terrify the people into abject compliance with the slightest whim of the new ruling class. No longer did you hear the ancient greeting, 'Gruss Gott' (God is good), but the aggressive 'Heil Hitler!'

Lew and I discussed it on the way back to St Anton the following morning. We both realised for the first time that Hitler had not finished with the takeover of Austria. The ease of this operation had fired him for more. Sooner or later the people of Europe who wanted to remain independent would have to face Hitler and stop him, and Hitler was very strong. He would not abandon his ambitions without a fight. It meant one thing only – war!

The sun shone brightly outside the carriage window. The Alps and the valley flats in their winter white were sights which normally filled my heart with delight, but there was little cheer in contemplating our own futures. War was the last thing we wanted. War meant death to almost all whose trade was flying aeroplanes. Once the pilot operated in a battle zone, his life expectancy dropped to days – a few weeks if he was very lucky. Neither Lew nor I had the slightest reason to believe that we enjoyed that sort of luck.

Back in St Anton after our Innsbruck visit, it was once more the carefree fun of the ski slopes. Our friends and guides, Paul and Fritz, disliked Heinie, the SS captain, and saw to it that Heinie and Helen were at all the parties. They also made sure that they had their share of the ski waltzes with Helen, making it very difficult for Heinie to get her alone.

For the last week the more experienced skiers, who included Lew, Bob and myself, joined up with the other experienced group, which included Helen, and we spent the days going on cross-country expeditions to other villages in the Inn Valley.

The days slipped past like a downhill ski run and before we knew it, on our last night of ski dances and merrymaking, Paul and Fritz sought out Lew, Bob and myself and we began what turned out to be a somewhat emotionally charged evening.

The two German boys were convinced that we would never see one another again in this world. They believed that war was inevitable and we would kill one another.

I had recovered somewhat from the Innsbruck visit and hoped fervently that they were wrong. We all got very drunk and swore everlasting brotherhood and friendship. I had not realised how emotional the Austrians could become and when the tears began to well up in their eyes I realised how deeply they felt. They were delightful companions and it was amazing how close we had become in such a short time.

We staggered off to bed at about three in the morning, and our farewells the following day were painful in more ways than one.

Back in England, I tried to interest people in the approach of war. The more socialistic press, which had for so long been opposed to any form of rearmament, continued a policy credited to the ostrich.

It was not necessary to interest the Air Force boys; they were already convinced and were already steeling their nerves for the coming struggles. The change in life in the mess became very noticeable at this time. Parties became more frequent and their temper became wilder. It was probably that the lads realised that collectively their time was almost up. Soon the old band would be split up and probably most of them would be killed. It was well known that the average life of a fighter pilot in the last war had been six weeks. It was highly likely in view of our numerical inferiority that we would not last much longer this time – if as long!

Some of our boys went over to Biggin Hill one day about a month later to hear a talk by Winston Churchill, who was visiting the aerodrome. They came back looking very grim. Winston had convinced them that the war was inevitable and he expected it to come in the early spring. We thought of our Gladiators and their chances with the Messerschmitts.

Towards the end of winter one ray of sunshine lit up the dark atmosphere of those threatening days. One misty afternoon, a small, sleek aeroplane of unprecedented beauty flew around our aerodrome and, after displaying a remarkable turn of speed, dropped down its wheels and glided in to a perfect landing. It taxied up to a hangar, a pilot in civvies got out, put on a civilian hat and walked up to the duty pilot and reported that he had delivered a Spitfire to 74 Squadron.

It was the first Spitfire for our station, the first ever seen by many of us and as this squadron was the second to be fitted with them they were still very rare. Within a month our entire station was equipped with these beautiful machines and we had parted with our old Gladiators. It was a sad day when we said goodbye to our old machines, as they had been our trusted steeds for nearly two years and had proved very reliable.

Our new aircraft were smaller and very nearly twice as fast. At first we were all a little frightened of them. After two large wings, one small wing did not seem sufficient to support us in the air. However, we soon found that we could do anything with a Spitfire that could be done with any other fighter, and a whole lot more. There was much intense excitement in learning to handle them and we became far more attached to them than we had ever been to any of our previous types. As a work of art, I doubt if any machine ever made approached it for its exquisitely beautiful lines. There was no hint in its profiles of the stark purpose for which it was conceived.

Reginald Mitchell, its designer, had forced himself to the ultimate of human endurance to produce the machine in time, for he was convinced that his nation and the world were in urgent need of it. His conviction was prophetic, and although his exertions caused his all too premature death, his creation lived on in the hands of equally devoted tradesmen and manufacturers arrived in the RAF just in the nick of time. Here they became the chief instruments, in the hands of similarly dedicated men led by Sir Hugh Dowding, who struggled against formidable odds at the political and Air Council level to prevent them being squandered in futile campaigns in France. On these few machines the fate of the entire world was to hang.

However, early in 1939 we had little knowledge that the strange new machines we were suddenly expected to fly would prove of such historic moment.

My first flight was on a squally, wet day with low cloud at eight hundred feet and visibility limited to a mile or so. A stiff, cold breeze blew in from the west and so I took off towards London at about three o'clock one afternoon in February.

The engine had a heavier, more penetrating roar than the Gladiator's radial engine and the greater acceleration was quite appreciable. The cockpit was tiny and almost cramped after the cockpits of earlier machines.

In a few seconds it was in the air, and I changed hands on the stick to pump up the undercarriage. This was achieved by means of a hand pump on the right-hand side of the cockpit which operated a hydraulic circuit.

The Spitfire was very sensitive in the elevator controls and the use of the hydraulic pump by the right hand produced a slight reaction in the left on the stick. I suddenly got one of the frights of my life. The Spitfire porpoised so violently that I was almost flung out of the cockpit on the up stroke and returned with even greater violence on the down stroke.

After an extremely uncomfortable period of experimentation, during which I became an airborne jack-in-the-box, I discovered that if I wedged my left elbow against my hip I could pump the wheels up without involuntarily abandoning the aeroplane.

This discovery led to the completion of part 'A' of the take-off technique. Part 'B' then demanded attention, for the engine was howling at maximum boost and revs and I had to operate the pitch control on the propeller (a new device) and so reduce the engine revs. Then the power had to be reduced to the normal cruising setting.

This considerably reduced the clatter and after pulling over the hood I looked around only to realise I was above clouds, so I descended cautiously until I saw the ground. I was over green fields, whereas I should have been over London. The next half-hour was spent trying to locate my position, which would have been easy enough in clear weather but in such conditions presented many headaches.

At last I located the Thames and realised that my preoccupation with the undercarriage had occupied sufficient time to pass over London, so I flew back while keeping visual contact with the ground. After nearly an hour I set it down on the grass of our aerodrome, very conscious that this new craft was just about twice as fast as anything I had ever flown before.

Pilots are human. Most of them like to show off when the opportunity permits, and our group was no exception. One showy piece of flying which became popular overnight was achieved by retracting the undercarriage on the take-off run while the aeroplane remained only a few inches above the runway. When done properly, the aeroplane did not appear to lift off in the usual way; the undercarriage simply came up. At the end of the runway the Spitfire was lifted abruptly into a very steep climb. It was quite impressive, at least to the initiated, because of the difficulty of pumping the undercarriage up with the right hand and maintaining level flight a few inches above the ground with the left hand while doing so.

Once the undercarriage was up, the lowest part of the Spitfire was the propeller, which, being twelve feet in diameter, was well below the underside of the machine. Of course, once a demonstration of this trick had been seen it was copied by every other pilot who thought he could do it.

I think Jack Kennedy, the other Australian, was the first to try it in our group, and his example was followed by Nicholas, who hated Kennedy and was determined that anything Kennedy could do, he could and would do better. Thus, before the interested audience of all the pilots of 65 Squadron and most of 54 and 74, Nicholas made his attempt to prove his superiority. Nicholas was a very capable pilot, but something went wrong – probably he misjudged the flying speed of the Spitfire's take-off in a nose-down attitude. In any event, as his wheels came up to the retracted position, Nicky sank a few inches into the grass strip, low enough for the tips of the propeller blades to hack an impressive shower of grass divots which were hurled out over a distance of about two hundred yards. Very impressive!

It looked as if Nicky was going to plough into the ground, but he suddenly hauled the Spitfire up and managed to keep going around the circuit. He came into wind and landed normally, then taxied up to the squadron workshop. When he switched the engine off, the metal blades of the propeller were all curved back like the petals of an overblown water lily. Poor Nicky! Was his face red! Every time he looked at Nicky, Kennedy laughed for the next month.

5

Phoney War

Our hopes for peace declined as 1939 progressed. I doubt whether any of the pilots in our station had the slightest desire for war. Those who had studied the subject knew that a fighter pilot's expectancy of life in the First World War was something under four weeks, and I am sure none of us had that sort of self-confidence which gives the assurance that we would survive when all others were dead. Nor could we anticipate any reduction of the cruel law of averages in a world conflagration. The drift to war was an unforgettable experience because, for us, war had this singularly unpleasant significance.

While we were being reequipped with Spitfires we paid several visits to the Supermarine works at Southampton. Here I met one of the outstanding personalities in the Spitfire saga – Jeffrey Quill, the test pilot who, with Mitchell, had nursed and watched over the Spitfire from its birth to its maturity when it took its place in the front line of the world's defences.

Quill was a wiry, athletic type of about average height, with a quiet, humorous voice. His looks gave no impression of the importance of the man in the scheme of things. I could not help thinking that this man, if he were doing the same job in America, would without question be hailed as a national hero. As it was, few outside the little world of those who made the Spitfire or flew it knew his name. Within that group, however, his name was already legend.

Jeffrey Quill and I had several pleasant hours in the course of the next few days as our eighteen Spitfires were collected and taken off to their new home. Much of my apprehension at flying this new machine was dispelled one morning when Quill gave a most polished demonstration of stunt flying, finishing the act by coming in to land upside down, pumping the undercarriage up in this position, then half-rolling out at the last minute to touch his wheels in a perfect three-pointer on the grass runway.

As the year rolled along we became very proficient at formation flying, and after a public demonstration one Empire Air Day in May the Air Ministry sent down a photographer to take some shots of our composite flight. This was usually led by Sam Saunders, with myself, Nicholas and McPherson making the second three. On the day of the photograph, Sam's place was taken by Bob Stanford Tuck, and the photos obtained became the standard formation photos for Air Ministry public relations for years to come.

With midsummer I hoped to get some leave and meet Helen – who had thrown over her SS boyfriend because he was too bossy – in London, but first we had to complete our August manoeuvres. We had exercises to carry out with the French Air Force. This, no doubt, was intended to boost the morale of the Allied powers and intimidate the Hun.

We went through all the motions of preparing for war and were advised that the French would put on a raid of bombers escorted by fighters. In due course the raid materialised and we were sent off on a 'scramble'. A terrific number of aeroplanes were eventually sighted, literally hundreds, it seemed. We had been briefed not to fly too close as the Air Ministry did not want any risks of collision. On approaching closer, however, we noticed that they were mostly old bombers of the biplane type and most woefully slow.

We stood some way off them and indulged in aerobatics, and even though we were looping and doing stall turns and other exercises which keep a plane more or less in the one spot, they still hardly seemed to move. The exercise may have heartened the French, but it did not provide us with much hope. If that was all the French could do, God help us!

Our squadron was given the role of day and night fighters with Spitfires. The weather was good most of the time but towards the end it deteriorated. Bomber Command sent wave after wave of their bombers, mostly obsolete, on raids on London, coming in from the coast of Holland.

Already some of us knew of the existence of radar, which we watched track a German Lufthansa civil aeroplane from Amsterdam to London, and we carried out some quite accurate interceptions during these exercises. The machinery of Fighter Command was in full swing though the number of squadrons was pitifully few and many were still armed only with Gladiators. Our exercises were conducted from all around the aerodrome in tents, the hangars being vacated.

On the last night of the exercise we had to test the first general try-out of flying in blackout conditions. London was to be blacked out and we were to check it from the air. The weather grew poor. There was no moon and heavy cloud had developed at ten thousand feet. The sky was completely overcast. Smaller clouds were scudding in at four hundred feet, which is rather low for night flying. Two lights were placed on the aerodrome by which to land, giving little more light than a candle.

Fortunately, just before the blackout was completed my flight sergeant friend, Macpherson, landed from a previous patrol. He came and said, 'The weather's not too good and you won't see a thing after take-off. Most of the lights were out when I landed and there was no horizon to go by. I think we ought to scrub it. There's cloud at four hundred feet too. It's too low. You know how quickly you lose height in a Spit if you get your nose down, well there's not enough room between four hundred feet and the ground on a night like this. Besides, flames from the exhaust pipes blind you.'

The CO asked me what I felt about it. I told him I had practised instrument take-offs as I had nearly come to grief once before on a dark night and had decided that they could be made in a Spitfire if necessary. I would have a go at it.

Macpherson said, 'Well, don't put your wheels up until you get to five hundred feet.' It was good advice.

'B' Flight commander, Sammy, and I had a short conference and decided we would take off before the weather got worse. Besides, it was essential to test the blackout.

We took off and it was indeed black. I flew straight to two thousand feet before I touched the retracting gear. In those days it required sixty pumps on the 'village pump' to get the wheels up on a Spitfire and involved flying left-handed. This was not easy on a dark night. The exhaust pipes threw out a blinding glare in front of me and I could see absolutely nothing but the arc of the propeller which, though painted black, looked white against the background of the sky. The blackout was a success all right, though to the south were two large fires which could occasionally be seen through the lower clouds. There was a similar one north of our aerodrome. I wondered what they were.

After an hour and a half of flying on instruments, I eventually succeeded in landing and made out a report. Sam landed about the same time. To my surprise, I found we were recipients of congratulations from the AOC. It was later that we heard that on the southern aerodrome they had not been so lucky. Both pilots who attempted the blackout take-off had crashed and were burnt to death while one of the two who took off north of us had suffered a similar fate. Altogether six pilots attempted to take off and three were killed. All were senior and experienced pilots.

The exercises were over and we half-hoped for a little leave. Our training for the last six months, culminating in the summer exercises, had been arduous. However, though a few of the boys were released, only two could go from the squadron at a time. Prospects were poor. My own leave was postponed as I was attached to an Army anti-aircraft camp in Devon in the middle of August.

By this time, the Danzig trouble was beginning to simmer. Mr Chamberlain had previously guaranteed the integrity of Poland after Hitler's annexation of Czechoslovakia, so it was a case of waiting and watching again. I admit I felt very anxious as I hated the idea of war. To me it meant all forms of unpleasantness, death and disaster. I could see nothing to recommend it.

On the opening day of the gunnery school a brigadier gave an opening address and his words struck dismay into many hearts. The Germans were expected to attack Poland at any time and were almost completely mobilised. Poland would not give way and we were to prepare for war.

The newspapers told the same story. After the day's work we adjourned to a coastal town nearby for a swim in a swimming pool as the day had been hot. There we made the acquaintance of two youths who announced that they were in the Merchant Navy and on the RN reserve. They were to report to their naval base immediately. The Navy was mobilising.

Two days later an urgent telegram demanded my immediate return to my squadron. It was on. There were still about ten days to go to the end of the month.

I returned from the Army to find Norman Jones had gone, posted to Training Command and myself as the new commander of 'A' Flight. A surprise all round, and my first command!

There were other changes. Several new faces appeared. Walker, an English volunteer reservist who had been called up, and Wigg, a New Zealander presumably there to keep the New Zealand content of the squadron up to normal now that we had lost Jones. Wigg, too, was a volunteer reservist (VR).

'B' Flight had some new faces too; Hart, an English lad, and Tom Smart;

both were VRs. As 'regulars' we had our reservations about the reservists – no full-time airman likes to think that a man can work for five days a week as an accountant or salesman and be an efficient pilot by flying for the other two days of the week. It was a slight on our professional status.

Looking back on it, our attitude was due to hurt professional pride rather than any cold logic. The average fighter pilot was not allowed to fly more than an average of two hours per week due to the pathetic shortage of aeroplanes and the sheer impossibility of getting any more hours out of those aeroplanes in the time available. Had we been permitted, we would have flown ten hours a week as a minimum.

For the three pre-war years I was with the RAF, we were desperately short of aeroplanes. Most squadrons were lucky to have twelve and at least two of these were continually undergoing some form of maintenance. Two more were kept as 'command reserves' and could not be flown, which meant that we were lucky to have four aeroplanes per flight to fly each day.

Normally we flew from 9.00 in the morning to 4.00 in the evening, except in winter when for the most part we did not fly at all, due to the impossible weather. Indeed, I had frequently seen the hangar doors shut for six weeks at a time, with no hope of flying. Even in the better summer weather we often had periods where we were unable to fly more than half the time due to incessant rain, storms or other normal inclemencies of the northern European weather. For those interminable days, when flying was impossible, we just sat around and shivered in wintertime and fretted in summer. There was nothing to do except talk flying, which for the most part we did incessantly.

Add to this that we shut the squadron down for a month each year in September and went off for our annual holidays, and it is not hard to see that we were very much underemployed. True, there was a certain amount of academic theory we were obliged to master, but this too could be covered in a couple of weeks of good, concentrated effort. The reservists for the most part flew on weekends. They flew obsolete types of aeroplanes. These were not only more readily available, but there were also more of them per squadron. They were mostly less complicated than the later models and their vagaries better known, their serviceability better and their productivity in terms of flying hours much better. They were only marginally slower than the front-line aircraft, but this, of course, was given tremendous significance by the professionals – yet looking back on it now, the difference both in performance and complexity was negligible. The important thing was that the reservists, by making themselves available for the 120-odd days which weekends and holidays provided, were able to average as many hours each per year as the regulars, who 'worked' for some 200 days, but who were flying at about half the rate per day. Generally the reservists were comparable in ability with the professionals, but because they were aware of an implied inferiority, they tried harder, and that too had its effect on their effectiveness. Thus, when the Hurricanes and the Spitfires became available, a pilot of an old Hawker Hart or Demon or Fury was equally able to cope with the new aeroplane as were the pilots of the Gladiators or Gauntlets, even if the latter were unhappy to concede the point.

However, as the threat of war became a certainty, the availability of pilots became the all-important factor. If there were no regulars to build up our numbers, then even the reservists were welcome!

The situation with Poland deteriorated and we moved our aeroplanes out into the aerodrome and all hands set to work filling sandbags to protect the aeroplanes from bomb blast. Tents were put up and for several days life was poor as we had nothing but cold food and irregular meals coupled with ugly warnings from the higher command.

London may be subject to raids of up to 500 aeroplanes simultaneously, they said. We reckoned up. We might muster 200 if we were lucky – five to two if every aeroplane intercepted. It was a bit hard, but it had to be faced.

There were no wild scenes when Mr Chamberlain soberly told the world that we were at war at eleven o'clock on that bright September morning. There were no shouts, only about a dozen very serious faces around a little battery wireless set one of the boys had bought from a second-hand shop. Those boys were too realistic to indulge in any sentimental or superficial enthusiasm.

Cookie, our CO, was unmoved and merely said, 'Well boys, we're on active service now' much as he might have said, 'Has anybody got a cigarette?'

We learned with disgust that Russia was going to side with Germany and had even volunteered assistance to the Huns in the attack on Poland.

There were several false alarms during the next few days but nothing very exciting happened at our aerodrome except for one episode. The war was just three days old when the defence system was tested. A searchlight battery on Mersea Island on the coast of Essex reported a flight of unidentified aircraft passing overhead in the direction of

London. At Hornchurch we were relaxing in the sun shortly before midday when the field telephone rang. Ron Wigg answered it and shouted, 'Squadron shamble, Angels 10!'

We raced to our planes, strapped in and taxied out, Cookie in the lead. We formed up and the twelve of us took off in a single formation into a cloudless blue sky. Control gave us a course to steer and we headed east towards the coast. My mind was in turmoil. This was probably it! Control turned us on to another course with instructions to look out for a formation of 'ten-plus bogies'.

'Bogey' was the code word for unidentified aircraft. With all the song and dance we had to go through before we were allowed to fly at this time, it seemed impossible to me that twelve aeroplanes over England could be unaccounted for. It had to be an enemy raid. Puffs of black smoke appeared in front of us. Our own anti-aircraft guns were shooting at us! It was crazy. A squadron of aeroplanes appeared near us but they turned out to be another squadron of Spitfires.

Obeying instructions, we turned north then west. More flak joined us from the guns below. Cookie's voice came over the radio as we altered course.

'Control! Stop those stupid Army bastards using us for target practice!'

Control replied, 'Say again Petal Leader.'

Cookie was so angry he bellowed into the microphone and overloaded it so nothing could be made of his tirade.

'Blue Two calling Petal Leader, we are being attacked by Spitfires, seven o'clock high!'

I looked over my left shoulder to see six Spitfires diving on us. The leader of the second section was firing at us. Black smoke trailed from his wings in eight narrow trails of sooty smoke. As Cookie turned left towards them they shot past us – the Tigers! 74 Squadron, one of our own Hornchurch squadrons, was shooting at us in conditions of perfect visibility. Somebody checked the letters on the plane firing the guns.

Cookie called Control again, 'What the hell goes on Control? Our sister squadron has just attacked us in anger. For God's sake stop this bloody nonsense before we are all shot down!'

A series of flustering orders came over the radio and we were sent off on one course after another. More aeroplanes were sighted but it was obvious they were more of ours. At last the order came to 'pancake'. We throttled back, nosed down and headed for base, four miles below.

We landed, taxied in and parked our planes, then gathered in the tent to hear Cookie pouring scorn over the controller.

'What the hell goes on there? Why are you sooling us on to one another? Why did the guns blast us? Doesn't any bastard there know what's going on?' And so it went on.

News came in that two Hurricanes from North Weald had been shot down by Spitfires from 74 Squadron! So they weren't satisfied with shooting us up, they had to attack a Hurricane squadron as well! Who was the trigger-happy idiot in 74 doing all the shooting?

The post-mortem went on for some days. Blunder had been compounded by blunder. No enemy planes were within a hundred miles of Britain that morning but that hadn't stopped the foul-ups. Slowly we unwound and got back to normal – if sitting out on an aerodrome on a hot summer's day waiting for a war to start was normal.

The Polish campaign came to an end, with it the announcement that Germany and Russia had partitioned the country and all military opposition had been overcome. As we moved into winter, except for an isolated raid or two and the raid on the Firth of Forth – where the Scottish auxiliary squadrons showed their mettle – there were no incidents. As the winter dragged on and it became clear that no major air action was likely against us, so our state of preparation and tension gradually relaxed.

In October we moved to Northolt on the other side of London. Here we almost froze to death in tents. Later, leaky wooden shacks were supplied. There was three feet of snow piled all over the aerodrome. It was bitterly cold but we had to grin and bear it and shovel snow off the runways.

Cookie developed appendicitis and went off to hospital. An Auxiliary Air Force squadron leader named George Pinkerton came down from Scotland to be our CO. This was indeed something new – a squadron of regulars, or mostly regulars, commanded by an auxiliary officer. Pinkerton, however, did have one moral advantage over all of us. He had shot down two German bombers during the big German raid on the naval base in the Firth of Forth, and in the process had been shot at. Some thirty-odd German bombers had attacked the fleet, presumably in the hope that it would not be very well protected, as two auxiliary squadrons were known to be defending the area. They never repeated the attempt, as most of the attacking force were destroyed and the few who escaped had a 400-mile strip of North Sea to traverse in bombers badly holed by bullets – an unenviable experience.

George Pinkerton had been one of the star performers and now that the opportunity presented itself he was rewarded with a DFC and the command of a regular squadron. At the same time, Bob Stanford Tuck and Brian Kingcome were posted from 65 to new squadrons which were being formed in the command, where they became flight commanders. Some of our sergeant pilots were promoted to officer rank and posted to new squadrons also. For a while they were not replaced and our squadron numbers were reduced accordingly.

When hostilities were declared, there were not many more than thirty squadrons in Fighter Command. In the next few months this figure was to be doubled as existing squadrons were milked of pilots and new boys coming in from the training schools took their places. All these new boys were volunteer reservists or auxiliaries. By this time our squadron was nearly half reservists.

At Northolt, I inherited the meteorological flights. They had a Gladiator for the purpose and most days, at dawn, midday and dusk, I took off and climbed to thirty thousand feet, taking wet and dry bulb thermometer readings at intervals of a thousand feet and calling these figures on the transmitter at two-minute intervals. In this way the operations room was able to work out wind velocities at the various altitudes, and from the temperature readings the 'Met Men' were able to amuse themselves for hours doing just what no one seemed to know.

It was, however, very exacting flying as the conditions were frequently almost impossible, with a cloud base below five hundred feet and visibility below half a mile. It was the sort of experience which was good for you if you survived, because you knew that there was scarcely anything worse short of fog. If fog set in, then the pilot was supposed to bail out, but not before all possible diversions to other aerodromes had been tried unsuccessfully.

Winter actually gave us more leisure time as our hours of duty were from an hour before sunrise to an hour after sunset. During that period we were tied to our aerodrome. That meant long hours in the summer time but in winter we could have quite a few hours to spend in the local pub or in the local town. We were fortunate in being close to London for we could catch an electric train and be in Piccadilly in thirty minutes. We were able to get to London and visit the nightclubs and theatres, see our girlfriends and make merry. Up to that time the rationing was hardly felt by anyone. Good food was still plentiful, so were beer and wines. The atmosphere of all our parties was 'eat, drink and be merry for tomorrow we die'. The pressure of living was rather high and many a party went through to the dawn.

The 'Phoney War', as the winter of 1939–40 was dubbed, was far from a dull time. Northolt was the centre of training for the pilots of Fighter Command in tactics. As the school was located at our aerodrome it only meant going to another hut every day for a week or two for me. Fighter pilots from all over England came down to do the course so it was really a good place to be as I met many of my old friends. Here we analysed the reports from France and tried out many experiments, a number of which were carried out by Johnnie Welford, Jack Kennedy and myself. These were intended to establish whether or not dogfights were still possible in Spitfires and Hurricanes.

The older school of pilots believed that speeds had reached a stage where dogfights were over, due to the excessive forces involved in turns at speeds in the 400 mph range. This was misleading as both the Spitfire and the Hurricane could fly at speeds below 100 mph and both would sustain a high rate of turn at about 140 mph. Due to the very low wing loading of these aeroplanes they could turn in very tight circles at this speed and continue to do so indefinitely. Over a series of experiments and demonstrations lasting about ten weeks we succeeded in convincing the experts that they were wrong and that dogfights were possible.

Camera guns were fitted to our planes which took photographs on cine film and these, after development, were studied in great detail.

We found out from an Me 109E that had come into our hands from France that its wing loading was almost twice as high as ours, so this augured well for our chances if we had to mix it with them. One advantage the Germans did enjoy was a constant-speed propeller, which in many ways compensated for their higher wing loading. This, in effect, gave them the equivalent of an automatic gear change. It also gave them the advantage of a better rate of climb and an almost ten thousand-foot advantage in their 'serious ceiling'.

Much of the work was tedious repetition of manoeuvre after manoeuvre and frequently involved the same drill day after day at varying heights up to twenty-five thousand feet, which was about our limit with the inefficient propellers we had at that time. It sometimes involved five or six flights a day to explore the possibilities of exploiting our advantages.

This bit of research attracted quite a deal of attention from the top brass at Fighter Command. We had several visits from the Air Marshals, who, being no longer personally in touch with the current problems of flying, were keen to learn as much as they could by closely following our tests. One exception in this regard was the Air Officer Commanding 11 Group, AVM Keith Park, who frequently flew his own Hurricane but did not have time to spend on the finer points of research.

When the experiments were over, I wrote a paper on our findings which recommended that we should function in elements of two aeroplanes, not three as was the established practice. The section of three was a legacy of the First World War. I might have saved myself the trouble because nobody took the slightest notice of it. It was filed away carefully and forgotten.

I did gain considerable experience in the theory of tactics, if not in actual combat, and this was to be of some use to me in the days which lay ahead.

One evening I met Hughie Edwards again. Hughie had been a cadet on my senior course at Point Cook. He was convalescing at Uxbridge, where he had been hospitalised for some months following a nasty accident the previous winter. He had been flying a Blenheim over the mountains of Cumberland one winter's night when he became trapped in a bad storm with acute ice formation. His plane had iced up and he lost control so he had bailed out. Unfortunately he tangled with the trailing radio aerial, which nearly cut his head off, but before he lost consciousness he pulled his parachute ripcord and this dumped him on the side of one of the Cumberland mountaintops.

Why he did not die from frost bite, exposure and loss of blood no one knows. Two days later a shepherd found him more dead than alive. He was brought down from the mountain and the slow process of patching him up and bringing him back to life began. To add to his problems, one of his legs was badly broken when he hit the rocky mountaintop.

Now, a year later, Hughie was struggling around on crutches. On one of his visits to the local pub I met up with him. Thereafter, we met two or three times a week. Poor Hughie felt very much out of it all and as he had been warned that he would probably not fly again, his spirits were pretty low. I did my best to cheer him up and assure him that he would make it again before long. However, he was still in such a mess I scarcely believed it myself.

Nevertheless, within two years, Hughie was back on flying and to such excellent effect that he collected a VC, a DSO and a DFC to make him Australia's most decorated airman. At the time I met him neither of us knew what the future held. It promised little.

During that winter some forty-two or more German reconnaissance planes were shot down over the coastal waters of eastern England virtually without loss to the intercepting pilots – one or two fighter aeroplanes were lost, but the pilots escaped by parachute.

Several squadrons had gone over to France to join forces with the French Air Force but the balance of kills over there was by no means so favourable as on the home ground. Our squadrons were equipped with Gloster Gladiators or Hawker Hurricanes and the German Messerschmitt Me 109s were far more efficient than the German reconnaissance planes raiding the British east coast and gave a much better account of themselves.

I had my own taste of drama at this time – I took off in a Spitfire to do a weather test one morning. The weather was marginal, and before the other pilots could be sent off one of the flight commanders had to try it out and see if it was suitable for the less experienced.

As I climbed away from the runway, the cockpit and the front of the aeroplane was enveloped in choking white fumes. Somehow the glycol which circulated through the engine and the radiator had burst a pipe and was boiling out everywhere in dense white clouds. The cockpit was rapidly becoming uninhabitable and in desperation I tried the side slipping technique which Sam Balmer had taught me years ago, should I be unlucky enough to be in an aeroplane on fire.

This consisted of flying around in a violent side slip which was generally only possible in an aeroplane enjoying a considerable excess of power.

A Spitfire had the sort of power necessary and by keeping one wing down about thirty degrees from horizontal and keeping the nose up, all the fumes blew over one side. The same was supposed to happen when a plane was on fire and it gave the pilot a chance to get out without being incinerated (providing, of course, the cockpit was not alight).

Thus I was able to see and make an emergency landing by side-slipping right on to the ground. I managed to get away with it, but, as I was to learn later, the great majority of glycol bursts resulted in mid-air explosions as the glycol/air mixture was almost as dangerous as petrol and could be ignited by the flames from the exhaust pipes. It must have been one of my lucky days!

Having passed the course in tactics, I was appointed tactics officer for the squadron. It was my job to keep up to date with what was happening everywhere and advise the CO on what tactics we should adopt. According to the book of rules, we were to operate in sections of three. In these we were supposed to shoot at formations, while maintaining formation ourselves. This was very difficult to achieve and on my recommendation we abandoned this idea in favour of a more individualistic attack.

In working this out we cooperated with a Wellington bomber squadron which had attacked Wilhelmshaven by daylight in the early days of the war. Their losses had been so great that Bomber Command decided to concentrate on night bombing. Jim Brough, an old friend of mine from the days at Point Cook, had been the only survivor out of a flight of six on two consecutive occasions. He had the experience of seeing all his friends on each side explode in mid-air and crash in flames as they were attacked by the Germans' new two-engined Me 110 fighters.

The advice that these boys were able to give us on tactics from the bomber's point of view was most useful. We spent many days at this work before we developed a technique which seemed both satisfactory to ourselves and was agreed upon as sound by the bomber boys.

Not long after this, Jack Kennedy was posted to 238 Squadron as a flight commander.

*

We returned to Hornchurch in the spring and for a few short weeks it seemed as if the war was just a bad fright and that really there was nothing to get excited about. Cookie, our regular CO, had left the squadron to have his appendix removed in October, but he rejoined us at Hornchurch.

The papers were still talking about a 'Phoney War', and there was little real action anywhere. Compared with the massive carnage of the First World War there seemed to be something wrong. It was once said that war is a time of prolonged boredom punctuated by periods of short but intense fear. We were certainly having our share of the boredom. We spent day after day sitting by our aeroplanes unable to fly them because no one could say when the emergency would start.

News filtered in from France where several Hurricane and Gladiator squadrons had been engaged in sporadic skirmishes with German fighters over the Maginot Line but this only emphasised our own inactivity. Some of the boys in France were beginning to knock down some German aeroplanes and in particular a New Zealander named 'Cobber' Kain had made a name for himself, but the army front was quiet, and so was the navy. The air force was busy dropping leaflets over Germany and already one of our Point Cook boys, John Allsop, had been killed in the process.

The Coastal Command boys were busy raiding enemy ports and trying to sink coastal shipping and two squadrons we knew reasonably well had lost most of their original crews in three months, but they were exceptions at that time.

We had one exciting moment to snap us out of our lethargy. One night about two o'clock in the morning the air-raid siren started to wail. I was snug in bed and it was raining outside. Drowsily my mind registered that there was a sound of aero engines fairly near, but I determined not to go to the shelter, and to take a chance and keep warm.

The sound of the engines grew louder and appeared to come from almost directly overhead. Without warning, the hut in which I was sleeping, or trying to, was lit by a brilliant orange flash. A series of explosions soon shifted me from my cosy retreat. Four more explosions were followed by a scream and a very heavy bang which shook the hut like an earthquake.

I charged down the corridor to the shelter at the end of the hut. The orange flashes and most of the explosions were coming from a battery of naval guns about fifty feet away from the hut. I had forgotten their existence. A large fire was burning about a hundred yards away.

As the clatter died down we emerged from our shelter to survey the damage. By the noise, most of the aerodrome should have been destroyed!

Dawn clarified the situation. A friendly bomber had been returning to base in difficulties as enemy fire had destroyed its radio. Caught in the bad weather, the pilot had tried to reach our aerodrome for an emergency landing. The hot reception he had from the naval guns convinced him to bail out with his crew, and the big explosion was the bomber and its load of bombs blowing up in a nearby field.

At least we had experienced our first taste of guns being fired in anger.

As April cleared the northern skies, news came through that the Germans had invaded Norway. Several squadrons of old Gladiators were reformed to go to Norway to try to help out. Volunteers were called for and I offered my services. To my disappointment I was not chosen, but several of my friends, including Caesar Hull, the little South African, went.

My reason for volunteering was that I still loved the old Gladiator and, as I knew I was probably as good a shot with it as any pilot in the RAF, considered I could give a good account of myself if necessary. It was just as well I wasn't picked – most of those who went were killed and the aircraft carrier which was their headquarters ship, the *Glorious*, was sunk in the campaign.

The RAF bombers were heavily engaged in this battle, which raged for over a month, and Bob Cosgrove, one of my friends from Point Cook, was killed. Duncan Good, who had occupied a room next to mine in those early days, was badly hit but managed to return to England.

The war was beginning to take shape – and to take its toll.

6

Hitler on the Move

Hitler intended that 10 May 1940 should go down in history as the day of the start of his 'new order' for the world. With a great blare of radio propaganda, he announced that 'the battle which would change the course of history for a thousand years' had begun at dawn. The BBC announced that a major battle was in progress in the Sedan area, and for many days little was heard.

Early on the morning of the 14th we were sent on a patrol over the Dutch coast, and as we cruised along our patrol line a single aeroplane was observed climbing up ahead of us flying towards England. We opened our throttles and climbed. The quarry did not seem to get any closer for some time but slowly sank down below the horizon as we gained height on it. Suddenly the object of our interest started to look larger and larger. It was a Junkers 88, one of Goering's new bombers – very fast and well armed. Black crosses and a Swastika became plainly visible.

Cookie ordered Red section, his own, to attack. Mine was Yellow section, while Sam Saunders led Blue section and Stan Grant led Green section. These four sections of three Spitfires each constituted our battle array. We normally flew in these four sections when operating as a squadron. The first section led, the second section flew just behind and below it, the third section behind and below the second and the fourth behind and below the third. Thus Cookie's order meant that the remainder of his squadron were to take no part in the action, just stooge around and wait.

I took over the lead of the squadron and Cookie and his two boys dived down on their victim. It had already seen them and had turned back, diving for home.

Cookie closed in, black smoke trailing from his wings indicating that his guns were firing. He broke off and Johnnie Welford followed him in. One engine of the Ju 88 seemed to explode, then the other, leaving long, thick lines of black smoke. Johnnie followed him down and I lost sight of them as they were so far below.

The rest of the trip was uneventful. Cookie found us, joined up and we all returned to our aerodrome. It was our first squadron kill. It was a very impersonal business and seemed almost too easy, yet a few days later No. 54 squadron, one of our sister squadrons, lost four out of six pilots trying to shoot down one of the same family of Ju 88s. They had a very powerful sting in their tail in the form of two .5 inch guns, while our .303 inch guns were shorter in range. When chasing the enemy we were further outranged because in effect we were shooting into wind and the enemy was shooting downwind. At speeds around 400 mph this reduced our range by nearly half, and increased that of the bomber by a similar amount. Thus, the initial disparity was very marked and gave a fast bomber a definite advantage.

Inevitably, there was much excitement and chatter on our return and Johnnie Welford joined the ranks of the very few in Fighter Command who had a confirmed kill to his name.

A few days later, about dusk, a very dirty Hurricane fighter landed and taxied in to the hangars. An equally dirty, tired-looking character struggled out. He had a week's beard on his face and a dirty pullover under his tunic. He stated that he had come in from France and said that the Huns had broken through. There was total confusion. All the aerodromes in his area had been captured by tanks or parachute troops and as far as he knew he was the only survivor of his squadron. His condition was terrible and his nerves were in tatters.

The station commander was not sympathetic and put him under arrest as he thought he was an enemy spreading despondency and alarm. He refused to believe that the Germans had broken through to the coast and that the British were cut off. Nevertheless, the visitor had a certain conviction about him, and we were worried.

The BBC still talked about a 'Battle of the Bulge', but true or false we were warned that the following dawn at 4.30 a.m. our squadron would be patrolling over the French coast near Boulogne.

Thursday 23 May. We took off at 4.30 after being called at 3.45, being briefed and generally floundering around in the dark. As the mists cleared we noticed dark-green, beetle-like objects creeping across the country towards Boulogne. We dived down and flew over them at low altitude. They were army tanks showing German markings and as we slid past them we flew through a shower of what looked like inverted rain. It was flak and tracer, our first taste of ground fire. It looked harmless enough, but of course this was purely an illusion.

We resumed our patrol line and saw a cruiser and a destroyer come fairly close to the shore and commence shelling the tanks. The tanks on the coastal strip looked as if they would take a nasty hiding from this little gesture of the Royal Navy.

After being relieved by our sister squadron No. 74, we returned to the aerodrome, refuelled and within an hour of landing were on our way to the patrol line again. Two trips before breakfast!

We arrived to find the two naval vessels on fire from stem to stern. Their guns were silent and they were surrounded by great patches of oil. Our orders were to stand guard over the ships and protect them from air attack, but obviously there had been a raid in our absence. Later we heard that sixty or more enemy planes had attacked the two warships and our sister squadron, though they had fought with all the gallantry they possessed, outnumbered as they were by five to one, proved unable to stop the attack.

We stood by in anticipation of a further raid, but after ninety minutes we had to leave as we were dangerously low on fuel.

We had a break for about three hours and had some food. Then at midday we were off again for the same area. This time we found only the masts of the warships showing above the shallow waters. Their hulls were below the surface. The dive-bombers had done their job thoroughly. After another uneventful patrol we returned, refuelled and took off to do the last light patrol over the same area.

As we flew up to the patrol line we saw two dots ahead of us, flying across our path. As we approached, two more dots were seen to be after them – two Hurricanes after two Me 109s. The British machines opened fire. Both 109s exploded simultaneously and began to spin down towards the sea. In the still air of evening there was a touch of tragedy in the sight of two small, lonely aeroplanes spinning down almost in formation, one leaving a trail of black smoke, the other a trail of white. I continued to watch them as they slowly fell to their watery tomb. No parachutes opened, and at last the two little objects disappeared in a momentary patch of spray in the purple waters below.

The squadron wheeled around and it was possible to see across

France towards the Rhine. A long line of smoke and fires visible in the dusk indicated where the front line stretched across to the German frontier. Our army was cut off all right, and down below the Germans were attacking with tanks, flamethrowers, shells and bombs, blasting their way to the coast opposite Britain. What next?

We landed in the dark. No interceptions all day for us, just flying around looking into the sun every few minutes in case of attack. It was 10.30 by the time we were on the ground, and 11.00 p.m. by the time we were in bed. The anticipation and excitement had been at fever pitch all day, and we were terribly tired.

Friday, 24 May. This morning we were called at 4.30 a.m. to relieve 54 Squadron, who had taken off for the dawn patrol. We would have to fly at two-hour intervals all day. The prospect was a bit tough as we were still all dog-tired from the day before. However, this was war. No argument! We took off and relieved 54 Squadron and saw nothing. After two hours we landed again, had breakfast and went out again at 10.00 a.m. This time we patrolled the Calais area and once again saw nothing. The other squadrons had all been actively engaged in the process, had acquired a score and had already lost several pilots. We seemed to draw a blank every time, all of the anxiety but no actual engagements.

We patrolled again at 2.00 p.m. This time we found a single Henschel Army Co-operation plane south of Calais and Sgt Franklin of 'B' flight shot it down after it had put up a significant effort at defending itself.

At 7.00 p.m. we took off again, by now all thoroughly exhausted and longing for sleep. Still no action; we landed at 9.30 and were in bed at 10.00 p.m.

Saturday, 25 May. With the rapidly increased tempo of operations some of the fighter squadrons which had recently formed and were training in central and northern England were brought down to the south-eastern corner to help out.

On the day the first of these squadrons arrived I was astonished, during a hurried lunch between flights, to hear somebody say, 'See that bloke there, he's got no legs.'

I turned around expecting to see some unfortunate in a wheel chair, and looked straight into a pair of bright blue eyes set in a handsome and strong face. Instead of being in a wheelchair, he walked somewhat stiffly across, sat down at our table and immediately took charge of the conversation. To my even greater surprise I noticed he was wearing pilot's wings and that from his conversation he had just flown into Hornchurch in his Hurricane. We were all introduced. His name was to become synonymous with courage and triumph over adversity, as well as belonging to one of the best-known aces of the war. He was F/ Lt Douglas Bader.

Apart from this short meeting, I did not see Bader again for the best part of a year.

Another personality who dropped in with his squadron was Bob Tuck. He climbed out of his Hurricane limping badly from a flesh wound in his leg, and proudly exhibited two bullets embedded in the armour-plated glass of his windscreen. We were all delighted to see him back, if only for a few moments. He had been flying as intensely as we had, but whereas we were tired and heavy eyed, Tuck's peculiar vitality was showing up and he was radiant with enthusiasm. He appeared to actually relish the job with all the danger and exhaustion which went with it.

We were all becoming very tired from long hours and almost no sleep. One of our new lads, a New Zealander, had failed to return. He had been seen by Johnnie Welford nodding off to sleep in the air. He called him up over the radio but it had no effect. He was too low for it to be an oxygen deficiency.

Under normal circumstances it would have been possible to roster some of the more experienced junior pilots to lead sections, but Jack Kennedy had recently been posted to another squadron, and except for Johnnie Welford and John Nicholas we only had green officers left. The chance of a rest for section leaders was slim.

Meanwhile, Saturday was less active for us for no apparent reason. Calais had been besieged. Johnnie Welford and I played a game of tennis in the afternoon.

Sunday, 26 May. 9.00 a.m. found us over Calais and a few minutes later we all saw a formation of some twenty or more Me 109s diving in on us from twelve o'clock high – head on. At last we were in it.

They had come from the general direction of the sun, and they were firing at us when we saw them. They slid by underneath us in groups of two and four, passing close enough to see the pilots' eyes. Their oxygen masks made them look like monkeys. I was more impressed by their toy-like appearance than anything else and by the thin, dead-straight, pencil-line white streaks of the tracer as they flashed across in front of us.

We opened up our throttles and broke formation. I turned right, climbing hard, and noticed a formation of Henschel Army Co-operation planes dive-bombing Calais.

I called up on the radio and flew towards them hoping to get a shot at them, but almost at once I was enveloped in a barrage of grey tracer. I turned violently to the right and saw two Messerschmitts on my tail, falling back as I tightened my turn. They were still firing.

I had just moved half a lap ahead of them with the prospect of soon getting on their tails when another, a big fat one, flew across my sights. I fired for the first time in action, and saw him roll over and dive into the layer of cloud below. Continuing on the turn after my original assailants, I soon had the rear one looming up in my sights. As I fired, a burst of tracer shot across my line of vision. My target gave up the turn and went into a vertical dive towards the clouds below. I turned even more violently to escape the tracer, but my Spitfire just refused to go tighter. The stick went sloppy and the nose flicked down vertically, the ground and cloud spinning like a huge gramophone record.

I had spun a Spitfire before, and knew how to get it out. As I pulled out of the dive I went into a layer of cloud which was about five hundred feet thick. I came out underneath and noticed several white scar-like patches on the purplish water below, then I used the excess speed I had from the dive to take me up through the cloud again.

Here I saw the mill still in progress. Aeroplanes were still wheeling around. Who said we could not dogfight? Spitfires with trails of black smoke pouring off their wings (the only sign of their guns firing), the German planes spitting the far more obvious streaks of tracer. I joined the mill and again a 109 appeared from nowhere and sat in my sights. I fired and he dived for the cloud. Another flew across my sights and surprised me so much that I was not quick enough to get in a shot. Suddenly the air was much clearer, and I chased one remaining greenish-grey fighter and got in a short burst before the cloud flashed up and we both went into grey opaqueness. I pulled up and chased an object which turned out to be MacPherson in a Spitfire. We joined up and hunted two more dots which turned into two more Spitfires.

Altogether eight of us joined up again and we descended under the cloud layer to see where the Germans had gone. We saw fighters all right, but they had the familiar brown and green camouflage paint of our own boys. The squadron was patrolling the cloud, and on approaching closer we noticed the letters of 54 Squadron, our relief. Below, on the surface of the water, were several light-greyish oblong patches of oil and foam.

As we were light on petrol, we returned to our aerodrome a hundred miles to the west.

It took us twenty minutes and I had time to sort myself out. I was soaked to the skin with sweat and very elated. I had survived my first big dogfight. I had been too busy to be the least afraid, and even though the German planes at which I had fired had shown no positive signs of damage, I knew that my camera gun had taken some very good close-ups of them. Gone was the tiredness, and in its place was a feeling of enormous satisfaction.

I had little idea of how long the fight had lasted, but on checking my watch it would seem to have been at least fifteen minutes. The whole affair had been very intense and my sense of time had been in abeyance. It could have been five minutes or an hour.

After landing we reported to the intelligence officer. Everybody shouted at once and we found that our other four members had flown back safely. No casualties, and no one claimed a kill. Most reported that the enemy, on being fired at, dived into the patch of cloud over which we had scrapped.

Only Wigg, the New Zealander in my flight, had seen nothing. He had been hit by cannon shells in the Hun's first attack, and thereafter had been so very busy flying his damaged plane back home that he had seen nothing of the fight.

We breakfasted and prepared for our next flight. Already a little reaction had set in, tiredness and a slight anxiety which vanished as the engine roared. This turned out to be a blank. Only an hour and a half of looking towards the sun in tense anticipation. We landed, took an early lunch and two hours later were over the same spot. Two aeroplanes were seen to the south-east, and I was instructed to investigate.

They were Me 110s. With MacPherson and Phillips I prepared to attack but then I noticed two bombers down below, and so I turned and dived at them. As I approached, large, fat lines of tracer streaked up towards me. Ju 88s! I closed in behind the right-hand Ju 88, waiting for his wings to fill the gap in my reflector sight which indicated the correct opening range. Because I was coming in just below him, his guns were blocked out by his tail but his partner kept up a fire of tracers which looked like tennis balls as they left the gun and suddenly shot past, leaving a slightly spirally trace just over my head and to the right.

At last I opened fire and saw the aeroplane suddenly loom very large in my sights. To avoid a collision I pulled up to the left and was accompanied by the familiar streaks of tracer, which flashed up now to whip past at right angles to my flight.

The whole of air warfare is one of illusion. One second the air is clear, the next it is full of aeroplanes. A few seconds later it is clear again, and everything has vanished as if by magic. Tracer starts from the bomber up towards you, but although it travels relatively fast, by the time it passes you the trail of tracer is no longer connected with the bomber, but begins several lengths behind it. Each bullet seems to leave the bomber slowly then gather phenomenal speed as it flashes past. It certainly lets you know that you are being shot at, and even when you fly through old tracer trails you have a feeling that they are alive and lethal.

I stood off, plucking up enough nerve to make a second attack. I felt as if I was about to jump into an icy cold lake from a great height. I made the next pass at the second bomber as the first had fallen back, but was irritated to see tracer still passing me as I broke away out of ammunition. Again I had no kills, but some good 'close-ups' of Ju 88s. The squadron was nowhere to be seen, so I returned independently.

MacPherson and Phillips had attacked some Me 110s and had lost me. We rejoined in the crew room. Here we were told that in our earlier engagement 54 Squadron reported they had just arrived over Calais to see six or more Me 109s go into the sea and crash. Just as they were about to climb up to see what it was all about we came down and identified ourselves. They confirmed six kills, but admitted that they had come in right at the end, and thought we might have got several more as there were numerous blobs on the surface of the North Sea at that point.

Apparently our earlier dogfight had not been so unproductive, even though our squadron had no claim. We were awarded six kills to the squadron, but none to individuals. Of course, it is possible that the score was higher.

Excitement soared and the next three trips that day were charged with anticipation, but as we landed in the dusk from the last trip, we realised the promise of the morning had not been maintained. Between flights we would just lie down on the floorboards and try to sleep.

The controller called for me as we landed for the last time and I wearily entered his office. I was to take off an hour before dawn to do a special job – no more information until I reported at 2.30 a.m. to the operation room in barely four hours' time.

Monday, 27 May. I was to fly over to France, land in a field at first light, pick up a British general, sit him in the cockpit, sit on his lap and fly him back to Britain. The navigational details were all worked out for me. First light of dawn would break as I was in the target area and a code of light signals was given to me on a card. It all sounded pretty hare-brained and I wondered how the devil I could fit a full-sized Army general into a Spitfire's tiny cockpit!

John Welford would lead 'A' Flight off on its first trip of the day, which would be leaving half an hour after I left. This would be the first time I had not led 'A' Flight but this particular exercise was vital as the Army headquarters was under attack and it was the only way they could get the general out. The entire area was surrounded by paratroopers.

I was still busily wondering how the devil I could fit a full-sized Army general in a Spitfire's cockpit as I started up the engine. As I rolled for take-off, the controller called me to cancel the operation and report to him. More drama? No. The general had already been captured so the mission was off. I could go back to bed.

As I dozed off I heard the squadron thunder off on its way to Dunkirk. How pleasant to have just a little more sleep.

The batman woke me three hours later to the news that Johnnie Welford was missing, believed killed. He had been shot down by a Ju 88.

We took off at 8.00 a.m. for another uneventful trip and were back on deck by 10.00 a.m. By then, news was in that Johnnie was dead. He had flown over a Navy convoy in an attempt to reach land and the Navy had finished him off. They shot him down into the sea. They picked him up, but he died on the destroyer's deck. We were all very upset at the news. Johnnie was a favourite with all of us, having been blessed with a happy, even-tempered nature, good looks and high intelligence. Like Ned Austin-Sparkes, his friend who had died two years before, he was one whom the gods must have loved – he died young. Things don't change much over the ages.

Such is life. If it had not been for the cancelled trip to the Army headquarters I would have led 'A' flight as usual and it would probably have been me, not Johnnie, who died on the destroyer's deck.

7

Missing over Dunkirk

It was like flying through some sort of vast black tunnel. The sky was black, the earth two miles below was black and to my right was a huge, twisting, sinister shape exactly like a tornado funnel – it, too, was black, but here and there were brilliant crimson and orange flashes from one of the greatest fires in history. A square mile of petrol was burning as Dunkirk's petrol installations went up in smoke and flame. This enormous black cloud above blanketed the sun and sky, and the wing of thirty-six Spitfires pressed on through the darkened zone.

It had been 5.40 a.m. as we climbed into our machines and coaxed the engines into life. A tight feeling of dull tiredness around my forehead from days of insufficient sleep would turn into a full-scale headache later in the day from continuous scanning of the sun for possible enemy approaches. We were third in the relay over the territory behind the beaches; the first detail had taken off at first light, 3.30 a.m., the next relay at 4.45 a.m. and now it was our turn. The previous evening we had been the last on patrol, landing after dark at 10.45 p.m. By the time we cleared the dispersal point area and got to bed it was after 11.30 and that left little sleeping time when we were called at 5.00 a.m. We taxied out, took off and climbed to ten thousand feet.

At Southend we were joined in the air by two other Spitfire squadrons and then we all set course for Dunkirk, climbing to fifteen thousand feet.

Over the Channel the sea was mirror calm, and across it, at irregular intervals of four or five miles, were vessels either going to or returning from the beaches with their decks crammed with weary troops. The air was crystal clear but ahead on the horizon the usual morning build-up of snow-white cumulus clouds was visible, with some sizeable turrets already at twenty thousand feet. But there was something else ...

Intruding into this peaceful early morning scene was one vast black storm cloud, perhaps ten miles in diameter at its base and surging upwards in huge, turbulent black billows to some thirty-five thousand feet or more, where it flattened out into an enormous black anvil. It looked evil, an overwhelming presence – perhaps the spirit of the conflict in the air, sinister, menacing and deadly.

As we approached, it dominated everything. It was composed of black smoke and soot from the hundreds of oil tanks in the huge Dunkirk oil terminals where much of the oil imported for Europe entered the Continent. Over the previous ten days German dive-bombers had systematically destroyed tank after tank and now they had almost completed their task. In retrospect, it was a stupid thing to do – the oil would have been of the greatest value to them in the months and years ahead – but destruction was the order of the day.

Some rays of sunlight from the east struggled through towards the beaches, where long columns of men were stretched from the brownish olive-green fields, across the sand dunes to the water – and out into the water where small craft were ferrying them out to the larger vessels standing some quarter- to a half-mile off the shore. The khaki of the uniforms was relatively undetectable against the grass of the nearby pastures, but they were most obvious where they crossed the sand dunes and the golden sand of the beaches. It occurred to me how much destruction we could inflict on such a situation if the roles were reversed and these troops had been hostile. A single Spitfire could have ripped down hundreds, if not thousands, with its barrage of 160 bullets a second along those ranks. It would be no trouble to get two or three five-second bursts at the first three rows of men and to line them up like sparrows on a telephone wire.

Obviously we had to try to intercept any would-be ground strafers well before they got to the beach areas and that could only be achieved by patrolling twenty miles behind the beaches and on the probable lines of approach from the enemy's known airfields. There the patrolling fighters had a chance to intercept the raiders before they reached the beaches and destroy them during the ensuing chase or in the inevitable dogfights. These tactics were paying off or the beaches would already have been strewn with thousands of bodies.

As we crossed the coast, one of the few rays of sun penetrating the scene lit up a pair of grey-coloured aeroplanes down near the docks of Dunkirk. They were heading in the opposite direction.

Cookie was wing leader. His voice came over the radio:

'Hullo Red Leader. Investigate two bogies below eight o'clock.'

After acknowledging, I rolled out of formation and spiralled down with MacPherson on one side and Phillips on the other. We positioned ourselves for an attack from the rear. Square wing tips; they looked like Me 109s. I turned on the gun button to 'fire' and waited for the wing tips of the leader to fill the rangefinder's 'gap'. The leaden tiredness evaporated as I tensed up with anticipation. As soon as I fired, the fight would be on. Anything could happen. Now!

No! At the last minute I held fire – there were blue-and-red roundels on the wings – British! I flew past our targets – Royal Navy Skuas, lumbering two-seater, single-engined fighters. They should not be in this area unless they wanted to die. They were lucky we had not fired at them. The Navy was like that, undaunted by its vulnerability. We waggled our wings in greeting and left to return to our wing.

Along the French coast from Boulogne to Dunkirk masts and funnels of dozens of ships stuck out of the water, mute witness to the efficiency of the German dive-bombers. Wigg, our New Zealander, said they reminded him of a suburban paling fence back home.

We wheeled around to the right and flew east along the beach for a few miles. The gloom was not so dense, but below were three hundred thousand men, beaten legions of the British Empire, all trapped! They had run out of land to retreat to and now they were done, hoping against hope to be rescued. I watched the long files from the grassy dunes across the beaches to the shallow water. Here dozens of little boats were taking them, a few at a time, out to the waiting transports, ferry boats and destroyers in the deeper waters. They were trying the impossible, to create a miracle to get that mob out.

My depression was profound. Having been brought up in the tradition of British military invincibility I now had a ringside view of their greatest thrashing in two hundred years. Less than three weeks ago Hitler had crunched into the Maginot Line. We had been outclassed, outgunned and, as far as I could see, rounded up like cattle for the slaughterhouse.

We turned inland, climbing. To my right the great black funnel dominated the whole scene. Despondency settled over me as I flew on course, a reaction to the earlier tension of anticipated combat. How tired I was! How tired could you get? For ten days now we had been 'flying to

Spitfire Ace

exhaustion' – an apt phrase of Air Force usage describing twenty hours of duty each day, followed by four hours' rest – if you could unwind your nerves enough to rest after twenty hours on duty, you might sleep for four. Actually we only spent ten hours in our Spitfires – two hours flying, two hours on the ground, then up again – throughout the hours of daylight, but it was twenty hours on duty without rest as midsummer approached in the northern latitudes.

The excitement was so tremendous that few of us had slept for the first few days, but after about three days we were so exhausted that it seemed impossible to stay awake another minute, even when flying – yet awake we had to be if we were to live to see tomorrow's dawn. We were approaching the limits of our endurance. Hell, how tired I was!

Dots ahead – fighters. There were ten, twenty, thirty, about thirty-four or thirty-five of them, probably our wing. Then I realised they were flying in three lines of twelve, not a pattern we used. The dots rapidly turned into aeroplanes, single-seater fighters, very like a Spitfire head-on. Theirs or ours?

Suddenly, five lines of tracer streaked out from the leader. They were Me 109s. The tracer came slowly at first, then flashed past close by at terrific speed. The centre line of tracer was fat and a bit wobbly – cannon shells.

I dived violently under their attack. MacPherson and Phillips broke outwards as I gave them the 'wash out' signal. Tracer poured harmlessly overhead and the lines of 109s flashed past – two, three, four, twelve. One row of twelve followed MacPherson, one followed Phillips and the centre row came after me. A thought of the hapless little Henschel I had watched destroyed by our squadron ten days ago flashed into my mind – it had been twelve to one then too.

God! I felt too tired to cope with twelve! God help me! Then I had another flash of memory – Kanga de la Rue's 'steep climbing turns to the right'.

'Always use a steep climbing turn to the right if the bastards get on your tail. Never fails to fool 'em.'

I lurched into a steep climbing turn to the right with the throttle wide open and 'through the gate'. The normally smooth Rolls-Royce sounded rough and savage. Speed dropped to 140 mph. I knew that was the Spitfire's best rate of turn.

We were now in a circle, the 109s in line astern behind their leader on one side, me on the other. We snarled around in our giddy circuits.

The Spitfire seemed to have the edge on the 109s and slowly I gained ground in the turn to where I could almost line up the tail-end Charlie in my sights. A few more degrees of turn were needed. I pulled back even tighter on the stick and felt a slight shudder – the start of a high-speed stall – I had to be patient. At last he was in my sights! A bit more for deflection – he had to fly into my bullet pattern. The leader was still about nine o'clock opposite me.

I pressed the button. The Spitfire slowed and nearly stalled again as the guns roared above the blare of the Merlin. The target was big and fat in my sights, his Prussian black cross my aiming point, but suddenly he vanished!

On to number eleven, in the same spot. Again the guns recoiled. He rolled over violently and fell out of sight.

Number ten came up for exactly the same treatment, the bead just ahead of his nose. He pulled up violently and vanished upwards and behind.

Number nine – I barely touched the button and he was off. Hit or just frightened I would never know. Each second my guns fired they pumped out 160 slugs to converge at 200 yards.

Number eight – he was closer than 200 yards and he lurched out to the left. Seven, like nine, left downwards and out of sight, under my nose. I doubt if he got more than half a second of fire.

Number six rolled left and number five half-rolled as the guns snarled again.

Number four was a beauty! As I fired he slowly straightened out and then, equally gently, dived. Perhaps I could get him to blow up or show some other signs of destruction. So far I could not claim a single one. Pieces flew off him as he dived more steeply. I thought I had him but by straightening out and going after him I had exposed my tail to the squadron commander.

CRASH! BOOM! Something exploded under my seat. The armour plate behind me rang like a bell, then there was a disgusting stench like stale urine – explosive shells bursting inside the fuselage. The Spitfire reared up like a wounded killer whale. I had no control as it hurtled ever upward in an oblique loop so savage that I blacked out. Coming out of my stupor, I realised that the plane was slowing down on top of the loop and rolled it into a tight turn again. The engine was vibrating violently but the rearmost of the remaining three 109s appeared just ahead of me. I lined him up and pressed the button – same formula as before.

This time there was no recoil. No noise, only silence! No guns! The odds were still three to one and now I had no weapons!

Number three knew I was on his tail and panicked. He flicked over and dived for the deck. What luck!

Number two did not wait to see what was happening, he followed suit. That left the Squadron Commander who had nailed me from behind. How I wished that I could have given him a squirt. Before I could get properly onto his tail, black smoke poured from his exhausts as he bunted into a vertical dive.

I flew around for a circle or so to make sure there were no others around. It was hard to be sure in the twilight, but I could not see any. Below were a number of fires, but these could be anything – even 109s. They could have been me, too, or MacPherson or Phillips.

Easing the turn, I took stock of the situation. I was still alive but there was a great sea of petrol in the bottom of the Spitfire. It was sloshing around and stank like hell, drowning the smell of burnt cordite. The fumes were so strong that a spark from the exhaust could have sent the whole Spitfire up like a bomb. A single tracer now through the plane would have caused an instant explosion and incineration. I slid back the canopy to let in some fresh air and pressed the petrol gauge. The needles flicked to eighteen in the bottom, nothing in the top.

I decided to fly around for a few minutes then try again, to see if it was still running out. I ran up over the beach at two thousand feet and took a look at the troops. There were thousands of them. No wounded or dead could be seen, so the 109s apparently had not attacked them. Perhaps we had chased them away after all. I hoped so.

What had happened to MacPherson and Phillips? There was no sign of them but there was a Spitfire on its belly on the beach. I went lower. By the letters on its side it was not one of ours.

Another check on the petrol gauge showed there was still seventeen gallons. The lowest hole in the tank had to be at about the eighteen-gallon mark. The Spitfire would do about eight miles to the gallon, so I could get back to England, providing the engine kept running. Oil pressure and temperature were normal, coolant temperature was normal and there was no sign of glycol leaks. It was probably worth a try. I climbed back to two thousand feet and set a course for Manston, flying parallel to the coast.

I looked again at the petrol in the bottom of the plane. The level had fallen, it was leaking out of the cracks and bullet holes. The

Spitfire wanted to climb into a loop, but pressure on the stick kept it level.

Suddenly there was a violent lurch and then another. A black puff appeared just ahead of my starboard wing. Flak! Dammit, the bastards were shooting at me. Even small arms fire could have blown me up with all those petrol fumes.

I altered course out to sea, diving and then climbing. The flak followed me above, then came below me. It dropped behind. I was out of range at last.

Near Calais I headed west across the Channel, only twenty-five miles to home. If the engine cut out now, I would have to jump and swim.

I realised that my right boot was soggy and squelchy and pulled up my trousers to see a mass of blood on the back of my leg running into the boot. Sweat was soaking me and there was a cramping pain in my side. I felt for more blood. No. It was only a cramp from holding the control stick forward all the time.

Ten minutes to cross the Channel and the engine was rougher now. Funny how an engine always got rough as you flew over water. It was jerking away at its mountings like a wet dog shaking itself.

I tried to get my mind off it. If the engine cut out, I would bail out rather than ditch. Spitfires always speared into the water and went to the bottom. They were no good for landing on the water – suicide. I did not feel like a swim with a shot-up leg.

If I had not been such a fool and stopped turning to follow the 109 that had straightened out, I would probably have got rid of them all without any bullet holes. As it was, I still had problems. The petrol had almost all leaked out through the bullet holes now – the stench was still overpowering, but the open canopy gave me a fair amount of fresh air. Land was coming nearer. I was tempted to open the throttle a little to speed it up, but to do so would have meant running out of petrol before reaching the coast.

Soon I had to land with no flaps and no brakes as the air pressure was gone. The flaps and brakes were worked by compressed air, as were the guns. Ahead I could just discern Manston aerodrome. If I could make Manston, the clear, grassy surface would help.

I was not sure whether to land on the wheels or on the belly. There was still a lot of petrol vapour in the fuselage. Sparks would cause the whole plane to blow up. I had to try the wheels, but I did not know whether or not my tyres had been hit by bullets during the dogfight. Burst tyres would mean a somersault or a cartwheel, more explosions! With no flaps the Spitfire landed at about 85–90 mph, and without brakes she would run for a couple of miles.

As I crossed the boundary the engine cut out – no more petrol! I fishtailed to lose speed and found myself landing on the same course as a Hurricane squadron which was taking off. There were some very close Hurricanes and a good deal of cranky fist-shaking, but we missed one another by sheer good luck rather than management.

The Spitfire hit the ground. My heart stopped as I waited for the somersault, but ... no! It ran swiftly across the aerodrome towards the cliff at the far end. No brakes. I had to try to do a ground loop without 'digging' in a wing, going into a cartwheel and capsizing. After a delicate piece of footwork with an injured leg, I made it. The Spitfire came to rest.

I sat in the cockpit for some time, too weary to move – too weary, almost, to think. My heart started to beat again – slow, heavy thumps. What a trip! I'd survived a twelve-to-one dogfight and an avalanche of crises, all incredible. Incredible that I was still alive! Incredible that I had been able to fight my way out! But most incredible of all that this could have happened to me.

I climbed out of the hot, smelly cockpit and walked around the aeroplane. The tail and rudder assembly looked like a bit of old lace. A bullet had half-wrecked and jammed the trimming tab on the elevator in a position which had caused the Spitfire to climb violently. No wonder I could not move it. That bullet had saved my life.

I slowly collected my parachute and looked around. No one was in sight. I was soaked to the skin. It turned out to be sweat, not blood, but my right boot was squelchy. The blood on the back of my leg had clotted, so I tied a handkerchief around the worst part and continued to work my way around the aeroplane.

Several bullets had gone through the main petrol tank, but fortunately the armoured sheet over the top tank had taken the ones meant for it and deflected them; bullets going into an empty tank can cause an explosion in the air and gas mixture. No bullets had hit the engine area but one apparently had knocked out one of the magnetos, and another had hit a sparkplug without damaging the coolant jacket. This was most fortunate, as a leakage of glycol would have meant an engine seizure over the Channel. The same would have resulted from any damage to the oil circuits.

The Channel crossing had taken about fifteen minutes, but it seemed more like fifteen hours. I suddenly felt very tired and not at all up to walking the mile back to the civilised part of the aerodrome, so I sat under the wing on my parachute and waited.

For a while I just rested from the ordeal, my mind flashing to various aspects – what had happened to MacPherson and Phillips? They must have taken their share of the wing. Perhaps two of the fires I had noticed were their planes burning, not Messerschmitts. And what of the troops on the beach? I had scanned them for a few moments when wondering about a landing. They would have constituted quite an obstacle to a wheeled landing as they traversed the beach in several places, barely allowing room for a landing. I had not noticed any swathes in their ranks or signs of bodies on the sand. Perhaps the three of us had sufficiently distracted the Germans' attention to draw them off from the troops on the beach.

I inspected my leg more carefully and decided that it looked as if it had been hit by a shotgun fired from some distance, as there were numerous punctures in the skin, none of them very large, but they made a bit of a mess. No doubt when the air bottle, which was under the seat, blew up, some fragments had gone into the back of my leg.

I had a look at the parachute. It was much worse than my leg, and the odds were that it would not have worked too well. Much shrapnel, either from a cannon shell or the exploding air bottle, had obviously gone through the seat. If it had not been for the numerous folds of silk in the pack (on which I sat) they would have made a much worse mess of my backside. Good old parachute! It had undoubtedly saved me a very unpleasant injury – perhaps my life. Other bullets had obviously been stopped by the sheet of armour behind my back. Altogether I'd had a very lucky escape.

My mind went back over the dogfight. Alan Deere and John Allen of 54 Squadron had both had solo dogfights with large numbers of Me 109s a week earlier over Calais. Both were credited with shooting down six of the opposition, but they were smarter than me, as they did not get shot up themselves. At least not that time.

I tried to figure out whether I had destroyed any of the fighters. There was no way of telling short of finding an eyewitness account from somebody who had seen it from the beach, and that was pretty unlikely. However, each fighter I shot at had presented the perfect target at very close range. I had spent months perfecting just such attacks at Northolt earlier in the year and had gone over the camera-gun shots time and time again. Each Messerschmitt should have collected the best part of 160 bullets or so, as I got in a good one- or two-second burst at each one. Well, I guessed that I would never know.

Still no one showed any sign of coming out to pick me up – maybe no one noticed my crazy landing – anyway, there was no point in just sitting there. I picked up the 'chute and set out like an outback swagman, back to the hangars.

Near the first hangar was a Skua identical to the two I had checked just before the dogfight. It had clearly been in a scrap as it was even more full of holes than my Spitfire. I climbed up and looked inside, then was violently sick – the rear cockpit had obviously been badly hit and blood and human fragments were everywhere. It brought home to me how close had been my escape – yet the pilot must have survived long enough to get back to Manston. The rear cockpit was the air gunner's, so maybe the pilot had escaped serious injury – not so the poor gunner. There was no sign of the other Skua – probably down at the bottom of the Channel – they had been flying in formation, so they would both have been involved if the Me 109s found them. They had nothing like the turning capability of a Spitfire and would have had no chance against such overwhelming numbers.

I found an office and the incumbent produced a car and drove me to the medical centre. The medical officer when I saw him took a careful look at my leg after cleaning it up and confirmed my opinion. It was not serious. He probed around and removed a few splinters which were near the surface, then wrapped the rest up in bandages.

To my inquiry about removing the other bits, he said he thought it was best to leave them in the muscle, as any attempt to cut around and find them would probably be unsuccessful and only make my leg much worse. He suggested I scrounge a trip back to Hornchurch and gave me a note for the local medical officer.

The problem of returning to Hornchurch was not great and F/O Joel, one of the Blenheim boys from 25 Squadron who had been at Northolt earlier in the year, turned on a Magister and flew me back.

It was late in the day and I found that the squadron was no longer there. They had been relieved as Group had decided we had taken enough punishment and were overdue for a rest. Furthermore, I found out later that I had been posted missing. MacPherson and Phillips had returned and had reported last seeing me in hot pursuit of twelve 109s! One way of looking at it, I suppose.

And all that time I thought they were chasing me!

8

Preparing for Invasion

Sleep was the most desirable commodity in my universe and for the first time in ten days I luxuriated in bed, sublimely conscious, or half-conscious, of the fact that I did not have to drag myself out and go out to the Spitfires for yet another sortie over Dunkirk. Nothing to do but sleep, if I wanted to – and did I ever want to!

I drowsed for some twenty hours and began to think back over the last ten days. I had survived some forty-five operational trips over enemy territory and had been involved in many vigorous dogfights. Dunkirk was a military disaster of a far greater order than anything suffered by the Allied forces in 1914–18. The land forces were beaten and the Navy, together with amateur sailors and fishermen, were managing to extricate them against frightening odds, achieving the impossible, but we had been defeated nevertheless.

France was clearly in a state of military collapse and Mussolini had now joined forces with Hitler.

During the past ten days we had seen ship after ship of the Navy sunk by air attack; we had seen the unprecedented destruction of Dunkirk's vast oil storage installations – indeed, they were still burning – and we had seen each day more of our small band of pilots join the ranks of the missing or killed.

My mind kept going back to the combats I'd had. Had I destroyed any 109s? Several of the boys of my vintage were already claiming double figures, but I had a strong aversion to claiming anything destroyed, as this most likely meant that a human life had gone. Those German fighter pilots I knew from my skiing days barely a year ago were close to me and I had no pleasure, only distress, at the thought that some of them may have been my victims. The thought plagued me considerably. I found I could take no pleasure in it at all. Yet, I had no doubt of the necessity to win the war. I could still vividly see that beer garden in Innsbruck and the stark evil of the prowling Gestapo.

Before it had seemed impossible that such a monstrous horror could descend on Britain, but now it was only twenty miles away across the Channel. A vast army was daily moving up with the avowed intention of crossing that strip of water and establishing the rule of that same Gestapo in England!

Around midday, I cleaned up and saw the station medical officer, who pronounced that my leg was best left as it was without further effort to extract the fragments of explosive shell and compressed air bottle. He considered that after a week I would be able to use it as if it had never been hit. Some of it would work its own way out and some may travel around a bit but the rest would probably become part of me. He was easily persuaded that I should rest my bad leg away from the station.

Alan Deere, the New Zealander in 54 Squadron, was back from Dunkirk where he had been shot down on the trip before the one in which I had run into so much excitement. He had been sitting on the beach watching my effort and told me that several of the 109s had been hit and had crashed into the sea off Dunkirk.

However, the squadron intelligence officer had gone north with the rest of the boys so I did not file any claims. The important point, anyway, was that I had survived, and I had promised Helen that the next time I was in London I would buy an engagement ring as we had decided to get married. So off to London town I went, light of heart and stiff of leg.

The purchase having been duly made, I still had to wait a couple of hours before Helen finished her work, so I took a taxi up to Lady Frances Ryder's place to pay my respects. I had kept in touch since her group had first arranged my leave for me in 1937.

Here I found a great deal of animation. Having announced myself, I was hurried into a room as fast as my bad leg would permit, and instructed to wait for a while. People scurried backwards and forwards and it was some time before I learned what was causing all the commotion. About a hundred Australian and New Zealand nursing sisters evacuated from Dunkirk had just arrived and the queen was coming down to meet them, hence the flap.

Her Majesty arrived a few minutes later and she spent about an hour walking around and talking to all the sisters and nurses. In due course she came into the room in which I had been waiting and I was duly presented. The queen at once asked about the fighting at Dunkirk and invited me to join her for afternoon tea at a table set for two.

At first, this so rocked me that it was all I could do to carry on a monosyllabic conversation with the queen doing all the talking, but soon the easy, natural charm of the first lady of the land had its effect. Swallowing my nervousness and several cups of tea, I enjoyed a pleasant half-hour chat with a very gracious lady.

I had not told Helen that I was coming up, as I thought I would surprise her. It turned out we both had a surprise. She had been advised that I was missing, but did not know that I was safe when I walked in on her. At that stage, I was not even aware that I had been reported missing. Thus it was a day of pleasant excitement all round.

The next few days were spent exploring the upper reaches of the Thames by paddling around in a punt. Helen managed to get a few days off, and join me. In the evenings we met up with Lew Johnston and some of his friends who were stationed nearby, and we whiled away the twilight hours sipping beer and ruminating on what had happened and what the future held.

The facts were obvious and grim. Hitler's powerful hordes were overrunning Europe in a conquest the speed and thoroughness of which had not been seen for a thousand years. Armies melted away before him. His use of air power and armoured forces had brought about the annihilation of the best troops in Europe. Resistance had collapsed just as fast as the German forces could maintain an organised advance. Now we had the enemy barely twenty miles away across a narrow strip of water and it was clear that but for that strip of water we would be, at this moment, desperately fighting an invasion force of the same magnitude as had crushed Poland, Holland, Belgium and now France.

I had seen from the air some of the horrors of war when a conquering army advances: houses and villages and crops on fire all over the country, and all the inhabitants fleeing down the roads. Everything in the path smashed, burnt or blown up. This of course, was no novelty to Europe, where armies had ravaged backwards and forwards with fire, sword and rape for centuries. The unfortunate country people had to rebuild their homes in their entirety once a century if not in each generation. The British had been more fortunate, thanks to that twenty miles of water in the Channel.

Our problem was how to prevent an invasion. For nearly a thousand years, all Britain had to do to achieve this was to retain a navy which could sink the invasion force that had to cross the Channel. Since the advent of gunpowder the island seafarers had been able to hold at bay any attempt by their Continental enemies to subject the island to fire and sword. This also had an effect on the prosperity of England. It meant that there was no necessity to maintain huge armies on the European pattern at the expense of the community. The Navy could do the job for a small fraction of the cost. Thus, taxation had been far less than on the Continent for centuries, and the saving of money and of manpower had far-reaching economic effects.

Now the picture had suddenly and dramatically changed. Air power now held the key. The Navy was threatened for the first time by the bomber and the dive-bomber. Cruisers, destroyers and aircraft carriers had already been sunk with astonishing ease by small formations of aeroplanes. The Navy had no effective reply to this new sudden death from the skies, and had to rely on cover from the RAF's fighters. Should the RAF be wiped out, the bombers could sink every ship in the Navy, leaving the narrow Channel waters wide open to invasion. A landing could then be effected by the crudest barges.

For home defence our Army was in a tragic state. British soldiers had been forced to leave France in such haste that most of their arms and equipment had been left behind. The exception was the Brigade of Guards, which refused to be parted from their rifles. Now we had no guns, no tanks and almost no rifles while the enemy, as we well knew, were equipped with all these weapons in abundance. In addition they had flamethrowers, automatic rifles and artillery of all types. Furthermore, they counted their soldiery in the millions where we had barely a few hundred thousand.

The struggle lay ahead. It would be fought in the air. The enemy's aim would be to smash the British fighters.

We knew from our intelligence reports that the Luftwaffe was probably four times as large as the RAF's Fighter Command. We also knew that the Navy had to be kept in existence because our Air Force was still too small to be able to destroy a landing force of invasion craft. That would still remain the job of the Navy, but the fighters had to survive the struggle if the Navy was to continue to float.

Protection of the Navy involved substantial forces of fighters being retained in areas where the Navy had its anchorages, such as Scapa

Flow, the Firth of Forth and other harbours. This meant that our fighter defences would have to be spread over a thousand miles and, therefore, the maximum force which could be concentrated in the south would be substantially below the theoretical strength of Fighter Command.

In addition, our lifelines, the ports and shipping lanes, had to be protected and the factories which were producing the aeroplanes to build new squadrons and replace those lost in combat would have to be defended at all costs. Thus if an all-out attempt to break the air defences in south-east England were made by Hitler, we could only count on about a half of our total fighter force for the purpose of beating him off. The other squadrons could be moved in to replace exhausted units, but the distances were too great for them so be able to render any tactical support during engagements.

As far as we knew there were about fifty fighter squadrons in the entire command and about five night-fighter squadrons equipped with obsolete Bristol Blenheims, which would be useless in day combat.

In contrast to our gloomy forebodings, the days were fine and warm as Helen and I paddled up the Thames. We relaxed mentally and physically in the pastoral splendour of that scenery which for informal beauty must equal, if not surpass, anything in the world. Duck and waterfowl paddled inquiringly past, and we tossed out the occasional crust which they always fought for with enthusiasm.

We came across a wild old mallard with a brood of the smallest ducklings I had ever seen. By chance I spotted her on a grassy bank. I approached very close for a better look. She sprang at me with so much energy and violence that I forgot myself for a moment, stepped back, tripped, and fell in the water. As I sorted myself out I remembered that I was not even remotely afraid of ducks, but the surprise and aggressiveness of the old girl's attack had been enough to give her the chance she wanted. Search as much as I could afterwards, I could not find her or her brood. They had just melted into the undergrowth. The lesson was a good one on the value of surprise and energetic aggression, but right then and there I cursed myself for a stupid fool.

I returned to Hornchurch to find the squadron just back from rest at Kirton-in-Linsey. Everybody was in fine form and there were new faces both among the sergeants and the young officers. One of the new boys was a bright-eyed, dark-haired youngster, quite short in build, who came to my flight to replace Johnnie Welford. His name was Brendan Finucane – we called him 'Paddy'.

Except for John Nicholas, all the officers in 'A' Flight were now volunteer reservists. Only MacPherson and Phillips were left among the sergeants. All the new sergeants were volunteer reservists too. Only four of the old pre-war regulars were left. We set to work to get the new boys into shape as most of them had not yet flown low-wing monoplanes.

After lunch on the day of our return, 11 Group Headquarters sent us off on an offensive patrol over the Calais area.

Over France I was far from happy. The recollection of the close shave at Dunkirk was still very vivid. We cruised around for an hour, but saw nothing except a large number of flak bursts which were surprisingly accurate for altitude and reasonably so for direction too. After the longest hour of my life we returned and landed. MacPherson had a hole as large as an apple in his oil tank, but fortunately it was in the top and so he was able to get back all right.

That evening I was summoned to the operations room to be briefed by the station intelligence officer. The senior pilots in each squadron were required by Group to carry out patrols over pre-arranged lines which would take them over Belgium and the north-east of France. The object of these patrols was to look out for any enemy activity in the form of construction work, repairs to aerodromes, railways, bridges and so on, and anything else which might look interesting. We were to fly singly or in pairs and the purpose was fact-finding, not fighting.

I did not fancy this very much as there were several aerodromes on the route with Me 109s in strength. To go snooping solo into their territory seemed to be asking for more trouble of the sort I had experienced before, and I was not at all confident of being able to scrape out a second time.

That evening saw me flying around my patrol line with the throttle as wide open as I dared keep it for the hour of the trip's duration. This first time around was merely to familiarise myself with the route. I navigated with one eye on the map, the ground and the instruments and the other watching behind. You had to watch for the devil at six o'clock.

On my return, I was advised that I would be required to do the trip twice a day until further notice! A happy thought! I had to traverse about one hundred and fifty miles of hostile France, entering at Dunkirk and sweeping around to Abbeville via Bethune, Lille and St Pol.

The next few days were mostly of significance to me in that I succeeded in slipping around without being shot down by the German fighters who were out to catch us if they could. I varied the height at which I flew and the time by up to an hour each day, so that a standing patrol would be busy knowing where or when to trap me. The other boys who were doing lines parallel to mine to give the complete picture did likewise.

After the first week I knew all the canals, rivers, hills, roads and railways by heart. They were etched on my memory by sheer concentration. Already I noticed strange scars appearing in many places on the French landscape. On doing a low sweep over them I discovered that they were huge sets of concrete and the Germans seemed to be mixing the concrete in the bare earth after scraping off the turf. Within a few days these strips of concrete were nearing a mile in length, and it was by then obvious that they were runways for aeroplanes. The astonishing thing was the speed with which they were set down.

Large army encampments were now appearing all over the countryside and I had to begin making detours as the 'inverted rain' was a little too heavy for comfort when I flew over these spots. Some of the landing strips were finished already, and aeroplanes were landing and taking off. Other scars showed where railway sidings had been brought up, roads extended and bomb and patrol dumps installed.

At the same time I noticed that one of the canals I checked my position by had disappeared. At first I thought I was slipping, but on my subsequent trip low down I saw a great strip of camouflage netting over the canal. The surface was covered with large barges. The invasion build-up was starting!

Each day the task of dodging patrolling fighters became more difficult and I freely admit that on more than one occasion I thought discretion much preferable to valour as I climbed madly for the clouds just ahead of the tracer of a bloodthirsty group of Messerschmitts.

On Saturday 22 June, three hours after being unceremoniously hunted out of France by these same German fighter pilots, I stood before the altar of the little church of St Mary's in Kensington, where Helen and I were married. Cookie and his fiancée were in the congregation, and Lew Johnston was best man. It was a quiet affair, and Cookie had arranged for me to have four days' honeymoon, which we spent at a remote hotel on the beautiful upper reaches of the Thames.

Four days later I was back in the squadron. Reconnaissance flights over north France were still the main items of interest. If it were not the necessity of doing these trips twice a day, we could have had a very pleasant rest. As it was, several of the aerodromes on my patrol line were now stocked with aeroplanes and they had lots of anti-aircraft guns and no shortage of ammunition.

With the capitulation of France, more large encampments of troops established themselves in various lush valleys. Many of the country chateaux were obviously being taken over by the German staff because several of them were now surrounded by guns with lavish supplies of ammunition.

It was estimated that in addition to the dozen or so French aerodromes within seventy miles of the English coast, the Germans constructed a further thirty or more in June and early July. With three squadrons operating off each aerodrome, this threatened us with well over a thousand aeroplanes.

Our fighters available for defence in that area were barely three hundred. Of course there were more in the centre and north of England, but they could not be brought down in time to engage in any one raid unless that raid made a very deep penetration inland.

Barges and tugs were appearing in the ports and it was obvious that an invasion was intended. The astonishing thing was how quickly it all took place.

Since the war it has been commonly asked why Hitler did not invade England immediately after the fall of France. Why did he wait three months?

The answer is that he did attempt to mount his invasion immediately. It was not possible to ship a hundred thousand or half a million armed men across twenty miles of water without ships or barges. These were produced with minimum delay. However, without some protection they would all have been sunk by the Royal Navy and the coastal guns as soon as they put to sea. That protection also was organised in record time by building bases for the dive-bombers and bombers of the Luftwaffe on French soil.

All that remained to be done by the second week of July, six weeks after Dunkirk, was to get this air force into action, destroy what was left of RAF Fighter Command, sink the ships of the Royal Navy as they showed up, and the invasion was as good as won.

We noted with some misgivings at this time the equipment of our own soldiery, who were allegedly guarding our aerodrome. It was one of the principal stations in the London area so we could expect the best. This was doubly necessary because the Germans had developed a technique in France of capturing aerodromes using paratrooper commandos and leaving the fighters up in the air with no place to go. If they landed they were easily rounded up and captured.

Our troops were mostly armed with 'pikes', a ludicrous contrivance made of electric conduit with an ancient bayonet welded to it. Various suggestions were offered by the pilots as to how the Army should best manipulate these weapons in an emergency, but the Army officers' sense of humour did not seem to be their strongest point in such discussions.

They also had a contrivance known locally as an 'armadillo'. This was an ancient truck surmounted by a square tank with four peepholes in the sides and a single door. It looked something like a mobile lavatory but it was intended to house machine-gunners who were to be driven to the seat of any trouble by a driver entirely encased in another steel cubicle with narrow slits to see through in order to drive. This contrivance took much mechanical ingenuity to be made mobile due to its great weight, and it frequently got bogged in soft patches of the aerodrome during exercises.

To augment this lamentable state of preparedness for the looming invasion, the local gentry, farmers and yokels were recruited into the 'Local Defence Volunteers'. All these people had in common were firearms which varied from sporting rifles to twelve-bore shotguns. All were trained by the local soldiery at target shooting, the target centre being a man in a parachute. Considering the odds we were up against, this collection of poachers and peasants was viewed by us with very jaundiced eyes, as the odds were that they would be giving us a blast of swan-drop or buckshot before the crisis was over.

Daylight was now at its longest. First light was about 3.30 a.m. and last light 10.50 p.m. or 22.50 hours as the RAF would register it. It was necessary for the squadrons to be at readiness each day at these hours as they were favourite times for surprise attacks. Four hours was the most sleep we could expect.

We had a supernumerary squadron leader named Sawyer posted to the squadron. He was attached to my flight to learn the tricks of the trade as he had been on staff work for some years and had to get back into the general feel of things. He was very easy to talk to and we soon became firm friends. When he was settled in he would leave us and take over command of a squadron which had lost a squadron commander in action.

He soon caught on to the general idea and was able to act as flight commander on alternate mornings, which gave me a chance to sleep in every second day. Cookie and Saunders had a similar arrangement in 'B' flight. Thus we began to enjoy life even if everything was likely to explode at any moment.

The press annoyed us all with a lot of ballyhoo about England not being invaded for nine hundred years. With our knowledge this seemed like carrying the ostrich act too far. Invasion was imminent, why not face it? Why encourage complacency at a time like this? What we needed was a furious effort to produce aeroplanes and guns before it was too late.

Perhaps I was wrong. The press no doubt soothed the taut nerves of those living in areas likely to be attacked and prevented a headlong panic on the lines that hindered the French so much in their campaign. As it was, everybody stayed put. 45 million people were holding their breath.

9

Channel Duels

We continued the daily patrols by single aeroplanes around the northern sector of France – the area from which enemy aeroplanes would work in an attack on Britain.

Our runs revealed more and more new strips being levelled and consolidated – one particularly large one near Bethune was quite an education to watch daily. The Germans ploughed up the subsoil after removing the turf and topsoil, which they heaped up around bays to accommodate aeroplanes. Then added some substance like cement, mixed it with rotary hoes, watered it and rolled it. They produced about fifty yards of runway each day and after a month they had completed a runway about a mile long. Within five weeks of starting they had their heavy bombers operating on it.

Similar activities were going on all over that area – some not so elaborate, just filling ditches and grading irregularities between fields. Aerodromes which had been severely ploughed up by their very efficient pattern bombings a few weeks before were graded up, cleaned up and readied for occupation. I now had to avoid the half-dozen aerodromes on my track because fire from the ground was too intense for safety. The area seemed to be almost one continuous aerodrome or army encampment. It was on one of these low trips that I had noticed that the canals and waterways behind Dunkirk were all covered with barges, in turn covered with camouflage netting – the canals had completely disappeared!

Abruptly, the pattern of life changed again. Convoys coming up the Channel – through the Straits of Dover into London – with all the vital food and fuel were suddenly singled out for attack.

These convoys, about twenty ships in each, were now being attacked several times each day by forces of sixty to eighty planes. To begin with they were Stuka dive-bombers with about two or three squadrons of fighters as escort.

When they started this effort we began escorting each convoy with six Spitfires throughout the hours of daylight, about eighteen to nineteen hours each day. With six or seven convoys in the Channel simultaneously plus another one or two making up the coast to Edinburgh, this involved some forty-eight to fifty aeroplanes.

With this number over the convoys, a similar number taking off to relieve, a similar number on their way back and a force on the ground, about two hundred Spitfires or Hurricanes were on duty all the time. With little more than three hundred available in the area, this left almost no room for reinforcement and none for rest or time off.

At this stage it would be worth describing the disposition of the fighter force in Fighter Command and how it was employed to cope with this problem.

Because of its small area, Australians are often surprised at the distances covered by the British islands. The distance from London to Edinburgh is some four hundred miles and a similar distance is covered going north from Edinburgh to Scapa Flow. At the Firth of Forth and at Scapa Flow the Royal Navy had concentrated most of the Home Fleet elements to attack any invasion and each of these had to be covered by a minimum of three squadrons of fighters.

Other squadrons were required to defend the Midlands, where the principal factories were located. These factories were contributing heavily to the war effort, making aeroplanes and aero engines in particular.

Last but by no means least, the ports needed some protection as through them came the all-important food and petroleum – so essential for the continuation of the struggle and our hopes of survival.

The whole of south England was now threatened from the north coast of France and so the squadrons which were not essential for the defence of the north were spread along this coastline, the greatest concentration being in the sectors around London.

By the time all this was sorted out there were more than half of the 600-odd fighters available for the defence of Britain, concentrated in the southeast quarter. This left the remainder of the island rather thinly defended and those outside the London area were virtually unable to assist in the battles which were developing.

In many ways operations covering the Channel convoys were the hardest and most expensive that summer. The defending aerodromes were sited at fifty to sixty miles apart, mostly along or near the coast. Only occasionally were the convoys conveniently close to the aerodrome. As they were usually about fifteen to twenty miles off the coast, their average distance would be fifty to sixty miles away from any one of the airfields.

The radar warning was hard pressed to be of much help. It could 'see' fairly reliably at about sixty to seventy miles, but again the convoys for the most part were halfway out towards the limit of their radius of search. When the attacking enemy forces were first picked up by radar, they were usually within forty miles of their objective and moving in at a fast cruising speed around 240 mph. They would thus cover the distance in about ten minutes.

The defending fighters, if they took off on the instant the radar stations received their first plot, would take on an average ten to twelve minutes to climb to the area of the convoy, for climbing was a slow business even in a Spitfire – it was less than half the cruising speed. As the pilots usually took three to four minutes to get into the air from the first warning, they usually arrived too late to help out the convoy's close escort. Because these escorts were seldom more than six fighters, they were hopelessly outnumbered from the start and disaster was always close at hand.

We moved down to Southend. This was about as far forward towards the east coast as we could get on the north bank of the Thames Estuary, but just to get a bit closer we spent all our 'readiness' time at Manston – an aerodrome about twenty miles north of Dover and the closest to the French coast.

'Readiness' was an Air Force term used in Fighter Command to indicate that a squadron or flight was on immediate call to take off and go into action. There was only one stage which was represented a more immediate state of preparedness, and that was 'Stand by'. At 'Stand by' the pilots sat in their aeroplanes with everything ready to go. Where the engine could stand it, this too was running. Fortunately or unfortunately, the Spitfires could not be kept at 'Stand by' with the engines ticking over as they would boil. (The radiator in the Spitfire was offset and clear of the slipstream and would not prevent boiling if the engine ran for anything longer than five minutes.) Thus we were seldom brought to 'Stand by', which was fortunate, as this could drag on for an hour or two. 'Stand by' was very restricting and boring for the pilots concerned, as the cockpits were cramped and uncomfortable and became very hot in the sun. 'Readiness' usually lasted for four or five hours or until the squadron was involved in a combat, at which time the next in line at 'Available' came to 'Readiness' and became the next to go into action.

In a three-squadron wing this allowed a third squadron to be resting at 'Released'. This was usually at an hour's call except in the evening, when it might be until dawn. When the 'Available' squadron was called to 'Readiness', the 'Released' squadron came to 'Available'.

At 'Readiness' the squadron was all set to get into the air within five minutes. Usually we succeeded in doing it in less. We were dressed for flying complete with life jackets and flying boots. The parachute, helmet and associated paraphernalia were arranged in the cockpits of the aircraft. The aeroplanes were nearly all spaced at about thirty-yard intervals in a staggered line to make it more difficult for a surprise attacker to line up several planes in his sights in a single pass.

When the order came to take off, this was normally passed over the telephone to one of the ground staff, who kept watch by the phone. He would shout the instructions to the crew room, where the pilots were sitting around, but to make sure the message got through he would rush down the corridor shouting 'Scramble Angels ten, base', or some similar crude code which simply meant take off and patrol at ten thousand feet over base.

The combination of the telephone bell ringing, followed by the sound of shouting, then pounding boots invariably sent us off at full gallop to our aeroplanes, where we strapped in, pulled on our helmets, etc. and pressed the starter button. A few seconds later and we were taxiing out to the downwind end of the runway for take-off. This pattern never varied except that sometimes it was a section, sometimes a flight and sometimes the squadron which was ordered off.

It became vital to protect the convoys by providing standing patrols of six or twelve fighters continually during daylight hours. It was not possible to protect them using the radar warning network because of the time factors and the distances involved. By the time the raiders were detected, the flights scrambled, climbed and directed into the vicinity, the attack could be over.

The first blows by the enemy were cautious but they hurt. Losses were often very heavy. One afternoon we patrolled in a formation of six fighters over convoys approaching the Dover narrows. Cookie took over the lead of 'B' Flight from Sam Saunders, who was away for twenty-four hours. He and George Proudman with four others relieved Sawyer and myself with our boys, over the convoy.

Half an hour after we landed two of Cookie's boys came back. They were two sergeants, Franklin and Curtin. Their machines were write-offs. The Spitfires were badly holed, and they said they believed that Cookie had been shot down and killed. Their story was that they had been attacked by seventy to eighty Germans, roughly half fighters and half dive-bombers. Cookie had attempted to attack the bombers, but had been last seen with six 109s on his tail. George Proudman had gone too, as well as one of the new officers and a new sergeant who was on his second operational trip. Four missing, believed killed, out of six in one trip.

Cookie's loss was a sad blow to us all. He had been our guide, philosopher and friend for four years, and it was as though we had lost a member of our family. He had turned down an offer of promotion to wing commander to stay with the squadron, and he was due to be married in three days' time – that made it doubly sad.

George Proudman had been one of my closest friends for the last four years. He was the son of a theatrical family who had been in the dramatic business for many generations. He had been a particular friend of mine and a great favourite with the squadron. He had been with us almost as long as Cookie. George and Johnnie Welford and I had a regular appointment for tennis whenever we had a few minutes off, although in recent weeks we'd had no chance to play. Now both were gone within a month. It was the end of a very happy association with two very gallant young men and I have never really played tennis again since that time.

Sam was back the following morning, and he led us as we covered a convoy about six miles north of Dover. With no warning, thirty Me 109s attacked us. The first impression I got was that the air suddenly became full of aeroplanes whirling around as if inside a huge invisible barrel. A climbing race set in, and I was reasonably certain that I had them, when of one accord they dived vertically, and I was unable to catch them. My engine cut as soon as I tried to follow suit, and by the time it caught on again they were rapidly vanishing towards France.

From now on the pressure mounted. Sawyer, who had been supernumerary in our squadron with the objective of taking over one of the new units, became our new squadron leader. However, as he still was feeling his way, either Sam or I led the squadron for the next two weeks of operations, until he felt that he knew enough about it to take over command.

The other two squadrons in our Wing, No. 54 and No. 74, had their share of disasters, 54 losing five out of six on one trip.

A couple of days later we were patrolling as a squadron of twelve over Manston at fifteen thousand feet when some twelve or so 109s hit us from the sun. We saw them in plenty of time and dived under their approach at the last minute. The air was thick with tracers and both formations whipped into tight turns. In a matter of seconds we were all milling around in a large circle about half a mile in diameter and about three of four thousand feet in overall height separation.

As the Spitfires pulled around on the tails of the 109s, they broke downwards – all except one, who was bent on out-climbing me. He had pulled up from the initial diving attack to about two thousand feet above me and was in a position to dive on me at any instant I tried to break away, so I climbed up after him.

The scramble went on between the two of us, and we milled around, up and up. The German plane looked noticeably different from the Me 109s and as I got closer to him I realised it was a Heinkel 113, a new and allegedly superior fighter which was still in the experimental stage.[1] It was cleaner and neater than the Me 109 and certainly could out-climb it. I had found no problem in out-climbing and out-turning the Messerschmitt, but this one kept his height advantage and because of it I could not get my gunsight up on him without incurring the certainty of a stall, followed probably by a spin from which, if he was any good, he would destroy me as I was committed to the check and the pull-out.

The climb went on and on interminably and the only advantage I could gain from it was that I was able to get around under his tail where I could see him but he could not see me.

Up we went – twenty-nine thousand feet, thirty thousand and still climbing. The Spitfire was sloppy now, but I was making little or no headway in catching him up.

However, he was obviously having qualms because I was under his tail and he would therefore be unsure whether I was making height or not. If I made height, I'd get him.

I guess he just could not bear the strain that I might be able to eventually get that shot at him. In any event, his relatively tiny wings must have been pretty sloppy in the rare atmosphere – they were only half the area of the Spitfire's. He suddenly rammed his nose down and dived vertically.

I half-rolled after him, but it was no use. I clocked some 450 mph on the speedometer by the time we were at twenty thousand feet, but he was still leaving me behind. The Spitfire was approaching the speed of sound and rumour had it the wings came off at that point, so I throttled back and pulled out. The Spitfire was almost rigid at that speed and did not like answering the controls. However, as the speed dropped back, control returned and at five thousand feet, I was flying level still with around 450 mph on the clock.

I lost sight of the He 113; whether he ever pulled out of that dive I'll never know. Certainly he was going much faster than I was, and could have gone through the sound barrier. Few planes could do that in those days without disintegrating when buffeting set in, and most just lost all control. Whether the 113 could, I know not. Anyway, I had seen my first He 113 and, as it turned out, the last; I never saw another in the air. Maybe it was just as well. It seemed more of a match for the Spitfire than the 109.

Our stints at Manston put us in an ideal position for escorting the convoys through the Narrows near Dover. It also put us uncomfortably close to the nearest German aerodromes at Calais only twenty-five miles away. Messerschmitt 109s were known to be stationed at Calais and at least three other aerodromes in the vicinity. At their top speed they could traverse the strip of water in four to five minutes if they decided to ground strafe us. We also knew that if they came in very low, they had a good chance of eluding our radar (which was still fairly primitive) until at least halfway across the Channel. This would give us only two minutes' warning. Unless we were in the air, we had little hope of avoiding disaster from this type of raid.

A couple of days after our 'mix up' with the 109s over the Channel and my encounter with the He 113, Sawyer was over a convoy south of Dover with five pilots of 'B' Flight. I was waiting with my 'A' Flight team to reinforce him if anything happened. Some Hurricane boys from Hawkinge, a few miles to our south, were covering another convoy in the narrows.

I was called off to take a section of three to investigate some activity near Dover, so MacPherson and Phillips took off with me and we followed the various directions from the controller.

About five miles south-west of Dover we suddenly saw a flash of instant drama – two dots were visible above and ahead of us. In a matter of seconds, they materialised into a Hurricane and an Me 109 which was stalking it. As they came within a few hundred yards of me (flying almost head-on) the Me 109 opened fire from immediately behind the Hurricane. Smoke appeared and the tail and rudder fell off the Hurricane. In the instant, the pilot popped out of the cockpit like a cork from a champagne bottle. His parachute streamed behind him.

As I watched this little act, I turned tightly to the right and kept the Me 109 in sight and chased him back across the Channel.

The Hurricane had apparently taken no evasive action to check if anything was behind him and had paid the penalty for his neglect. Now the victor was on his way home, equally careless of the fact that I was giving chase. He must have been so intent on watching his quarry that he had missed seeing us altogether.

Whatever the cause, he was now flying a perfectly straight course for Calais in a fast downhill run at about 450 mph. Perhaps he thought he was faster than we were. MacPherson and Phillips formed in behind me in line astern and at full throttle we waited for the gap to close.

The coast of France was getting very close when his wings filled the gunsight rangefinder and I opened fire. Pieces large and small came off him and flashed back dangerously close, but he made no move to escape or turn. The wings rocked from side to side very rapidly for a second or so as my sixteen seconds of ammunition ran out. In disgust, I broke away and immediately realised that I was within inches of the water.

MacPherson and Phillips reformed on me, which I thought was strange, as they normally would have gone in to finish off what I had failed to do.

I called control and reported my position and was told to land. Before doing so I took a look around to see if I could see the pilot of the Hurricane who had bailed out. I had a rough idea of where he would land, and as only seven or eight minutes had elapsed since he was hit and I had returned to the English coast I reckoned I would have a fair chance of finding him.

I located his parachute in the middle of a field of ripe wheat. A track through the wheat followed a bizarre zigzag and about a quarter of a mile away was the pilot in his yellow 'Mae West' running like a hunted stag. Two rustic members of the Home Guard were taking pot shots at him with rifles or shotguns – presumably because he had come down by parachute.

This was a mounting danger – the threat of invasion which now emerged had resulted in the hurried formation of the Home Guard.

These stalwarts had been given some crude instructions in defending their localities if attacked – the most dangerous and the most difficult threat to counter being from paratroopers, who had spearheaded the German attacks in Poland and France. Thus considerable effort had been put into alerting the Home Guard to take action in such an extremity. Their target practice included targets with a parachutist as the aiming point and no marks were given for filling the silk canopy with holes! The body was the bull's-eye!

The more dedicated of the Home Guard now viewed all parachutists as either hostile or excellent random target practice. It was open season for parachutes and we were the bunnies.

I made a series of low passes over the two intrepid defenders of the realm and cursed the fact that I was out of ammunition as a series of bursts in their direction would have kept their heads down in the ditch long enough to let the pilot escape.

When the latter seemed sufficiently out of range of the Home Guard I returned to Manston and landed. I raced into the crew room and rang up the local police and told them to call off their jolly yeomen and alerted the Army and other people to try to help the Hurricane pilot.

It was after all this that I noticed the excitement on MacPherson's and Phillips' faces. It seemed that as I broke away from the Me 109 it knifed into the water. They said that they were afraid I was going in with it, as I seemed to be concentrating on my aim and was getting awfully low in the process.

It must have been another lucky day for me. At least they could confirm the 109. I thought it had flown on back to its base! It was the first one confirmed for me.

10

Fatigue and Fire

We soon took to Sawyer, our new squadron leader. He was a big man in every way and unusually good-looking. I had seen him a couple of years before when attending a camp concert at Cranwell where he took part in the evening's entertainment. He had been the outstanding performer and was a very able artist. He probably would have made a star in the theatrical world had he chosen it instead of the Air Force, especially with his physique and his good looks.

He also had a delightfully generous and happy nature and it was a rare bonus for a unit to have such a type as its leader. We knew we were lucky to have him.

He took it in turns to fly with 'A' Flight or 'B' Flight. When he flew with 'A' Flight I led the squadron, when with 'B' Flight, Sam led. However, as most of the work at this stage was escort of convoys by flights, there was little opportunity to employ the whole unit.

It was his turn to fly with 'A' Flight one afternoon about four weeks after Cookie's death and on this occasion he was going to lead if we took to the air. The weather clamped down as a warm front came in from the Atlantic. Flying conditions became progressively worse and the forecast was that it would deteriorate into heavy rain, with little possibility of a clearance until morning. For the first time that summer the weather had broken and reverted to the average foul English day. For the first time since I had arrived in England I welcomed that murk and drizzle – it meant an early night and some sleep.

We were released early, about three o'clock in the afternoon, and Sawyer invited me to join him in his little sports car and we took off for an hour or so at the local pub.

Over a few beers we talked of many things, but mostly about the other pilots. Sam Saunders, MacPherson, Smart, Franklin and Phillips all came in for a mention. We philosophised about life and the shortness thereof in our trade. In particular he was interested in the attitude shared by Sam and me, neither of us believing in claiming kills.

Sam and I both felt that it was the urge to confirm a kill which led so many boys to follow a stricken plane down and in the process make the perfect target of themselves for the ever-growing enemy. If we were going to survive, let alone win, we had to abandon all forms of claims and never give them a thought. This of course was hard when others subscribed to the opposite philosophy and some impressive scores were already being tallied up. Franklin, Sam's most experienced sergeant pilot, claimed no less than twelve kills at this stage, and Sam and I knew that if we had accepted the same standards of certainty for kills, we could both match him. In Sam's case he would be two or three ahead. Nevertheless, the prospects of survival were too grim to alter our attitudes and we would be very lucky indeed to come through the onslaught which was steadily mounting. No deviations were to be encouraged, and in a matter such as this examples were all important.

Sawyer was very unhappy that neither Sam nor I had a gong. Already most flight commanders were wearing at least a DFC and many already had bars or other recognition added. He knew of Cookie's unpopularity with the station commander and felt that but for that fact Cookie would almost certainly have had a DSO and Sam and I something too. We both already had some sixty to seventy operational trips, including forty-odd over Dunkirk. Being on the forward aerodrome was no help either – out of sight was out of mind where decorations were concerned, and the station commander never ventured to Southend, far less to Manston.

As we parted company for an early night he announced that the first thing he would do the following morning would be to recommend both Sam and I for a DFC.

I made for my cot in the caravan by the Spitfires with a pleasant feeling in my middle. It was not just beer – Sawyer was one in a million and it was pleasant music to hear some appreciation for all the blood, sweat and tears. Anyway, I was really dog-tired.

As the German attacks on the convoys had become routine, we had reverted to a routine of flying to exhaustion. This was similar to the situation at Dunkirk when we were flying turn and turnabout on the patrol lines behind beaches. Now, however, we flew cover over the convoys being relieved every hour or so. When there was a fight the tempo would step up. Thus tiredness had once again become the all-consuming sensation of life, and we were lucky indeed from this point on to get four hours' sleep during a night.

The German High Command must have been aware of the exhausting effect this would have on us, so they began a programme of bombing our airfields at night in order to ruin what little sleep we were able to snatch.

Every night, one of our more experienced night-flying Spitfire pilots had to sleep fully dressed in a caravan near the Spitfires. In the case of our squadron this was Sam, MacPherson, Phillips, Tubby Franklin or myself. When the night 'sleep disturbers' came over, we were called to make some sort of effort to intercept them.

Sailor Malan had the record so far. Searchlights had picked up two in the one trip and Malan had destroyed them both! Thus whoever was detailed for this job consoled himself with the hope that if he were lucky, he could match Sailor's feat – it was largely up to the searchlights.

It came around to my turn every fourth night, and I was sleeping in the caravan on this night, which followed the drinking session with Sawyer. Suddenly I awoke to hear a Spitfire start up. After a few seconds the engine roared to full throttle for take-off.

Strange, I thought, as I rang the controller to find out what was happening.

Oh, it's all right, said a voice at the other end, Squadron Leader Sawyer said you hadn't had a decent night's sleep for weeks and that if there was a 'scramble' he would take your turn.

The roar of the Spitfire's engine suddenly stopped in an abrupt explosion and I looked out of the caravan window to see a fierce fire blazing about a mile from the end of the runway.

It was a very dark, murky, moonless night after the day of rain and there were no stars. It was easy to see what had happened. Sawyer had never flown a Spitfire on a truly dark night. He had been dazzled by the exhaust flames, losing his orientation and crashing. It had almost happened to me over a year ago and had happened to the three pilots killed on the night of the London blackout test just a year ago. It was not his lucky night.

I jumped in the flight truck and drove to the scene of the crash. The ambulance and firemen were in the process of extracting Sawyer's body from the blazing inferno which was all that remained of the Spitfire.

After being violently sick I returned to the flight caravan and reported to the controller.

Oh, it wasn't a raider after all, he said, so you can go back to bed.

To bed, yes, but not to sleep after that. Poor Sawyer, trying to do me a kindness and let me sleep a little longer had paid for it with his own life. He had a beautiful wife and two little children – oh! The tragedy of war! It seemed that it was always the Sawyers and the Cooks who were killed. Eventually sheer exhaustion put me into a fitful sleep and I awoke at 6.30 – three hours after first light. It seemed impossible – the weather was clearing and a strip of blue sky was visible to the west.

I had some breakfast – almost unheard of these days – but I was still feeling sick from the sight of the crash the night before, and ate little.

Eventually we were brought to readiness at 11.00 a.m., and as Sam was away for a forty-eight-hour leave pass I was acting as squadron commander. The sun was shining and once more it was glorious summer.

At 11.30 we were alerted to take off and patrol Manston at twenty thousand feet. After the patrol we would land at Manston and stay at readiness for the remainder of the day.

I led the squadron off. In those days the twelve Spitfires took off simultaneously in two groups of six, forming up in the air in four sections of three, each flying behind and below the one in front. In this way we could fly through thousands of feet of cloud and still keep together.

At five hundred feet, as the last two sections steadied down in line astern, I wheeled the squadron around in a turn at full climb and turned on oxygen supply as we were going to twenty thousand feet.

Immediately there was a sharp explosion and the oxygen regulator dial blew up. I could see a fierce flame burning behind the instrument panel on the petrol tank. Sparks and dense smoke filled the cockpit and I realised with horror I was in trouble.

My first thought was that perhaps this killed Sawyer – I had to think of a way out. The Spitfire would obviously blow up in a few seconds, as soon as the oxygen fire heated the petrol tank to flashpoint.

If I rolled the Spitfire over and fell out I would be blown back through propellers of the following section leaders. If I turned they were so well drilled they would follow me. My radio was dead – wrecked in the explosion – so I could not tell them what was had happened.

I could see MacPherson on one side and Nicky on the other, and I realised that they would act on hand signals as we had done months of formation aerobatics by hand signals, so I decided on giving them the 'breakaway' signal – that would at least give me a chance to get clear of the squadron and those churning twelve-foot propellers.

It worked – they peeled off and I pulled up into a vertical climb. Five hundred feet was too low for a parachute to open, so I had to get extra height, if possible.

The Spitfire rocketed vertically. I unfastened the straps of the harness and tore off my flying helmet. Many pilots had broken their necks trying to abandon an aeroplane with the helmet still attached. It worked like a hangman's rope. As the Spitfire stalled on the top of its climb, I kicked the left rudder hard and put it into a stall turn. This blew the flames over to one side of the cockpit as I pulled the canopy back, and, jumping up on the seat, pushed out into the cool, sweet, fresh air.

I could see the Spitfire rapidly separate from me, and then the tank blew up with a huge orange flash.

I lost interest in it at that point and pulled the parachute ripcord and waited for the jerk. Nothing happened. I looked down and saw the parachute all caught up around my legs, not streaming out as it should. With some horror I tried to free it and found that the little pilot 'chute, an umbrella-like device with springs to flick it open, had fouled my flying boots and was not doing its job, pulling the silk out. I grabbed it and tore it free, then threw it clear.

After what seemed an age I felt a most violent jerk and for a few seconds could see nothing but stars. These cleared and I realised I was now supported by the parachute.

As my vision improved, I took stock of the situation. A violent crump told me the Spitfire had hit the ground and the main petrol tank had exploded. I could see it clearly, not far below – it had crashed next to some high-tension cables which carried 330,000 volts across the countryside. I was dropping, as far as I could calculate, precisely on those cables, too!

The experts claimed a parachute could be guided by partially collapsing one side and side slipping. This, I told myself, I must do. The important thing was to avoid collapsing the canopy too close to the ground, and I was getting awfully close.

I looked up to take stock of the effect of pulling on one of the main straps, when I received my next nasty fright. The parachute looked like two half-moons! Two complete panels forming a diameter across the canopy were just not there – a couple of fragile seams kept the whole from completely disintegrating.

Now I remembered – I had not had that parachute aired and packed since before Dunkirk. It had been sitting in my cockpit for almost four months, in water and damp, and was in no shape to be used.

Miserably, I abandoned the idea of a sideslip. It would fall to pieces if I sneezed. With a cold, clammy feeling I watched the high-tension wires come up. I missed them by inches.

Before I hit, I heard a loud thunk-thunk report then braced myself for a heavy arrival. The parachutes we used were supposed to break our fall to the equivalent of jumping off a fourteen-foot wall. The thump I made as I hit was equivalent to considerably more, but I was lucky – I landed on a beautifully heaped up row of potatoes – my feet, hands, face and bottom making quite an interesting pattern in the loam.

I got my wind back to find myself surrounded by Land Army girls.

'Ee luv,' said one chubby lass, 'be you one of us or one of them?'

I was wearing my RAAF uniform which was dark blue and they were justifiably uncertain.

So was the Home Guard who ran up and, rightly or wrongly, was going to finish me off with a shotgun full of swan-drop. That was the thunk-thunk I'd heard on my way past the high tension cables! Fortunately, a bit of the Australian vulgar tongue was readily identified as friendly. That problem resolved, we were soon all very matey.

The tubby one rolled up the parachute. 'It's a luvly bit of stuff,' she said. 'See 'ere Gert,' to one of her mates, 'make luvly knickers, wouldn't it?'

Gert: 'It's not much good, luv, it's all ripped to ruddy ribbons. Better take it back and trade it in for a new one.'

All the drama had been acted out in the circuit area of the aerodrome and a sudden crescendo of ringing bells announced the imminent arrival of the station fire engine. In its wake was the ambulance.

I put the parachute into the ambulance and we set off but did not get very far. We ran into a ditch which was invisible as the grass had been scythed flat with the rest of the field. The ambulance rolled over. Fortunately, nobody was hurt.

Next, I mounted the fire engine and with bells ringing madly in my ear, we charged at full throttle down the country lane to the Spitfire. It was still burning furiously and we still had some stubble which had to be doused.

This done, we turned back for the aerodrome. Apparently our fire engine drivers seldom had a run outside the aerodrome, but when they did they liked to open the engine up. Their philosophy was a simple one – fire engines must proceed at top speed! We thundered down a straight stretch of road, the wind in our faces making the tears run from our eyes while our ears were pounded by the bell, which rose to a crescendo as the speed mounted.

The driver did not know the road. Around the corner was a bridge in the centre of a hairpin bend. At our speed there was no chance of making the turn. As we crashed down the embankment, I hurled myself into the air once more and landed for the second time with an even greater crump on the far bank of the creek. The bank was rock hard.

Looking back, the fire engine was upside down, slowly disappearing in a great doughnut of foam. The driver called his crew together and established that all were safe. No one was in the foam or under the engine.

I set off along the road to walk the mile or so back to the aerodrome. A local farmer passed me in his old bullnose Morris, stopped, and as I caught up to him, offered me a lift.

'Not bloody likely,' I replied, 'I'm going to walk!'

He did not seem to understand that I'd had enough. I just wanted to walk back under what was left of my own steam.

Between us the camp doctor and I took stock of my condition. Eyebrows, eyelashes, moustache and hair mostly missing. Skin burnt but not badly. One damaged foot (it turned out I broke a bone in the right one) and a considerable assortment of severe bruises. In his opinion I would be little use for forty-eight hours so I'd better get to bed. I explained that I had a wife up in London whom I hadn't seen since we were married nearly a month earlier, so I was given a pass for forty-eight hours. One of the new boys flew me in the Maggie up to Hornchurch, where I caught a train to London.

Before I left I heard that Wigg had taken two boys up at Manston to investigate a raid above the overcast. They broke through the clouds immediately under a German fighter formation which promptly shot the three of them down. Warrant Officer Phillips and one of the new sergeants were killed; Wigg escaped once more by parachute.

It was a bad day for 'A' Flight, five Spitfires down, all destroyed by fire, the squadron commander and two others killed, Wigg and myself out of action – that just about eliminated 'A' Flight for a couple of days. It was a day I am unlikely to forget.

When I arrived in London I immediately rang Helen. She was working in St Thomas' Hospital as a social worker and was not expecting a visit from me.

We met at Leicester Square and, regardless of my burns and bruises, made for a restaurant called The Queen's Brasserie, known to all fighter pilots in Fighter Command as 'The Queen's Brassiere'. It was a delightful spot with a distinctly Austrian atmosphere. It was popular with the boys because it reminded them of their skiing holidays. Skiing was a generally popular sport with the RAF and Austria had been cheap and unspoiled. Thus most of them found their way there in the balmy days of peace – because of its decor and its associations, The Queen's was thus our peacetime rendezvous and this had continued on into the war.

We walked straight into Hilly Brown, a Canadian flight lieutenant who was stationed at Tangmere – Hilly's face was the colour of beetroot and about twice its normal size. His ginger moustache and most of his ginger hair was gone and his hands were bandaged up. I knew him well from other get-togethers in the relaxed days of peace. He was a great friend of Bob Tuck and Caesar Hull, the South African.

We joined forces and compared notes. Hilly, too, was on forty-eight hours' leave – he had been shot down and his Hurricane had caught fire. He had been burned on his way out, but it was not sufficiently incapacitating to keep him in bed either.

Others joined in the noisy reunion and we had quite a party. No doubt the civilian patrons of the restaurant thought the rowdy red-faced fighter pilots who got so drunk and sang songs out of tune were a raucous nuisance and behaved like that every evening – getting off with the prettiest of the girls, too. Well, such was life. They had no idea what it was like working each day from Manston, nor that it was our first night off for a drink for over a month and we would not have had that if we had not both been burnt that morning.

For all the noise and enjoyment we turned in early. It was the last time I saw Hilly; later he was killed on Malta.

Two days later I was back on the job. Sam Saunders was acting squadron commander again but we were told a new CO would be posted to take Sawyer's place. While I had been away one of 'B' Flight's officers had been killed and my boys were desperately tired from lack of sleep.

Except for the party on the first night I had slept most of the forty-eight hours, so I was feeling much refreshed, if still bruised and stiff. I arrived back at Hornchurch by midday, had a meal in the mess, then flew a new Spitfire back to Southend.

Within half an hour I was climbing up to the east with Nicholas on one side and MacKenzie on the other – we were ordered to investigate some plots which had appeared near Dover, estimated at twenty to thirty thousand feet.

We climbed in perfectly still air towards France at twenty thousand feet and the view as always was superb. Below was the Channel, seemingly no bigger than a large river – in fact, the Thames Estuary seemed wider. As we flew down I looked at Nicholas and he waved back. Then, as usual, I glanced at my other companion. He seemed to be looking down at the floor of his cockpit. I waited for him to look up, but he did not move.

Gradually his left wing dropped and he slipped away from the formation. I turned towards him and called him on the radio.

'Red Three – you OK? Over?' No sound. I called again – by this time his Spitfire was going down and with full climbing power he was gathering speed rapidly.

I called him more urgently. 'Red Three – what the hell's the matter? Wake up Red Three! Red Three! Wake up!'

He continued to roll to the left and dive. The speed was mounting to the high 400s. In a few seconds I would have to break off or hit the speed of sound, which could break up the Spitfire. Obviously MacKenzie had gone to sleep. They were all so tired it was amazing how they kept awake.

I called Control. 'Red Three's gone to sleep – I can't wake him. If you can't wake him in a few seconds, his wings will come off and he'll be killed.'

I listened as the more powerful radio of control called.

'Red Three. Wake up! Red Three wake up! Wake up – do you hear me? Wake up.'

The tone got more urgent, but it was no use. The Spitfire was now diving vertically and slowly spiralling to the left. There was nothing more I could do. I lost sight of him in the haze over the Channel.

Nicholas and I continued on the patrol to thirty thousand feet, but apart from a very remote vapour trail over France there was nothing to be seen.

Half an hour later we returned and landed. No response from MacKenzie. He had gone to sleep and that was it. It could happen to any of us – we were a depressed flight that afternoon. Only Nicky and I were left of the officers and Nicky was in pretty bad shape. He was becoming even more nervy as he became more weary – he desperately needed a rest. Wigg was still away for a couple more days recovering from the effects of being shot down in flames two days before.

MacPherson, who had been one of my best friends over the years, had risen to rank of warrant officer. He was easily the best of my bunch, so I had to appoint him as my deputy to lead the other section of three in the flight. The only problem was that we were now down to five pilots in total – no rests and no time off unless one of us was hurt.

The following day at about three in the afternoon, the five of us returned from an escort job in the Straits of Dover – already I was feeling exhausted again, and we had seven more hours to go before we could be released. We landed at Southend and taxied in to our dispersal point. As I climbed down from my Spitfire, I saw MacPherson's machine still out on the aerodrome where it had finished its run.

I leapt in my little truck and drove out to see what the trouble was. MacPherson usually taxied in without delay and a Spitfire could not be left with the engine ticking over like other aeroplanes, because its radiator would boil within five minutes.

I reached the Spitfire and climbed up on the wing. MacPherson was out cold – fast asleep. He had gone off between landing the Spitfire and coming to rest at the completion of the landing run. I woke him up and he looked around stupidly, shook his head, opened his throttle, finished his taxiing and switched off.

In the caravan we discussed it. MacKenzie, we knew, had gone to sleep in the air. Now MacPherson had missed doing so by moments. Yet with five pilots to fly six aeroplanes, none of us could get any rest. It was some problem and the fatigue made us feel so damned miserable all the time – yet the real fighting, we knew, was still to come.

That night three new pilot officers showed up, two for 'A' Flight and one for 'B' Flight. We welcomed them wearily and Sam shot a few questions at the senior boy – or rather the one among them who seemed to be an old-timer. He was at least thirty or so and had a very mature look about him. The others seemed to be children.

The new boy smiled self-consciously as Sam paused for'him to reply and said, 'Sorry, Sir, I do not understand very well.'

'We are Poles,' said one of the younger members of the trio with fair curly hair. In fact, he looked too young to be in long pants, far less in an Air Force officer's uniform.

'We do not spik the English too good – pliss to talk very slow and I think I understand.'

Hell, I thought, it's come to this – we have no pilots left, only bloody foreigners who can't talk to us.

I suddenly felt too tired to cope but Sam took up the interview.

'You are Polish,' very slowly. 'Good, I'm very glad you have come – we need you very badly. Can you fly Spitfires?'

'Oh yes,' said the curly-haired boy with a grin which lit up his whole face. 'Very good aeroplane – I fly for two hour – Szulkowski he fly for one hour, Gruszka fly for one hour, too.'

So. Their names were Szulkowski and Gruszka. It turned out the boy's name was Drobinski. One hour, two hours on Spitfires – what the hell – and unable to communicate with us!

I won the boy and the short, stocky, fair-haired Gruszka. I explained to my pair very carefully to get to bed and get plenty of sleep, because it might be the last they would get, and to see me at midday the next day when I returned from the morning visit to Manston. Then I would see if I thought they could fly Spitfires.

When we got down to business next afternoon, I was pleasantly surprised to find that they knew all the controls of the Spitfire and that they knew the various procedures for take-off and landing perfectly. They could even locate every tap and switch with their eyes shut. Further, I learned that they had four hundred hours' flying to their credit, albeit in somewhat less advanced planes. Also, they'd had many hours in combat and could fly formation and do aerobatics.

I sent Gruszka off and he started by doing a circuit and a landing, the latter a perfect job. I waved him off and he disappeared for half an hour, returned and landed. Drobinski then did the same. Then, with one on each side, I took them off in formation. They obviously knew their business. I gradually stepped up the manoeuvres until we were doing aerobatics. Both of them sat either side as if riveted to my main planes.

We landed and I had a new respect for these boys. They were really good. The phone rang in the caravan. It was Sam.

'How are your Poles?'

'First class. Yours?'

'Same. Most capable.'

That was all we said but I knew we both felt a little more hopeful about the immediate future.

11

Ordeal at Manston

MacPherson returned from a convoy engagement with an assortment of bullet holes in his Spitfire, and when it came to the point where he lowered his undercarriage for landing the wheels would not come down. Mac went through all the emergency and 'panic' procedures, but still no wheels, so with much reluctance he landed in the centre of the aerodrome on his Spitfire's belly. This grieved him considerably, because he had flown the same aeroplane for some eighteen months and had formed quite an affection for it.

So now he had to go and collect another Spitfire as a replacement. This was an inconvenience because we were again short of pilots as well as aeroplanes. Nicky was off on necessary leave to give him a bit of rest, and we had lost one of our new sergeants. A couple of hours later MacPherson was back and he was very unhappy. His trouble was, he told me, that his new aeroplane was virtually unmanageable – it would only fly with its wings about ten degrees down to the left unless an effort was made to force it to fly level. In Air Force parlance, it was 'left wing low'.

I took the Spitfire up for a test flight. Mac was quite right. It was useless.

While the aeroplane could be flown, this defect was a great curse to the pilot because it flew along like a ship with a list to one side and the only way to correct it was by continual pressure on the control column against the tendency to lean. This could be tolerated for a few minutes at a time, but if the machine was in the air for an hour or more, the effect was like holding a small weight at arm's length for that period. You hardly noticed it for the first five minutes, but at the end of ten the weight felt like a hundred pounds. In half an hour the weight was quite insupportable, an hour meant cramps and general muscular agony – two hours was pure hell.

Another result of this defect was that as soon as the wing dipped, even a degree or so, the aeroplane side-slipped quite significantly. With a five-degree list the slip was far too serious for continuous formation flying, as the aeroplane tended to 'slip' in and ram the leading aeroplane. If, on the other hand, the 'list' was to the other direction, the aeroplane tended to float away from the formation.

'Why did you accept it, Mac?' I asked him.

'Remember that bloke Quill who was the Spitfire test pilot at Southampton? Well, he was up at Hornchurch for some reason or other and when I rejected it the engineer officer appealed to Quill who stated that he had flown it two days ago and it was quite OK.'

Thus overruled, Mac had been obliged to fly it down to Southend. As it was only flyable in an emergency I gave instructions for it to be put at the end of the line until I had a chance to sort it out. It seemed odd to me that Jeff Quill could pass a machine so badly rigged. I was moodily contemplating this latest annoyance when who should walk into my caravan but Mr Quill, all fitted out in a flight lieutenant's uniform.

'I was just thinking about you,' I said. 'What brings you down here to this forsaken outpost?'

'The Air Ministry has agreed that a few of us test pilots can fly with operational squadrons to see what goes on under battle conditions. Bad luck old boy, I've been attached to your flight.'

'By the way,' as an afterthought, 'have you got an aeroplane I could fly?'

'I certainly have – there's one over there at the end of the line – you might recognise it,' I said.

'Isn't that the one Warrant Officer MacPherson was bitching about this afternoon? That's a good aeroplane.'

'Fine', I said, 'it's yours. I suggest you collect your bits and pieces and put them in the cockpit – taxi it up here near mine and you can fly number two next to me for a few trips until you feel you have the score.'

It was late in the day and we were let off the 'Readiness' list to relax at 'Available' so Jeff and I talked for some time about the finer points of the fighter pilot's trade and in particular what to do when the dogfights set in.

At 4.30 the following morning we were ordered into the air to patrol Manston at twenty-five thousand feet. Jeff took off with me, and with Wigg on the other side we climbed to our altitude in a cloudless sky. We spread out to about ten spans and every now and then I glanced at Quill to see how he was going. For the most part his Spitfire remained on an even keel though now and again I noticed it sliding in towards me.

We were ordered around the sky on various courses, but after two hours of scanning the horizon and the sun, we landed at Manston. Jeff was some time before he climbed out of his Spitfire and I was just beginning to think that I must have been imagining its imperfections when he slowly struggled out of the cockpit and eased himself gingerly onto the ground.

He was not smiling when he announced, 'I'll condemn that bloody aeroplane if it's the last thing I do – where's a phone – I want to ring up the works.'

He disappeared wearily inside the crew room for a phone to ring the Spitfire factory at Southampton. I don't know what he said, but we never had a Spitfire from the works which flew other than perfectly level in flight from that day on.

For the most part Spitfires were superbly well put together and could be flown 'hands off' at most speeds. Occasionally one would need a small adjustment to make it fly level. This was usually achieved by attaching a piece of cord along the top or bottom of the aileron trailing edge. Occasionally the trouble was a warped aileron, when considerably more rectification was necessary. Usually this was done, but in the case of this particular Spitfire it was necessary to send it back to the works.

The exchange was arranged and in a few hours Jeff had a new aeroplane, or rather MacPherson had it as he had the prior claim to the machine.

It was easy enough to understand. Quill normally tested the Spitfires as they came off the assembly line for only a few minutes. He was very experienced and could tell almost immediately if there was any serious fault in the assembly. During these tests he seldom flew them for more than a minute or two in a straight line and a tendency to drop a wing slightly on one side or another was common in most makes of aeroplanes and was not viewed as a serious fault, especially in the heavier aeroplanes, where trimming controls were available in the cockpit to correct the tendency in flight. There was no such control on the Spitfire. Having spent most of two hours wrestling with this imperfection, Jeff was physically a very tired man and it was quite unnecessary to mention it again.

Two days later Jeff and I landed at Manston. Paddy Finucane and another pilot were with us. As there were only four planes to refuel, we took a chance and landed together. The intention was to refuel quickly and then continue escorting a convoy a few miles out in the Channel.

The tanker had just started to refuel the second of our Spitfires when we heard an unusual snarling growl from an unfamiliar aero engine. We looked up to see six Me 109s coming in over the hedge with rows of tracer squirting out of their guns.

We scattered at tremendous speed, most heading for the nearest dugout shelter, about a hundred yards away. Our yellow life jackets were obviously noticed by the attackers, as two of them turned off from shooting at the parked aeroplanes to try to hit us on our run to the shelter.

We hit the back of the shelter mound as a barrage of cannon shells and bullets zapped into the other side of the low earth mound over the trench. The 109s snarled past only a few feet above me and hauled up into a steep climb. Another and another screeched past and I judged from the absence of missiles slamming into the mound of earth that I might have time to make the entrance and safety.

Above, the 109s stall turned and came down on the opposite side. They were after me, but I whipped around to the other side in time to get down the 'funkhole'. I was second in.

As I made it, a shower of cannon shells and slugs spat filling the shelter with the stench of exploding cordite.

There was silence for a couple of minutes during which Paddy Finucane hurled himself down the entrance. He only just made the tunnel as another broadside hit the opening – Quill arrived shortly after Finucane, and we were all safe.

The roar of Mercedes engines faded and we emerged into the sunlight. Two of our four Spitfires were burning furiously – the other two were unharmed.

Jeff was furious. If there was one thing which made his blood boil, it was to see Spitfires being destroyed on the ground by Me 109s. He was even more livid on account of the undignified scramble necessary to avoid being massacred by the ground strafers in their efforts to kill us.

We had learned a lesson – never refuel without a top cover. The 109s had come in fast at wave height from Calais. They were so low that the radar had not had a chance to pick them up and warn us.

We continued our convoy patrols but, for some reason we could not understand, there was a lull in these attacks for a couple of days. In between escorts, we were alerted regularly and sent scrambling into the air only to return as the alleged raid disappeared, and according to Control dispersed. After five or six such false alarms, we became sceptical about the reliability of the radar. The controller insisted that they were unusually large concentrations of aeroplanes according to the radar screens, thus we were anticipating a dramatic increase in enemy effort, but each alarm was a fizzer.

The days were hot and we were irritable at being endlessly disturbed as we tried to snatch a few winks of badly needed sleep on the dusty floor of the crew room. Each hour and each day made us feel worse. Already Jeff Quill was looking like one of the old-timers. He too was tired and sported a two day's growth of black beard which somehow made him look like a pirate from a bygone age.

Things changed dramatically late in the morning on Monday 12 August.

According to Adolf Hitler's favourite English-speaking radio personality, Lord Haw-Haw, Britain would lie in ruins by 15 August, in just three days' time. It was a hot, still, humid morning – the light breeze blowing in from the west had dropped and clouds had begun to build up over the Straits of Dover. Nature, it seemed, was holding its breath.

We knew that Hitler had smashed all air resistance in Poland in two days. The same pattern had been repeated in Holland and Belgium, again in a couple of days. France, one of the most powerful nations in the world, had collapsed after three days of air onslaught and the complete and unconditional surrender had been achieved in under six weeks, about the time it took the infantry to walk across the territory. Now, according to 'the Voice', whose prophesies had proved so right each time, it was our turn!

As it was, our fighter defences were desperately thin. More than half of the force was necessarily dispersed north to protect the major fleet installations in Scotland and Scapa Flow, as well as the vital Rolls-Royce factories, the bomber bases and the industrial heart of England, which could not be left unguarded. They were all at least two hundred-odd miles to the north and beyond effective range of help.

What remained, some two hundred and fifty pilots and fighter planes, was dispersed around the south of England from Cornwall to Kent and Essex, a distance of around two hundred and fifty miles. Opposite us, across the powder-blue waters of the English Channel, Hitler had ten times that number of planes poised to strike, or so our intelligence experts had told us – so too did Lord Haw-Haw. Directly across that strip of water, which we could see through the crew-room door from Manston, was the hazy outline of the white cliffs of Calais, barely twenty-five miles away. There, although we could not see them, were six squadrons of Me 109s on the airstrips near the town.

All we could do was wait.

The squadron's pilots looked a motley bunch as they sought relief from the deadly weight of fatigue. We had virtually no reserves so most of us had been on continuous duty since the Dunkirk fighting twelve weeks earlier. The hours of duty were from first light to last light, a spread of twenty hours, with an average of four hours' sleep each night. This was exhausting even in good times, but when the stresses of continuous operational flying and battle were superimposed, the effect was overwhelming. Sleep – just eight hours of peaceful sleep – represented the most precious commodity in life.

There was MacPherson, the tall, spare warrant officer pilot who would not accept a commission because the medical examination involved would risk detection of his secret. One of his eyes was virtually useless. He had tricked his way into aircrew four years earlier and knew he could not do it a second time. He was a superb pilot and incredibly courageous. He never claimed a 'kill', although his score was already in double figures.

Remarkably handsome, Paddy Finucane was a veteran already. He was only eighteen and looked younger because he did not yet shave. His beard had not begun to grow and I suspected he was even younger than he claimed. Yet such was the superb vitality of the boy that he always appeared bright-eyed and full of fun.

His boon companion was Dave Glaser, another eighteen-year-old who was as tall and blond as Paddy was short and dark. He too did not shave, nor did he have any fear. He and Paddy produced the only real sign of life when the squadron was on the ground, horsing around tirelessly like a couple of playful pups. It was a classical David-and-Jonathan friendship and under the most impossible conditions they seemed determined to get the most out of what little life they could anticipate.

'Sam' Saunders was, at twenty-three years old, in temporary command of the squadron. Tall, thin and blond, he was rude to everyone except one or two of us who were spared his barbs. I was one who was excluded, as was Jeff Quill. Sam had to be the shyest man I have ever met and without exception the bravest of a very brave lot. He led us most of the time, except on odd occasions when his duties as de facto squadron commander demanded his attendance elsewhere. Then I led the team. In our eyes Sam had already earned two VCs, but it seemed that fighter pilots did not qualify for this rare honour as the number of witnesses and other conditions required by the charter could never be met. He would earn half a dozen more in our eyes before the crisis was over.

Tom Smart was a plump, easy-going Englishman of twenty summers. He had the joviality of a fat man and was as friendly and outgoing as Sam was introspective and reserved. They were great friends – no doubt their personalities complemented each other in some way.

'Butch' Franklin was a tough, prematurely balding warrant officer who claimed twenty-odd kills already. He alone of the squadron kept a jealous tally of his victories, which he collected with a savage and ferocious satisfaction. His father had been killed in the First World War.

Drobinski, one of the Poles, was another youngster, with blond, curly hair and a pinched look due to enduring fantastic hardships in escaping overland from Poland, then from France. He had the appearance of a prematurely old man who had suffered greatly. We called him Gandhi-ski, but he was a most intrepid boy. He was later to receive the Polish 'VC', which was richly deserved.

Szulkowski was another Pole, a much older man who had great difficulties with the language, but none at all with a Spitfire. In his thirties, he had over 3,000 hours flying to his credit, more than three times the flying Sam or I had, more even than Jeff Quill. He was in Quill's class as a pilot, probably one of the best in the world. He had been a squadron commander in Poland whereas now he was a humble pilot officer in the RAF, but there never was a better one, nor a more cheerful one.

Oh! How we wished we had an extra thousand Spitfires just to back up our meagre waiting twelve. According to Jeff Quill, he had been loaned to the RAF partly to help offset the appalling losses of skilled pilots and partly because of the failure of the main Spitfire shadow factory to supply a thousand or more fighters to date. This was due, he said, to communist subversion and obstruction in the works. This latter achievement of the comrades was part of their contract under the Hitler–Stalin pact of non-aggression and mutual friendship and assistance signed on the outbreak of hostilities against Poland a year earlier. It was the joint socialist contribution to the struggle against British capitalist imperialism led by Winston Churchill, the arch-warmonger!

Spitfire Ace

What we could have done with another 1,000 Spitfires! We had a bare 250 out of the 700-odd fighters available, but the Spitfire was unquestionably the best.

It was eleven o'clock. Saunders, Quill and I were discussing the villainy of the industrial sabotage at the Spitfire works. A sudden clatter of boots running on floorboards jerked us out of our chairs and off towards the aeroplanes a few yards away outside the crew-room door.

'Scramble!'

We were all half-asleep and wearily dragged ourselves to our planes. There was no ginger in our stride, though from so much practice we were all taxiing briskly across the aerodrome for a take-off into the west within a couple of minutes of the call.

'Scramble Base Angels Ten,' shouted the voice as we jumped into our Spitfires. I took my flying helmet off the control column where I always left it attached to its wires and tubes and pulled it on. An airman had jumped up on the wing and handed me the straps of my parachute over my shoulder and I clicked them into the main coupling box; next the webbing belts of the safety harness were secured. I turned on the petrol cocks, switched on and pressed the starter button.

A cloud of bluish smoke appeared and the Rolls-Royce engine growled into life with customary staccato belches and coughs – I opened the throttle enough to roll away and out on to the field. There was now a light wind blowing from the west, so we taxied across the aerodrome to the opposite side and as we did so Sam called Control to check that radio contact was normal.

'Control – Petal Squadron taxiing. Scramble one minute.'

The twelve Spitfires turned into the wind and formed up as we had done a hundred times in the last month. We paused a moment for Sam to call the usual take-off command over the radio. We would take off all together as four sections of three, Sam leading the first six, I following with the second six. Sam's six aeroplanes were ahead and to my left.

We had not begun to roll when there was a violent 'crump' and to my amazement I saw two hangars near the hut we had just vacated erupt into the air in two vast geysers of black smoke and earth. Two more crumps in quick succession sent two more buildings skyward. I could not believe my eyes. We had never been bombed before and I had never seen a large bomb explode except on films.

Two vast fountains of dark-grey earth suddenly erupted thirty feet away to my right, eclipsing the first explosions, and a fraction of a second later the shock wave hit the Spitfire like a huge, invisible hammer. It seemed to move two yards to the left.

Sam called over the radio in his usual calm voice.

'Let's get out of here.'

He need not have said a word. Already each Spitfire was at full throttle. I glanced up as we started to roll, scarcely daring to look, and saw a huge massed formation of some two hundred bombers about five hundred feet above us. The black crosses of Prussia were quite unnecessary to tell us they were hostile; their bomb bays were open and the bombs were right there in front of us and above, falling down exactly above us.

At first it seemed they would all land in front of us, but as we gathered speed they drifted back in their path. I watched fascinated as stick after stick raced along and speared in about twenty yards to my left, chasing Sam's flight as they gathered speed. They seemed to explode in a solid line, rushing right up to the Spitfires and bursting among them. For a moment they were completely lost in the smoke, then the Spitfires were out in front again. One was hit and trailed back behind me, its propeller stopped.

I looked in the rear vision mirror to see what was happening to Jeff Quill and his two boys. They were inches in front of a huge cascading wall of black smoke and dust which reared up like some huge tidal wave about to catch up, crash down and engulf us all.

I knew just one of those bombs in front of us now would kill us all, yet for some curious reason I felt no fear, only a tremendous interest in getting into the air as quickly as possible to avoid that pursuing tidal wave of disaster.

The time dragged but the Spitfire leapt into the air at last. At full throttle plus override, I forced it up to hang on its propeller as I clawed for enough height to escape the bomb blasts if they came.

A pair of Me 109s streaked past, going at twice our speed. Fortunately, we must have been obscured from their approach by the bomb blasts as they had obviously not made a pass at us. They could not have missed.

I looked back and was amazed to see both my wing men, MacPherson and Drobinski, in position and Jeff Quill, imperturbable as ever, moving into his station under my tail. Ahead of me Sam continued to climb with four of his five followers in immaculate formation. I moved in behind and below his rear section.

We could still see the bombers too far ahead to be in range of our guns and they wheeled around and turned east. It was an impressive sight. The clouds had massed up now and were almost a complete cover

over the Channel so once the bombers reached them we had no chance of seeing them again.

Two Me 109s broke through the cloud in front of Sam. They had no idea they were just in front of eleven Spitfires and paid the price. Both blew up as Sam got one and Paddy Finucane the other.

For the next half-hour Control wheeled us around, but it was all over. We returned to Manston and flew around for a while. The entire surface of the aerodrome was covered in white chalk dust. Six hundred large bomb craters were visible, over two hundred of them in two distinct straight lines marking our recent take off run. From start to finish the bomb lines were over a mile and a half long. Just one of those bombs, had it dropped in front of us, could have destroyed our entire team.

We returned to Southend as it was impossible to land at Manston. Later that day we heard Lord Haw-Haw's version of what happened from Germany. He boasted that over three hundred bombers had struck Manston in the most massive attack in history and that twelve Spitfires caught taking off had all been destroyed on the ground!

We had already heard that the Spitfire pilot who had failed to take off was safe. A bomb blast had stopped his propeller but done no other damage. He would return when it was possible to use the aerodrome again.

Well – it was on – the massive attacks on the aerodromes of which we had been warned. The mystery of our few days' respite was solved too. The Germans, with their Teutonic thoroughness, had been practising forming up large formations to provide a hitting force of three to four hundred aeroplanes, roughly half fighters and half bombers. As there would be ten or more of their aerodromes involved in each raid, the organisation and timing could not be taken for granted. They had been practising the art of marrying up three large formations of the size they had been employing against our convoys with such success.

Such a massive onslaught on our aerodromes could reduce us to ruins in a few days, just like Poland, France, Holland and Belgium.

This new turn in events woke us up from our weary exhaustion. If we thought the prospects of survival against a hundred or so of the enemy were slim, our prospects against forces four times as large were much less. That attack on 12 August marked the beginning of the main assaults of the Battle of Britain.

It was a notable day in my life, too, for from that day on I believed in miracles.

12

Death in August

By the following morning it was clear to everyone that this was a new phase in the fighting. 54 Squadron had been bombed at Manston that morning in almost identical circumstances to our own. They made it with a few more yards to spare than we did, as they were alert to the dangers.

To my dismay I found we were to go down there again at midday to relieve 54 Squadron. It seemed impossible that anyone could operate off Manston after the mess made by the carpet bombing of the previous day and that very morning.

When we arrived I discovered how the miracle had been achieved. An Army gentleman in a new device called a bulldozer had succeeded in filling in enough bomb holes to give us a clear strip a hundred yards wide to land and get off on. It was flagged out like a runway and we were back in business.

It seemed to me the height of absurdity that we should risk Spitfires for another attack by the German bombers. We were only twenty-two miles away from their nearest aerodromes and our hopes of surviving by another miracle were nil in my opinion. It took the bombers less than five minutes to cross the Channel at that point. But it seemed the politicians had decided that Manston would be held and operated regardless of danger and inconvenience to the pilots.

Right or wrong, we were on Manston at 12.00. The place was a greater mess than I had imagined. All the dozen or so huts had been destroyed except for two. Two Me 110 fighter bombers had been caught by the explosions of their own bombs. They had crashed and rolled themselves up in front of the crew room in an unrecognisable tangle of metal and wire. Four bodies were still trapped in them – dead – but it had so far defied the resources of the ambulance and rescue teams to extricate them.

Sergeant Franklin came in sporting a pair of very smart German flying boots. He had managed to get them off one of the corpses! They were much dressier than ours.

A belly-landed Me 109 was a few yards away. It was in quite good shape and we spent some time studying it. It was almost the same size as a Spitfire but the petrol tank was behind the pilot instead of being in front of him, as in the Spitfires and Hurricanes. This was a big advantage from the pilot's point of view.

An aeroplane was a structure full of petrol, oil, inflammable engine coolant and explosive bullets or bombs. Once a bullet holed the petrol tank the fumes of petrol and oil in the fuselage became highly explosive. A single tracer bullet was more than enough to explode the lot.

Once the petrol tank was set on fire a vast sheet of brilliant orange flame trailed back from the tank, rapidly melting and consuming what was left of the frail aluminium structure. No human could survive the heat of the burning petrol. The few who made it through the flames were always terribly burned.

The Germans, on the other hand, had a reasonable chance to get out without too much personal incineration unless they were hit by bullets, in which case their end would be somewhat slower than that of their opposite numbers in the Spitfires and Hurricanes.

One disadvantage of the Me 109 was that the pilot sat immediately over the wing and this gave him a much greater blind area below him than was the case with both the Spitfire and the Hurricane. This meant that he would miss seeing some of us, especially if we were underneath him. That was worth remembering!

Already the ground crews at Manston had got themselves organised. A slit trench was dug to the side of each Spitfire's parking area, the starter batteries were plugged in and as soon as the engines started the crews slapped shut the plug covers (where the battery plug was inserted) and dived into their foxholes.

Now that we knew the real heat was on, we took off every time a sizeable plot was picked up by the radar, even at extreme range. There was no more taxiing out into wind and forming up. We just opened up as soon as the engine was firing evenly and took off straight ahead. This cut down our take-off time by about three minutes, and although we did not know it at the time this was enough of a margin to prevent the Germans catching us on the ground again.

The aerodrome now looked like a white desert with thousands of bomb holes everywhere. A bulldozer growled and creaked away in the bright sunlight as we sat around at 'Readiness', more or less holding our breath waiting for the phone to ring.

The crew-room table had to be manhandled down from the roof. It was a big table and it took some manipulating to get it back inside the hut and through the narrow doorway. It was the mystery of the week how it had been heaved out through the door in the first place, although once out it was not hard to figure how it had got up on the roof.

Wigg had a theory that during the bombing raid even the table legs had turned to jelly and that was how it had been blown out of the room in the first place.

The laugh of the week had been provided by the duty pilot. His hut was drunkenly perched on the side of the biggest bomb crater of the bombing, which was some thirty feet or more across and about fifteen feet deep. A huge pile of chalk was heaped on its roof like some crazy mass of snow. It seemed the duty pilot had taken cover under the table during the bombing raid and somewhat predictably everything shook and rocked like a violent earthquake. When the noise had stopped and all was quiet, he gingerly emerged head first from under the table like some prehistoric tortoise and as he did so the electric clock, which had broken loose from the wall and was swinging back and forth, finally broke its wire. It fell on his head, knocking him out cold. Nine stitches and a week in hospital after surviving some thousands of bombs – one, the largest, only inches from his own head.

I think the remaining duty pilot felt his mate was the lucky one. He had no great hopes of surviving many more such bomb raids – and there were bound to be more.

About three o'clock, pounding boots from the direction of the phone sent us all headlong to our Spitfires. Mine was already ticking over as the orderly shouted, 'Base ten thousand feet.'

We took off in some sort of loose order, but squadron formation on take-off was now out of the question as the chalk dust blinded everyone. This time we took off in threes and formed up in the air. The sky was clear this time, and the attackers would not be able to elude us by making for the clouds.

At seven thousand feet we could see a great cloud of aeroplanes. They were well above our level. There were several hundred bombers in a mass with little packets of fighters everywhere. Sam turned away and we climbed at full throttle. They did not seem to take any notice of us as we continued to climb and eventually we were about five thousand feet above the top bombers and to their south.

We headed in towards them, still climbing, and I felt my stomach curl up into a hard knot. There were twelve of us and about four hundred of them. Slowly they came down below us at about two o'clock ahead. We were almost over the top of them when Sam called, 'Number One Attack go.'

We nosed down one behind the other, the speed mounting rapidly. Perhaps they did not see Sam as he started his dive, but before he got within range of the nearest bomber, most of the 250-odd bombers were firing tracer at him or at us. He and his wingman, Tom Smart, were virtually obscured by the crazy maze of tracer. As we flew down along parallel paths, the tracer grew as thick as rain and it had a curious negative effect on us – even the old trails somehow seemed lethal. It seemed quite impossible to traverse that barrage with any hope of survival.

All of a sudden large bombers were everywhere in front – big ones – with endless streaks of tracer coming from them at point-blank range. Then we were in the clear blue sky again and the attack was over. I had fired as I went past one of the bombers in such a way that I should have hit him and another which was in line with him, but the whole attack had been futile as far as I was concerned.

I pulled over to the side and found myself flying along with six or seven groups of Me 109s. They seemed to be more interested in the bombers than in me, so I lined a group of four up and fired at the leader. If my deflection was out, some of the slugs should have found their mark on his followers.

They wheeled off wildly towards the main formation and I made a pass at a group of three. I don't think they even noticed me and I ran out of ammunition as I pulled around behind them. There was not much future in sticking around without bullets, so I made a tight turn and, satisfying myself I was not being stalked, opted out of the fight.

I was more than a little pleased to still be alive, and as I made for the aerodrome I called Control to see if it was still possible to land there. It was, so I made for it without too much haste because I wanted to be sure that the bombers were not going to clobber it as I landed just for a change.

I wondered how many of our boys would be alive after that suicidal attack of Sam's. It would not have surprised me if only half of them made it, or so I decided before I landed. Half an hour later we were all back or all accounted for. Wigg and one of Sam's boys were walking back from some remote Kentish village, but we were all in one piece as a squadron. It seemed incredible.

The refuelling over, we discussed the raid at some length. Sam had made a pass at the leader, or the one he thought was the leader, but this had left the rest of us to dive through the main body of the tightly massed bomber formation, where the risk of collision seemed overwhelming. We had somehow missed each other and at the same time had been unsuccessful as far as we could see in hitting any of the enemy machines. Sergeant Franklin claimed two Me 109s, but that was routine with him.

Apparently the target of the raid had been Eastchurch, and the raid had made quite a mess of that aerodrome, but before the attackers returned to their bases other Hurricane and Spitfire squadrons in the group had destroyed about a score of their machines. There was another raid that evening, but it was a hundred miles or more to the west, near Tangmere, and although we went over to give a hand the bombers were back in France by the time we arrived.

The first two days of the big blitz were over. The much-advertised 'Eagle Day' was about to be launched. 'The practices had been run, now it was to be for keeps.' So said the German radio in their English broadcasts, and Lord Haw-Haw laconically claimed that the squadron of twelve aeroplanes taking off from Manston on the 12th had all been destroyed by the invincible Luftwaffe. Well, that was us, and we were still all alive and kicking, even if we were not landing too many kicks at this juncture.

We were dreary with the fatigue from insufficient sleep next day when we landed at Manston at midday to do our turn at 'Readiness'. There had been some attacks in the morning, but by the time we had been mobilised from 'Available' and despatched to the area the scraps were over.

I sat on the floor in the chalk dust, too tired to read and too tense to go to sleep. Our aerodrome was due for another blitz. As soon as the telephone bell rang, we would have to reach our Spitfires in even time and make no mistakes starting off or we would be in for real trouble.

At three o'clock the controller rang. A warning had come through that the German crews were getting into their bombers in France and that another 'carpet raid' was underway. The French Resistance were getting warning messages through on their radios so we checked to see that all was set and waited.

A quarter of an hour later the controller warned that the radar was registering a build-up about sixty miles to our south-east, but not to go yet as it might be a feint – aimed to get us into the air long enough to have to land and refuel – the main attack would then hit as we were refuelling.

A few minutes later and it was clear that it was on. We took off and climbed out over the Channel, then turned back to the west, climbing over England. At twenty thousand feet we turned east again and after about five minutes we could see them – somewhere between 400 and 500 aircraft. 200 to 250 of them were bombers, which made quite a spectacle. As we rapidly drew nearer on a head-on approach, the much smaller fighters could be seen rather like wasps escorting a large flock of pigeons. The bombers were rock steady except for the odd ones out on the flanks, where formation flying was most difficult. The fighters, on the other hand, gave an impression of movement as some, if not all, were weaving around using their superior speed to turn continually in their search for us.

There were several large cumulus clouds towering up to thirty thousand feet and the formation leader would have to avoid these or they would wreck his fine formation. We had decided that I would try to cover Sam's attack this time to cut down the risk of hostile fighters attacking him as he attacked the leader.

We closed rapidly, within a couple of minutes or so, and Sam was on his way down. Two Me 109s had seen him and were after him, so I gave chase and opened fire on the leader. He must have seen me or the bullets registered on his machine, for he hauled up in a full-powered climbing turn with me and four other Spitfires on his tail. Several groups of Me 109s came in from both flanks and we were forced to break up and take evasive action.

Thus I found myself surrounded by about forty-odd fighters with no visible friendly support. They were above, at the same level and below me, while a mile below again the great armada of bombers ground on its course up the Thames Estuary.

The fighters all seemed to have their eye on me. No matter which way I looked they were all turning in my direction. The most immediate threat came from the leader of twelve 109s, who had tightened up his turn so that he was almost able to get a head on attack on me. As he was almost straight ahead of me, at this instant, I straightened out abruptly and flew straight at him, the eight guns snarling. I was out of range at first, but in four or five seconds he was only a couple of hundred yards away, closing fast.

He lost his nerve or I hit him, because he suddenly nosed down under my attack. All his squadron followed him. They were all firing their guns but they had no chance of hitting me as they followed their leader. Why they did not break up and attack me separately I'll never know. That reduced the odds, so I then fastened on the next nearest and he opted out together with a friend who was trailing him.

There were still half a dozen other groups still above me and I had no chance of out-climbing them while they could all get down on to my tail. At this stage I could see no chance of surviving the odds, so I suddenly dived on one of the few below me and, as I passed him, kept on going.

The bombers had vanished, and I made the safety of one of the large clouds before my pursuers could open fire effectively. The cloud was rough and threatened to pull the wings off the Spitfire given the high speed at which I dived into it, but I had no chance of surviving a thirty-to-one fight with most of them above me so the cloud was my only hope. A dozen seconds later I broke out of the cloud only to see more clouds banked up in front. I could see no sign of my pursuers, so I weaved around the clear spaces on the off chance that I might find something to expend the remainder of my ammunition on, but everything had vanished. I called Control and they told me to return to Manston.

One of our Poles and one of 'B' Flight's new boys were not accounted for. Later that evening we heard that they had been killed. The odds were too severe for all of us to escape unscathed.

The following day the events were almost identical. This time, however, the skies were clear except for a few thin strata patches over the Channel and one or two at higher levels around the twenty thousand feet – no big cumulus to play hide and seek in or to use as escape hatches!

Once again we had plenty of warning and were above twenty thousand feet when we saw them coming. The only difference was size – this time there were almost twice as many bombers. The fighter strength was more difficult to estimate as they were hard, if not impossible, to see at first.

Sam called up, 'Red Leader, you go in as high cover and try to occupy the fighters – I'll have another go at the leader.'

'OK,' I replied, and climbed for height over their topmost fighters.

As the raid came towards us in its massive grandeur, the fighters became visible. I seemed to be well above the highest of the escort. Realising that for the first time I was up sun, and therefore probably not visible to them, I cautiously closed in. Six 109s were flying along quietly just below me so I slipped down and in behind the rearmost one. It was a perfect shot, and as I pushed the button the 109 dissolved in a huge puff of black smoke.

'Bullseye!'

I pulled up in case the flight tried to attack me, but to my surprise the leader just put his nose down and dived for France, firing all his guns. His four remaining stooges dived and fired also. They disappeared from sight.

As if by magic, four more, flying almost line abreast, appeared from nowhere in a perfect position for a repeat performance. I did the same thing again. To my amazement my target exploded again, but before I had time to pull up the other three dived abruptly, wheeling back to France.

There was another group a few hundred yards to the right. I went across and opened fire on the nearest and down he went, back to France, closely followed by his mates. He did not oblige by exploding.

A single Messerschmitt below was too tempting to ignore, so I dived on him. He saw me coming and dived. I was close on his tail, so I sprayed him for about five thousand feet. We went through two layers of cloud and by this were down to ten thousand feet. I pulled out as the speed was very close to the speed of sound and the Spitfire was believed to disintegrate if this speed were attained. The 109 continued on its dive to the cloud layer over the sea. It showed no sign of pulling out or slowing down as it entered the cloud.

I allowed the speed to drop as I circled at four thousand feet, then descended through the cloud. It was a thin layer and directly below was a large patch of white on the dark water which could have been left by my quarry. There was no other sign of aeroplanes, so I climbed up to see if I could find the large raid again.

Above the top layer the air was absolutely empty of all aeroplanes. I called Control and was given a course to steer; a minute later and I saw a dot on the horizon. I was flying straight at it and it was not moving. Either it was going the same way as I, or it was coming towards me.

A few seconds later and it was clearly a single-engined fighter – either a Spitfire or a Me 109. Which? It answered the question for me and dozens of tracer streaks flashed towards me. As we did not fire tracer I instantly knew he was not one of ours, but before I could make a move to put my sights on him, he flashed by overhead, tracer still pouring out of his guns. He was travelling at his full speed, I should think, and running slightly downhill at about 400 mph. My own speed would have been around 350 mph, so our combined closing speed would be about 750 mph or twelve miles a minute. As neither the Spitfire nor the Me 109 could be seen five miles distant from head on, this meant that he had come from a position beyond my range of vision to point blank in thirty seconds. He probably opened fire a mile away when he still could not be sure of my identity about five seconds before he passed me. I turned as rapidly as I could through 180 degrees, but as this took about a minute at my speed he was out of sight by the time I was going in his direction. It was a good lesson on the speed at which things happened – out of sight to point blank in thirty seconds, with five seconds to identify friend or foe, then out of sight again in the same time. It meant that at any time a clear blue sky could produce an enemy who could destroy you in half a minute – much less if he came from the sun.

I was ordered to return to Southend as Manston had been savaged again.

When I told my ground crew that two of my victims had blown up and another had crashed into the sea in all probability, they were almost delirious with excitement. They took my success as part of their own – and very rightly so! These two youngsters, both in their early twenties, were fanatical in the care they lavished on my aeroplane. In addition to being on duty whenever I was (which was about eighteen hours a day), they worked through the night as well, and usually slept on the ground under the plane's wing during the day once they had the machine checked over and serviced to their satisfaction. They were the most loyal and devoted boys with whom I have ever had anything to do. The proof of their work was in the performance of the machine they serviced.

However, while I basked in their elation, I could not help thinking that it might so easily be my turn to be blown up next. I had destroyed other aeroplanes and the men in them, but it was kill or be killed. These formations had to be destroyed or we ourselves would suffer the same fate.

*

Our duties as interceptors of the enemy's fighter screens took us up to greater and greater altitudes. A week or so before the battle began, the de Havilland people who made the variable-pitch propellers on our Spitfires had turned up with a supply of little boxes which they attached to an oil tube on the back of the Rolls-Royce engine. This was a constant-speed unit and it weighed about a pound or so. The effect it had on the Spitfire was truly magical.

Prior to its attachment, a Spitfire was staggering at twenty-four thousand feet and was only just flyable at twenty-five thousand feet and it took some twenty minutes to make that altitude. Now it shot up at twice the speed and reached twenty-five thousand feet in less than ten minutes. It continued to climb beautifully to thirty-eight thousand feet, when for some reason the spark plugs started to give trouble and the engine ran roughly. New plugs were provided and the Spitfire was able to make forty thousand feet comfortably and still climb if necessary.

However, other problems immediately plagued us. Intense cold in what was essentially an unheated and unpressurised cockpit froze hands and feet in minutes. If we put sufficient clothes on to combat the cold it was impossible to move around and keep a reasonable lookout. Worse still, after reaching thirty thousand feet, the Perspex and windscreen frosted up badly due to the condensation of the water vapour in the breath and it was only possible to see at all by continuously scraping off the frost as it formed.

Even though we scraped away furiously, the little patch of clear Perspex quickly refrosted and the combination of ice crystals and frozen leather scratched the canopy badly, making it even more difficult to see. As it was, we could only see through the hole in the frost for a few seconds before it fogged over again and we could only get an all-round view by progressively scraping the frost off in patches all around the canopy from left to right, a peephole at a time!

What we could see of the other planes in our own formation revealed that we were leaving vast streamers of vapour behind us as if we were some kind of rocket. If the opposition were not similarly cursed with frost, they would have no difficulty in locating us and closing in for a kill. We would not even know they were there, and we would not even get the warnings of seeing the tracer go past.

Sometimes we would spot other vapour trails and we would set off after them. However, it was most difficult to keep them in sight and as we approached they would usually dive for the lower altitudes and that would be the last we saw of them. It was a curious game of blind man's bluff – we could see, but only just and then only for a few seconds at a time.

I was going through this routine at thirty-five thousand feet one afternoon when I suddenly felt a delightful sensation of relief from all the tensions of the combat area surge over me. It was a lovely afternoon for a little snooze. I was weary and at last I was at peace with the world and not the slightest bit afraid. To hell with the Kraut, and frost, and the ice crystals, and the damn cold.

The engine noise changed and I could not care less – the rush of air grew to a shrill scream, but I loved it – I was so happy and relaxed. Then I realised – I must have run out of oxygen! My brain faintly registered I was passing out. The oxygen must have given up or perhaps the pipe to my mask had become disconnected. Faint fear began to register and I blanked out visually as I felt around for the pipe. I found it and managed to push it clumsily over my nose – I took a couple of deep breaths and began to come back to reality. I could see again. The nose was down – the speed well up over the 400 mph, altitude fifteen thousand feet and the engine screaming – I had dived some four miles in the process. I pulled the throttle back and eased out of the dive. There was plenty of time and no danger at all, but I was very lucky that I realised I was passing out and found that oxygen tube, or it might have been the North Sea for me.

The oxygen attachments were crude and far from efficient. Mine had become caught up around the back of my neck, where it passed so as to prevent undue clutter in front of the pilot. As I turned my head from side to side to keep a lookout, the tube had come off the little pipe attachment on the gas mask and thus, in a few seconds, at thirty-five thousand feet, I was due to pass into unconsciousness.

Others had similar experiences. Alan Deere of 54 Squadron actually passed out, coming to in a shallow dive at very high speed at about five thousand feet, where there was enough oxygen to revive him naturally. He was lucky that his aeroplane was not by then in an unmanageable dive, which no doubt happened to many others in those days.

1. 28 May 1940. Spitfires of 65 Squadron on their way to patrol over Dunkirk. 'Intruding into this peaceful early morning scene was one vast black storm cloud, perhaps ten miles in diameter at its base and surging upwards in huge black turbulent billows to some thirty-five thousand feet or more, where it flattened out into an enormous black anvil. It looked evil, an overwhelming presence.'

2. Supermarine Spitfire K9903, YT-A, of 65 Squadron, Gordon Olive's regular aircraft in the early days of the war. He flew this machine in the desperate air battle of 28 May 1940. After repairs it did not go back to 65 Squadron. It was delivered to 64 Squadron at Leconfield, Yorkshire, on 3 September 1940, but was then involved in a crash just three days later on the 6th. K9903 was finally struck off charge on 7 October 1940.

3. Amid the swirling thick black smoke from oil fires at Dunkirk, Gordon Olive's painting depicts vivid memories of his desperate air battle of 28 May 1940. The Australian's wingmen last saw him *chasing* no less than a dozen of the formidable Messerschmitt 109s.

4. Scramble at Manston, 12 August 1940. Looking to the right and behind: 'They were inches in front of a huge cascading wall of black smoke and dust which reared up like some huge tidal wave about to catch up, crash down and engulf us all. I knew just one of those bombs in front of us now would kill us all.'

Above: 5. Ideal RAF tactics of the Battle of Britain. Because of their higher performance, Spitfires (of 65 Squadron) climb to engage the escorting German fighters, while Hurricanes attack the bombers. 'Our role had become almost exclusively "anti-fighter" as distinct from "anti-bomber". One reason was because we were the most easterly squadron and therefore first to intercept when the raids made their way up the Thames Estuary. Another reason was that we were equipped with Spitfires and were accordingly better fitted for taking on the Me 109s, which were superior to the Hawker Hurricanes in most respects.'

Right: 6. Gordon Olive just prior to the fighting over Dunkirk.

7. 'We nosed down one behind the other, the speed mounting rapidly. Perhaps they did not see Sam as he started his dive, but before he got within range of the nearest bomber, most of the 250-odd bombers were firing tracer at him or at us. He and his wingman, Tom Smart, were virtually obscured by the crazy maze of tracer.'

8. Scramble at Manston, 12 August 1940. 'I watched fascinated as stick after stick raced along and speared in about twenty yards to my left, chasing Sam's flight as they gathered speed. They seemed to explode in a solid line, rushing right up to the Spitfires and bursting amongst them. For a moment they were completely lost in the smoke.'

Above: 9. 25 August 1940, Me 110s flying in defensive circles. 'Sam led in with an attack on the leader of the uppermost wing of fighters and followed on towards the formation on the outer flank. He appeared to be lining five or six aeroplanes up in his sights simultaneously. His attack must have panicked the fighter leader, for all four elements of the fighter escort began flying around in defensive circles. They went into it so simultaneously that it must have been a radio command. I remained five thousand feet above the formations. I was puzzling over the best way to attack these defensive circles when a flash of inspiration showed me a better way ... While they wheeled around in their merry-go-rounds, the fighters were rapidly losing their bombers, who were flying on up the estuary unescorted.'

Right: 10. About to leave Australia on the P&O liner *Narkunda* in January 1937. Gordon Olive is second from the top, near the front rail of the steps.

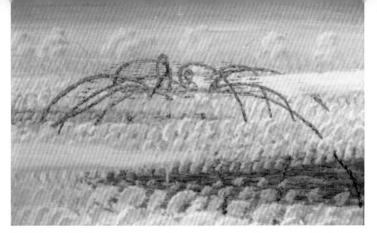

11. 25 August 1940. 'I noticed several smaller dots diving in – the Hurricanes and Spitfires from the squadrons closer to London. As I watched, column after column of black smoke appeared and arched over down through the strata clouds. I counted about a dozen. Bomber after bomber exploded and dived out of the formation. Within a few minutes, scores of smoke trails, the bombers arching downwards, made a pattern in the sky like the ribs of a gigantic umbrella.'

12. 'Early in the afternoon of 25 August we made contact with a smaller than usual formation of about 250 aeroplanes. To begin with I thought they were unescorted bombers, but as they came in towards us, we realised that there were about 150 to 200 Dornier bombers escorted by about 120 Me 110 fighters.'

Opposite: 13. Attacking from above. 'We had plenty of warning and were above twenty thousand feet when we saw them coming. The only difference was size – this time there were almost twice as many bombers. The fighter strength was harder to estimate as they were hard, if not impossible to see at first.'

Above: 14. 'It was clear that it was on. We took off and climbed out over the Channel, then turned back to the west, climbing over England. At twenty thousand feet we turned east again and after about five minutes we could see them – somewhere between 400 and 500 aircraft. 200 to 250 of them were bombers, which made quite a spectacle. As we rapidly drew nearer on a head-on approach, the much smaller fighters could be seen rather like wasps escorting a large flock of pigeons. The bombers were rock steady except for the odd ones out on the flanks where formation flying was most difficult. The fighters, on the other hand, gave an impression of movement as some, if not all, were weaving around, using their superior speed to turn continually in their search for us.

Below: 15. Olive family memorabilia – Gordon Olive's flying goggles.

Above: 16. Dogfight! 'All of a sudden large bombers were everywhere in front – big ones – with endless streaks of tracer coming from them at point blank range. Then we were in the clear blue sky again and the attack was over ... I had fired as I went past one of the bombers in such a way that I should have hit him and another which was in line with him, but the whole attack had been futile as far as I was concerned ... I pulled over to the side and found myself flying along with six or seven groups of Me 109s.'

Below: 17. Me 109E under attack. It is damaged and one wheel of its undercarriage has dropped down.

18. Climbing above the enemy. Such beautiful tight formations were ideal for peacetime air show flying demonstrations over Hendon but they were wrong for air combat. Only the leader's eyes were free to search the sky for enemy aircraft; the attention of the other pilots was more on maintaining formation! RAF tactics needed to change.

19. The pilots of 'A' Flight talking tactics in February 1941. David Glaser is second left and Gordon Olive, with back turned, is second right.

Above: 20. 'We headed in towards them, still climbing, and I felt my stomach curl up into a hard knot. There were twelve of us and about 400 of them.'

Below: 21. Head-on attack! Go!

Above: 23. 'We climbed at full throttle. They did not seem to take any notice of us as we continued to climb.'

Below: 24. After the outbreak of war, 65 Squadron's identification letters were changed from 'FZ' to 'YT'.

Opposite: 22. Attacking bombers out of a clear blue sky. At the end of August, 65 Squadron was sent north to Turnhouse for much-needed 'rest'. Gordon Olive recalled, 'The weather helped quite a bit too. Gone was the unbroken Australian summer which had proved so helpful to the Germans and so tiring for us. Several days of dirty weather blew in from the North Atlantic and gave us a chance to stop flying and rest in the Mess. At every opportunity. we slept. There was very little interest in parties, for a start, we were all so thoroughly exhausted. When flying was washed out for the day we just went to our rooms and slept.'

Above: 25. 13 August 1940. 'Now we knew the real heat was on, we took off every time a sizeable plot was picked up by the radar, even at extreme range. There was no more taxiing out into wind and forming up. We just opened up as soon as the engine was firing evenly and took off straight ahead. This cut down our take-off time by about three minutes and although we did not know it at the time, this was enough of a margin to prevent the Germans catching us on the ground again.'

Below: 26. A 'scramble' staged for the camera.

27. The RAF was unprepared at the time of the Munich crisis in 1938. 'We were issued with some old overalls and paintbrushes and were directed to paint our lovely silver Gladiators brown and green. This was a messy business but all hands had to get at the job. Urgency was extreme. In the evenings we had to load ammunition belts by hand as there was no machinery on the camp to do the job.'

28. Olive family memorabilia – Gordon Olive's medals and awards. From left to right, his CBE; DFC; 1939–1945 Star with Battle of Britain Clasp; Air Crew Europe Star; Pacific Star; Defence Medal; 39–45 ASM; Coronation Medal; Air Efficiency Medal; and Cadet Force Medal.

Above: 29. 'We were almost over the top of them when Sam called, "Number One Attack go!" We nosed down one behind the other, the speed mounting rapidly.'

Below: 30. Dornier Do 17s on the way to the target.

Above: 31. A section of Spitfires preparing to dive onto a box of Heinkel He 111 bombers. (Detail from 29.)

Below: 32. Cockpit of the Heinkel 111 bomber. The pilot is on the left, the bomb aimer/front gunner is lying down looking out for RAF fighters. 1940.

Above: 33. Escorting Me 109s make a head-on pass to disrupt the Spitfire attacking their bombers.

Below: 34. Messerschmitt Me 109E. (Refer to Notes section.)

Above: 35. Although the ideal situation was for Spitfires to hold off the escort fighters while Hurricanes attacked the enemy bombers, sometimes because of circumstances the roles had to be reversed, as the painting shows.

Below: 36. Hurricanes peeling off to attack. A work unfinished by Gordon Olive. Pencil lines indicate where the enemy bombers would have been painted into the scene.

Above: 37. Spitfires diving in line astern to carry out a Number One Attack on the incoming bombers. 'We nosed down one behind the other, the speed mounting rapidly.'

Below: 38. A bomber gunner's view of a pair of Spitfires closing in for the 'kill' (this time it is on a friendly Hampden bomber during exercises).

Above: 39. 'The German ace of aces, Adolf Galland, writing about the Luftwaffe air offensive in 1940, claims that he took part in raids of more than 1,000 aircraft at this time. I reported raids of more than 600 but my method of counting was somewhat sketchy. Few on our side had the time to be thorough with their arithmetic. On one occasion, I merely divided the "gaggle" into four. Next, I halved one of the quarters mentally, then tried to count this segment. I got up to eighty in a rapid count before a rain of tracers from behind, and above, diverted my attention. As I got busy with the chore of turning on to their tails, I made a quick calculation of at least 650, perhaps 800 machines. This was considered highly improbable at the time but in retrospect, these guesstimates of mine were not far out and were probably conservative.'

Right: 40. W/Cdr Gordon Olive DFC in a caricature by Dubois.

41. An air fighting rule of 1940: 'Beware of the Hun in the sun.' On one occasion, 'they ... were firing at us when we saw them. They slid by underneath us in groups of two and four, passing close enough to see the pilots' eyes. Their oxygen masks made then look like monkeys. I was more impressed by their toylike appearance than anything else and by the thin, dead straight, white pencil line streaks of the tracer as they flashed across in front of us.' Commenting on tracer bullets, Gordon concluded that there 'was an advantage we enjoyed by not using tracer in our ammunition. My original target did not know of my attacks until the bullets began to clang around his machine. My initial attack from behind was not detected. On the other hand, the formation of six that attacked me ... gave me a most welcome warning by the masses of parallel lines of tracer, which not only told me of their unsuccessful attack, but also indicated which side was free of bullets and therefore safer to turn to.'

42. Pat Hughes in a quieter mood.

Above: 43. Air fighting rule: 'The advantage of height is half the battle.'

Right: 44. A gathering of 65 Squadron pilots in 1938–9. Gordon Olive is second from the end on the left of the line and John 'Jack' Kennedy, the other Australian in the unit, is the tallest man in the centre.

45. Gloster Gauntlets at RAF Hornchurch at the Empire Air Day in May 1937.

46. Cadets of the Point Cook class of 1936. Left to right, back row: Cadets Paine, Rogers, Robertson, Dillon, Cooper, Jackson, Sladin, Fowler, Kinane, Good, Cameron. Centre: Cosgrove, Yates, Hullock, Hughes, Armstrong, Wight, Grey-Smith, Gilbert, Power, Kelaher, Sheen, Brough. Front: Johnson, Kaufman, McDonough, Boehm, Allsop, Hartnell, Olive, Marshall, Mace, Campbell, Eaton. Most subsequently had careers of distinction in the RAAF and RAF. Of them, Gordon Olive, Pat Hughes, Desmond Sheen and Dick Power flew in the Battle of Britain.

Top: **47.** A line-up of Heinkel
He 113 fighters. This type
was actually the He 100D.
It was generally believed
that this fighter had entered
service with the Luftwaffe,
when in fact only twelve
were produced and none
were accepted for service.
In a successful bid to fool
Allied intelligence, the dozen
were painted with different
insignias several times over
for propaganda photographs,
thus creating the impression
that they were in widespread
use. On numerous occasions,
Me 109s were mistakenly
identified as He 113s – an
easy error to make in the
heat of battle – and were
entered as such in many RAF
combat reports and official
records.

Middle: **48.** An Australian
student in Germany, Pete
Bjelke-Petersen, walking
through the streets of
Berlin, the trappings of the
Nazi movement evident
everywhere.

Bottom: **49.** 'Stuart Walch
from Tasmania was killed
off Portland Bill. True to his
nature he went back to try to
extricate two new boys out
of trouble when they lagged
behind and were caught up
by a large force of German
fighters. He saved his new
boys, but lost his own life
in the process. If any of the
boys were mourned by their
fellows, Stuart was.'

50. A line-up of 65 Squadron pilots, left to right: Robert MacPherson; John Nicholas; Stan Grant; Gordon Olive; Lord Balfour, Secretary of State for Air; Henry Sawyer; Gerald 'Sammy' Saunders; Tom Smart; and Richard Kilner.

Left: 51. Gordon Olive at 'Readiness' at Tangmere in December 1940.

Right: 52. No. 456 Squadron's last CO, S/Ldr Bob Cowper, DFC and Bar.

Above left: 53. 'Another tragedy was the loss of Pat Hughes. Those who knew Pat well were all agreed that he typified the best of the Air Force pilots. Virtually without fear, he had a sense of humour which never deserted him in the worst moments. After being credited with six kills by his fellow pilots (and sixteen by his commanding officer), he was killed one day as the wing of a bomber broke off because of his determined and excellent shooting. Unfortunately Pat was so close up behind the bomber that he flew into the wing, and it wrecked his plane and no doubt killed him instantly. Pat died at the height of his prowess and in the full bloom of his manhood. There was no more typical Australian in the fight than Pat. His end was a personal loss to all who knew him.'

Above right: 54. Desmond Sheen considered himself one of the luckiest pilots in the Battle of Britain, being shot down twice and surviving. He also survived the war and afterwards had a distinguished career in the RAF. He has been credited with up to six enemy aircraft destroyed, including one of the few night victories scored by a Spitfire pilot, this occurring in March 1941.

Right: 55. Robert Bungey, the CO of 452 RAAF Squadron in the second half of 1941. 'His dual performances in France and in the Battle of Britain alone must rate Bob Bungey as one of Australia's truly great airmen. His heroism had gone unheralded at the time as his COs never seemed to survive long enough to put him up for the gallantry awards he had earned so often.'

Left: 56. Dick Power, from Gordon's 1936 Point Cook class, also survived the war. He flew Bristol Blenheims as night fighters but they were ineffective, being too slow to catch the German bombers even when equipped with primitive airborne radar. His squadron was transferred to Coastal Command.

Above: 57. 'The latest bomber, the Bristol Blenheim, was fifty miles an hour faster than the fastest fighter in service and popular opinion amongst the young pilot fraternity was that the bomber was now faster than the fighter and that was the way it would stay.'

58. The first twin-engined fighter flown by Gordon Olive was the Westland Whirlwind, as his logbook shows, for experience of the type on 4 September 1940, after 65 Squadron had moved north out of 11 Group.

59. Messerschmitt Me 110. Although this type failed as an escort fighter in the Battle of Britain when confronted by the RAF's more manoeuvrable Spitfires and Hurricanes, it was still a formidable machine and proved deadly as a night fighter against RAF bombers later in the war.

Left: 60. A portion of one of the honour boards of presidents in Brisbane's United Service Club. It shows that Gordon Olive was president 1970–71. Another board shows that Colonel R. J. Olive, Gordon's eldest son, Richard (Rick), was president 2000–01. To date they have been the only father-and-son combination to hold the position in the club's long and distinguished history.

Right: 61. Wing Commander Gordon Olive DFC RAF, prior to him rejoining the RAAF.

62. September 1986. Gordon Olive inspecting a Battle of Britain display at Mudgeeraba in Queensland.

63. A Bristol Beaufighter IIF powered by two Rolls-Royce Merlin engines. No. 456 RAAF Squadron was re-equipped with the type. This necessitated retraining and conversion to twin-engine aircraft. The squadron's first victory came on the night of 10/11 January 1942, when a Dornier Do 217 was shot down in flames.

64. Inter-service athletics. Gordon Olive, described as being of fair complexion and five feet six inches tall, was a champion javelin thrower in service and inter-service athletics. He is shown here second from the left in the front row with other RAF winners. Next to him on the very end of the row is Adolph 'Sailor' Malan, who was destined to become one of the RAF's most successful aces of the Second World War.

Left: 65. Famous pre-war photograph of Spitfire Mk Is of 65 Squadron RAF in formation. Closest to the camera is the machine flown by Robert Stanford Tuck. Gordon Olive is at the controls of aircraft FZ-A, fourth in the line.

Right: 66. The twentieth anniversary of the Battle of Britain and the reunion of members of 'A' Flight, 65 Squadron RAF. Left to right: Gordon Olive, David Glaser and Spitfire test pilot Jeff Quill.

67. Junkers Ju 88, the first German type to be shot down by 65 Squadron. Ju 88s were treated with respect. 'They had a very powerful sting in their tail in the form of two .5 in. guns while our .303 in. guns were shorter in range. When chasing the enemy we were further outranged because in effect we were shooting into wind and the enemy was shooting down wind. At speeds around 400 mph this reduced our range by nearly half, and increased that of the bomber by a similar amount. Thus, the initial disparity was very marked, and gave a fast bomber a definite advantage.'

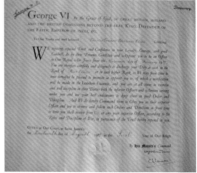

Left: 68. Acknowledgement by letter of leaving the RAAF, March 1946.

Above: 69. Gordon Olive's Short Service Commission, 19 February 1937.

13

Fight to the Death

A session at Manston was a very anxious occasion, much worse than sitting in a dentist's anteroom anticipating a torture session. It lasted longer, too. As it turned out we had to continue to operate from there, for ten days after the initial attack, and on three occasions got off the ground just a few yards ahead of trouble.

We had to abandon our old hut as its place had been taken by a large hole after one raid, so we went and waited for our call in the duty pilot's hut on the other side of the aerodrome.

The morale of the ground troops was surprisingly good. While squadrons took it in turn to operate from Manston for half a day at a time, the ground crews stayed there throughout. A small Army detachment armed with a bulldozer kept a round-the-clock battle going with the bomb holes. As soon as the bomb holes appeared, the bulldozer went out and, after pegging out a track for a runway, filled in all the holes on the track. Then we returned to operate again. The chalk dust over the 'drome became about six inches deep and, apart from the general dust-storm effect caused by the propeller slipstreams, it contained numerous shell fragments which punctured tyres on take-off and landing.

The following afternoon, we took off and contacted a force of fighters worrying the balloon barrage at Dover. After an ineffective quarter of an hour I found myself with Sergeant Harold Orchard flying next to me. We were instructed by radio to make for Southend. As we headed in that general direction, we saw the remnants of a raid returning from the direction of the Thames Estuary. There were a couple of Ju 88s escorted by a squadron of Me 109s. As we approached I dived at the leader of the fighter squadron and he led his squadron into a defensive circle. This manoeuvre was executed by the squadron flying around in a continuous circle, each man following the other's tail.

Such a formation is very hard to attack successfully as, no matter the angle from which it is approached, two or more of the enemy can always obtain a good shot at the attacker. We used it on occasions when we were severely outnumbered, and at a tactical disadvantage, but it has several disadvantages, not the least of which being that the squadron stays more or less over the same geographical point as long as the circle is maintained.

Thus, while I sat over these boys they were rapidly being separated from the bombers they were escorting. I told Orchard to stay over them and keep them nervous, and I would make a pass at the Ju 88s. This I did with the result that one Ju 88 went into a steep dive at two thousand feet. I did not follow it further, as tracer indicated that I was being shot at, and I turned to meet a head-on attack by a lone Me 109. We flew at each other all guns going, and I ducked under him at the last moment. I could see no damage but that was not surprising considering our closing speeds.

Orchard still had his school following each other's tail, and I toyed with the idea of seeing how long we could keep them there, only we were so low on petrol I decided to make for base. Had we had more fuel, it might have been possible to keep them there until they ran out of petrol. As it was, we were too low ourselves to experiment.

On landing, MacPherson told me that he had seen the little drama and that my Ju 88 had crashed somewhere south of Rochester. It was a bit of luck, MacPherson being around at the time, as I had already claimed a damaged only. I altered my claim to one destroyed.

The German ace of aces, Adolf Galland, writing about the Luftwaffe air offensive in 1940, claims that he took part in raids of more than a thousand aircraft at this time. I reported raids of more than six hundred but my method of counting was somewhat sketchy. Few on our side had the time to be thorough with their arithmetic. On one occasion, I merely divided the 'gaggle' into four. Next, I halved one of the quarters mentally, then tried to count this segment. I got up to eighty in a rapid count before a rain of tracers from behind, and above, diverted my attention. As I got busy with the chore of turning on to their tails, I made a quick calculation of at least 650, perhaps 800 machines. This was considered highly improbable at the time, but in retrospect these guesstimates of mine were not far out and were probably conservative, as I then believed they were.

These huge formations, if they could be so called, required relatively clear conditions for their operations lest the risk of collision among themselves exceed the risk of destruction by us.

The weather had been fine for almost four months, a real summer in the Australian sense of the word. Cloud, when it appeared, was only an insignificant layer of broken cumulus about three thousand feet thick. This often gave the retreating enemy formations and straggling bombers some measure of protection on their return flight to their bases.

Fine weather only added to our strain. With a normal English summer the frequency of attacks would have been halved; as it was, even the fickle English climate was against us.

Eight weeks of incessant attacks, increasing in severity, was a long time. It was eight weeks of intense strain during which many of my best friends had been killed, mostly in blazing meteorites plummeting to earth from those clear blue skies. Some had escaped with mutilated bodies or horrible burns. Those of us who had survived Dunkirk and were still with the squadron were indescribably weary. Nineteen or twenty hours of duty a day is exhausting enough when times are good. With the tension which accompanied this battle, the effect was beyond description. It already seemed an eternity.

The great classical battles of history, battles like Marathon, Agincourt, Waterloo or Trafalgar, had been resolved in a day. The Spanish Armada dragged on for a week. This battle had already lasted for eight weeks and there was obviously much more to come. In terms of protracted nervous strain, this battle had no historical equal.

The long days of August rolled on. The other squadrons from our main aerodrome were sent up to the north of England and Scotland, where there was relative peace and quiet, but we seemed to have been entirely forgotten. A squadron of Defiants was sent down to relieve us but they were not good enough. The Defiants were too slow and not sufficiently armed. Only two crews were left alive and whole at the end of their first day. Our relief had to be postponed. A squadron of Spitfires was sent down but their pilots were green and they met almost as swift a fate. We were told we would have to stay on as moving a new squadron in without seasoned leaders was proving far more expensive than was tolerable in such extreme emergency. The squadrons in the front line would have to remain there and the losses made up from inexperienced squadrons in the Midlands and the north.

So we were to be the sacrificial goats!

The weather broke for a day towards the end of the third week of August. As the rain system moved from west to east, this gave us almost two days' rest. I needed the break very badly. We all did. I had never expected to welcome the dull, wet days of English weather, but this time it meant life. It meant a day to live without the hollow fear of high-altitude incineration, a day to live as once we had lived in those remote days of peace, even if it were only a wet day. I felt I would not really complain if every day were a wet day, if only I could enjoy a little more life. There had been many times when I had been bored to distraction with wet days. Now I could not even imagine such a situation. Life on a wet day was infinitely better than no life at all. A lifetime of wet days was infinitely preferable to no lifetime at all.

That was my reaction to continued fatigue and danger. For three months I had been reducing my knowledge of flying and tactics to the simplest rules of thumb. Now my whole outlook on life was subjected to the same process. I knew with certainty that the simple things were the only important things. Those were the things which we took so much for granted when times were smooth and safe. Our friends, our fellow men, our fellow creatures, the sparrows and the trees, the green grass and the good earth; these were the things which gave life its meaning. If we were fortunate enough to see the sun shining sometimes, and to live without fear for a little while, then we knew life at its best.

Our experience of life was the personal miracle of each one of us. How it all happened was of no importance. It was irrelevant. It could occupy the tedious investigations of the boffins, but they would never discover in their telescopes or their microscopes just how good life was. I had discovered that in the frightening battlefields of the skies. To my mind it was impossible to discover it in the suburban security of the laboratory or the library. Furthermore, the boffins would never understand from their formulas or their slide rules that life is a gift; that it is the most incredible gift of space and time to each of us for it is a gift in a medium wherein we are allowed complete freedom of will. We are even free to reject the gift of life itself.

When seen in this perspective, our gift demands that we in our turn recognise the basic nature of the principle of giving, and develop the art in our own turn. Neglecting to do so must brand us as forever unable to grasp the simplest fact of existence and as totally lacking in gratitude and appreciation of our good fortune in sharing in the experience of living.

This view of life is the starting point of most worthwhile religion, and makes the demands of Christ as valid and as intelligible today as nineteen hundred years ago. The man in the street back then lived much closer to disaster in his daily life and consequently kept his ideas from being tarnished by the dust of too much security.

The sun shone brightly again, the operations phone bell rang and within minutes we were back in the sky, searching intently for the first glimpse of the approaching armadas from the east. By the fourth week of August, we were again reduced to eleven aircraft and pilots. We had lost twelve killed and several others wounded. Some had collapsed under the relentless tension. Three of the Poles were dead. Each had accounted for four or five of the enemy before being lost. Dave Glaser was the only one of the 'schoolboys' left.

Our role had become almost exclusively 'anti-fighter' as distinct from 'anti-bomber'. One reason was because we were the most easterly squadron and therefore first to intercept when the raids made their way up the Thames Estuary. Another reason was that we were equipped with Spitfires and were accordingly better fitted for taking on the Me 109s, which were superior to the Hawker Hurricanes in most respects.

This form of activity was in no way profitable to us personally. Apart from the fact that the enemy fighters were much faster and more difficult to hit than the bombers, they were also very nimble and extremely dangerous. They appeared from nowhere, struck hard and then vanished.

As the Germans stacked their escorts higher and higher, we found we were forced to climb up seven miles or more in order to keep above or on the same level as them. This was unimaginably cold in an unheated cockpit as the outside temperature was sometimes as much as 70 degrees below freezing. We were unable to wear much in the way of clothing as the cockpits were very tiny. As a result, after a few minutes we were very miserable and painfully cold. Cold is a terrible demoraliser and I always felt very unhappy as well as uncomfortable.

Apparently the enemy were not much happier, as they usually lost their nerve when we attacked them and we were now able to send reasonable numbers panicking out of the fight by an attack on the leaders of the small elements operating at those heights. If we could attack from above, they seldom waited for us to get close enough for a good shot before they rammed their noses down vertically and vanished.

This type of action was not conducive to good scores, which was the official yardstick of the fighter pilot's merits. The fighters we attacked were either over the Channel or over France, and even if we scored a hit there was absolutely no future in waiting around to see the results. A fighter is invisible fifteen thousand feet below and we were at least thirty-five thousand feet up most of the time. As a result no one in our squadron had an impressive score, though we had undoubtedly made it a lot easier for the 'anti-bomber' boys further inland to reap their rewards without undue danger from fighter escorts.

One instance provides the perfect illustration. A new pilot was taking off from Hornchurch. He was late as his engine had not started promptly and he was five minutes behind his squadron. As he was about to pump up his undercarriage, a dozen Stuka dive-bombers struck the aerodrome. Their escorts had been driven off but they pressed on with their attack regardless. The new boy shot down three in the circuit of the aerodrome before he pumped his wheels up, then he shot down two more, completed the circuit and landed out of ammunition. His victims were all burning within a few miles of his base!

Such a feat in the presence of escorting fighters would have been impossible. If the raiders had been Me 109's instead of Stuka dive-bombers, it is doubtful if the pilot would have got his wheels up before he himself had been picked off. That was the luck of the game, but it did seem a bit hard when our efforts were judged by the same yardstick as those operating against the slower, and far more vulnerable, bombers.

A raid materialised and we were able to attack the uppermost fighters from slightly above. There was no surprise as we were all leaving endless plumes of cloud behind us – so were our targets. As we closed in, with little speed advantage at such altitude, they dived away in groups of four or six, wheeling around and making for France. We continued to threaten their escorts by climbing above and diving at new elements each time. Perhaps thirty or more in sections of four or six had removed themselves when one lone fighter appeared ahead of me. He was flying slightly across my path and as I closed in I pressed the button.

The guns produced their usual harsh roar, but nothing happened. I moved the dot of my reflector sight out on to his wing tip to compensate for his turn as we were both travelling fairly fast and in a slight turn.

Again the guns blew their raspberry and this time a few bits came off and fluttered in the air like playing cards. Simultaneously, a streak of grey-white tracer squirted out behind him. It stopped, so I squirted a bit more lead at him and this time he really turned the gun on full and fishtailed his rudder, producing a hose effect with the tracer bullets. None of them were very close and I fired again, feeling very entertained at the way he just sat and trusted in his blind squirt gun.

As I opened up again, I was enveloped on the port side by what seemed an impenetrable barrage of grey tracer. To the right the air was clear, so I turned right as violently as the altitude would allow. As I did so I saw six Me 109s with red markings following me around in the turn. Every machine was firing; they were forming on their leader and apparently firing on his word or command.

They were no match for the Spitfire in the turn, and after about one complete circle I was almost on their tails. They bunted vertically and vanished miles below in a few seconds. It was no good trying to follow them in a bunt as they had a fuel injection system which was never upset by inverted leads. Their engines continued at full power, whereas ours flooded the carburettor and for a few vital seconds the engine died. This made it impossible for us to catch an Me 109 once he committed himself to a violent nose-over dive. Perhaps it was a good thing, as following down was so often fatal.

This episode was a good example of an advantage we enjoyed by not using tracer in our ammunition. My original target did not know of my attacks until the bullets began to clang around his machine. My initial attack from behind was not detected. On the other hand, the formation of six which attacked me while I was chuckling at the blind tail gun gave me a most welcome warning by the masses of parallel lines of tracer, not only alerting me to their unsuccessful attack but also indicating which side was free of bullets and therefore safer to turn to.

The remainder of the sortie was spent trying to get close enough to the Me 109s to score an effective shot, but they seemed to be avoiding me. The vapour trail was the main trouble, as it advertised my presence and ruined any hope of surprise. When they saw a Spitfire approaching, they did not wait. Its reputation was already established.

Early in the afternoon of 25 August, we made contact with a smaller than usual formation of about 250 aeroplanes. To begin with I thought they were unescorted bombers, but as they came in towards us we realised that there were about 150 to 200 Dornier bombers escorted by about 120 Me 110 fighters. The Me 110 was a two-engined fighter. It had superior firepower to the Me 109, but was about twice or perhaps three times the size of the latter. It was even slower in a turn than the Me 109, so was rather vulnerable to Spitfires or Hurricanes. Their formation was very neat and businesslike. The Me 110s were flying in four well-defined formations covering the flanks, rear and top of the bombers.

Sam led in with an attack on the leader of the uppermost wing of fighters and followed on towards the formation on the outer flank. He appeared to be lining five or six aeroplanes up in his sights simultaneously. His attack must have panicked the fighter leader, for all four elements of the fighter escort began flying around in defensive circles. They went into it so simultaneously that it must have been a radio command. I remained five thousand feet above the formations. I was puzzling over the best way to attack these defensive circles when a flash of inspiration showed me a better way.

While they wheeled around in their merry-go-rounds, the fighters were rapidly losing their bombers, which were flying on up the Thames Estuary unescorted. It was clear that if I could keep them in their defensive circles long enough, they would become completely separated and this would give our own fighters further inland a rare opportunity to rip into an unescorted formation of bombers.

I waited until the formations began to break their circles then attacked the leader again. He immediately reorganised his merry-go-rounds for a few more circuits. I pulled up to my original position about five thousand feet above and up sun. I called up Control at this point and told him that I had the fighter escort completely occupied and that he should tell the fighters from Hornchurch and North Weald who would be going in now that they could go for the bombers without fear of fighter interference. I doubt if the controller believed me – I could hardly believe my own eyes myself!

After some five minutes or so, the fighter circles broke again. They all did this together, obviously obeying a radio order, so I sent each of my blokes down to each attack a leader, as now they were undefended by their circles. I personally took on the one I took to be the leader of the escort. The move worked, and as I pulled up from the dive the four circles were reformed and obligingly chasing each other's tail.

After some seven or eight minutes had elapsed, the bombers were just about out of sight but I could still see a greyish patch against the snowy backdrop of the cumulus clouds. Then I noticed several smaller dots diving in – the Hurricanes and Spitfires from the squadrons closer to London. As I watched, column after column of black smoke appeared and arced over down through the strata clouds. I counted about a dozen. Bomber after bomber exploded and dived out of the formation. Within a few minutes, scores of smoke trails made a pattern in the sky like the ribs of a gigantic umbrella.

The next time I looked west, there were twice the number of smoke trails. Those boys of ours were really having a party. As the bombers had been flying in a straight line away from me, the smoke trails looked as if they came from the same spot of sky, but in reality of course they were probably spread over several miles.

MacPherson called up on the radio and asked me if he could go down and try an attack by flying around the inside of the formation. I had heard him a few days before expound on this theory of his. He believed it would be possible to 'explode' one of these circles by flying around inside it and continually firing his guns. I refused as I wanted to hold them all in their 'circles' as long as possible. I still needed MacPherson.

The fighter escort at last decided they would have to make a dash for it or run out of fuel over England. They broke their formation sooner this time and wheeled away in four long lines. When I attacked they just stubbornly kept flying east in the direction of France. We gave chase and this time I emptied my ammunition at a tail-end Charlie. His tailplane and rudders broke off and flicked back towards me. Fortunately they missed. Meanwhile, what remained of the 110 nosed over towards the ground.

The five of us landed. We still found it hard to believe what we had just seen. MacPherson was quite impressed. It had not occurred to him that we could hold all of the escort away from the bombers so successfully for so long. I had to admit that I too did not expect such success, and it was hard to understand why well over a hundred fighters were taking such extreme defensive measures against five Spitfires. No doubt they thought we would all press home our attacks swiftly, after which they could rejoin their bombers using their superior speed for the purpose. That I delayed my attack until they were hopelessly separated, then forced them into a further panic, completed their discomfiture. Perhaps the greatest single factor was their inordinate fear of the Spitfire, married to their inability to grasp the fact that we would attack even when outnumbered by twenty to one. I think they reasoned that there must have been a great many more than five of us if we were game to attack over a hundred Me 110s. That they could not see the others only made them all the more nervous.

I later heard that some forty bombers were destroyed from that formation for the loss of two fighters. The arithmetic was improving. Our squadron, however, only claimed three 110s.

We were no doubt getting some very good ideas out of all this. The only problem was whether any of us would be left alive when it was all over, for as fast as one formation was broken up and sent home, another mounted up to take its place. It seemed absolutely endless and hopeless.

Two days later we were up in Scotland. Relief had arrived in the form of an auxiliary squadron from Turnhouse, and after they survived two days without crippling losses we were sent out of the line for a rest for seven days – perhaps a fortnight if we were lucky.

14

North

New faces met us on our arrival at Turnhouse. Fifteen of them, and it turned out that none of them had flown a monoplane. This also meant that they knew nothing about retractable undercarriages either.

There was nothing difficult about retractable undercarriages, providing you remembered to put them down to land, but flying a new aeroplane, especially one which didn't seem to have sufficient visible means of support, could be a bit disconcerting. When people get disconcerted they tend to forget things – vital things – like wheels to land on. Failure to put wheels down meant the aeroplane tobogganed along on its belly. It also smashed the propeller up and usually wrecked half the engine in the process.

We had a Miles Master trainer, a two-seater monoplane with retractable wheels, and we checked each pilot out in it, with Sam or myself acting as instructor and ensuring that the wheels were not forgotten each time. In spite of all the precautions, some of the new boys still kept landing the Spitfires on their bellies, the wheels neatly tucked up in the retracted position.

This seemed incomprehensible – there were several warning devices in the Spitfire to prevent this. Firstly, there was an array of red lights in the centre of the instrument panel. These turned to green when the wheels were down and locked for the landing. Then there were two little 'tabs' on the wing which retracted flat into the wing when the wheels were up, but came out about three inches when the wheels were down. These were pretty much in the line of sight as the pilot looked over his wing for landing. Also there was a klaxon horn behind the pilot's head which made an ear-splitting noise if the throttle was closed in flight without the wheels being down.

There was the radio, too. We kept a radio out on the landing strip during flying practice for new boys so that we could call up and warn them if it was obvious that they were doing something wrong. If someone was coming in with their wheels up, we could call them on the radio and warn them to go around again.

Finally, there was a Very signal pistol which was also kept out on the end of the strip. This was kept loaded with a red flare and was fired if all other efforts failed to alert the pilot that he was doing something wrong and should try again.

In spite of all these safety measures, several Spitfires were wrecked in that first week by belly landings. One character who flew in and landed in spite of flares, radio warnings, horns, lights and his flight commander (me) doing a crazy war dance to try to get him to go around again insisted he hadn't noticed a single warning. To the question, 'How is it you didn't go around when you heard me on the radio telling you "go round again, Yellow Three – no wheels – go round again, Yellow Three no wheels"?', his reply was he could not hear the radio for the hell of a noise the klaxon horn was making!

No. 13 Group Headquarters was very rude about these accidents. Spitfires were desperately scarce and to break one was to achieve what every fighter pilot in Germany was dedicated to doing. MacPherson suggested we should mint a few Iron Crosses and award them to the blokes who broke a Spitfire. This suggestion was somewhat neutralised by Wigg, however, who claimed he should be given an Iron Cross and three bars for all the Spitfires he had lost. At least he had not landed on his belly because he forgot his wheels!

This nerve-racking process went on for two weeks, after which the new pilots became fairly normal in their behaviour. All this time we were officially described as being on rest. Nevertheless, it was much less exhausting than the combat down in the London sector.

The weather helped quite a bit, too. Gone was the unbroken Australian summer which had proved so helpful for the Germans and so tiring for us. Several days of dirty weather blew in from the North Atlantic and gave us a chance to stop flying and rest in the mess. At every opportunity we slept. There was very little interest in parties, for a start; we were all so thoroughly exhausted. When flying was washed out for the day we just went to our rooms and slept.

*

Slowly the exhaustion left us. The auxiliary squadron which had taken our place at Hornchurch had left a Spitfire behind which was having some repairs completed. I flew it down for them when it was ready for delivery and took forty-eight hours leave with Helen. It was the first time I had seen her since my singeing a month before and only the second time since we were married.

London was being bombed. By the time I reached her flat in Kensington it was dark and the sirens had wailed their warning across the roofs of the capital. I had been bombed at Manston but this was the first time I had been in a raid with nothing to do – just sit it out. Helen asked me if I thought we should sleep in the basement and before I gave my opinion I decided to look at it first. I was out on the stairway when the first stick of bombs came down.

A distinct high-pitched whistle rapidly descended to an ear-splitting din as frightening as a close clap of thunder. As each bomb in the stick struck, the scream of the others mounted and the building rocked with each explosion as the bombs went off. I found myself in the basement wondering how I had got there. Helen was highly amused. She had never seen anyone get down stairs so fast. We sat and looked at each other as stick after stick thundered down. It was incredible that so much noise could keep going on without one of the bombs demolishing our building.

I elected to sleep in the basement. All night the bombs kept coming down. There would sometimes be a lull for half an hour – once for an hour, when we got a bit of sleep, before the drone of the bombers overhead, the whistle, the screech, the crash, screech, crash, screech, crash. By midnight I was beginning to have hopes of surviving the night. By two o'clock I was so uncomfortable and cold I decided to go back to our flat and chance the risk of a direct hit. I began to treat it like a bad thunder.

We slept fitfully till dawn, when the bombs stopped and we slept on late into the morning. After we surfaced we went for a walk around the district to survey the damage. To my astonishment we only found one demolished house and Helen assured me that it had been hit a few nights before. She had at this point been through some ten nights of these bombing raids and was already quite adjusted to it. I think she had quite a chuckle at my expense at my reaction.

Those first few raids are a terrific shock to the system until you realise the actual significance of the event. Ten million people had been enduring these shocks for nearly two weeks without complaint. They did not know it at the time, but there would be at least another hundred nights of such raids before we found some answer which placed a check on these nightly terror attacks.

I now discovered further great pleasure in wet, misty days. It meant the enemy could not achieve his objective and finally destroy Fighter Command. Each day meant more fighter aeroplanes produced and more fighter pilots trained. For me it meant more rest and I still felt I would never get enough of it. I would be tired for the rest of my life.

Two days later I was back in Scotland. It was still raining, although there was a report of a clearance in the south. The news was good. Instead of having to go back after a spell of two weeks, we were given an extra week. The wet weather had stopped our losses.

Whenever there was a fine spell we would get our new boys up in the air. Their formation flying was good, their confidence had soared. Now they realised that they did not need two wings and a mass of wires to fly and that the Spitfire was quite safe and would not misbehave providing they always put their wheels down for landing. We took them up and made them follow us around in imaginary dogfights. I taught them right-hand climbing turns and by the end of the third week I felt confident that we could fight as a squadron once more when we went south.

*

Lawrie Holland, our CO, developed meningitis and was off so long that we had to have a new commanding officer. At last Sam Saunders was promoted and formally took over the job he had been doing since Cookie's death. Sam and I were both awarded a DFC and we started to think of having a party or two. Sam's promotion was the first excuse – we followed this with another a few days later when the DFCs were announced. We had forgotten what a hangover was like.

The Duke of Hamilton was in command of Turnhouse. He was a pleasant, friendly man who mixed freely with all of us in the mess. He ran a very efficient station and was popular with all ranks. He was one of the Auxiliary Air Force pilots, having joined the RAF when a student in his university days. We called him 'the Duke', but not to his face. The Duke decided that we should get in some leave, as neither Sam nor I had had any during the year apart from some convalescence after being burnt or shot. Sam went off for seven days and I took command of the squadron in his absence.

Two days later the Duke sent for me. He had a letter marked 'MOST SECRET', which he handed me to read. This document stated that we were about to be visited by a German spy of the top echelon. He was a colonel in the Spanish Air Force. He was officially in Britain as a Spanish observer, so they could not shoot him, but he was most friendly with the German high command and his mission was to find out whether there were any reserves left in the RAF.

The Germans believed that they had virtually destroyed the RAF's fighter forces and that all that was left were the few squadrons in the south and that these could be blotted out with a few more massed attacks. His information, as it turned out, was not too far out, but it was important that the Germans should not know this. In fact, our squadron was one of two out of some thirty-two squadrons which were in the north that were assessed as fit for further operations in the south. (We were unaware of this fact at the time, but Lord Dowding's despatches on the Battle of Britain made this quite clear later on.)

We were to put on a flying display for the colonel, calculated to impress him with our efficiency, and entertain him in the mess with all the pilots who had been in action against the German formations in the south. Other efforts would be made to mislead him. We had two days to prepare a flying display.

I rounded up all the old hands, except Sam, which made six of us, and with six of the new boys we designed a squadron formation-flying routine along the lines of the old Empire Air Day displays. Our first fly-past would be four sections of three in line astern, the sections stepped down. This was our normal battle climb formation. The next would be sections in a diamond pattern. Then we would fly sections in line abreast. Then, if we could do it, we would fly the twelve aeroplanes in an echelon starboard, which meant the twelve aeroplanes flew in an oblique line.

On passing over the centre of the aerodrome, they half-rolled in rapid succession and dive-bombed a point on the aerodrome at low level. This was a bit risky with green pilots and only half the team had any experience of display flying. There was always the risk that the last ones in the dive past would fly into the ground simply by trying to get lower than those in front. It tended to become competitive. The leaders had to know their job exactly; each man had to know his job exactly. After the last individual dive past we reformed, flew past in sections line astern and landed in succession in threes on the runway.

First we ran through the whole plan on the blackboard in the crew room and then we did it on the parade ground, each pilot walking along in his relative position for each manoeuvre. The orders to be given over the radio were used at this stage. Then we had our first trial flight for half an hour, landed and talked over the mistakes. We practised this routine for three hours each day for the next two days and did nothing else – it had to be good! The weather was fair and we soon became reasonably efficient. The most difficult part was to keep the continuity going and this meant fairly tight turns in the vicinity of the aerodrome; the pilots had to change from one pattern of formation to the next in the turns. This was hard for new boys.

The great day dawned and the weather was rough and unpleasant. The clouds were low and there was intermittent rain. We waited in our crew room and the Spanish colonel eventually turned up in an old Anson. He had been flown up from London via most of the east coast aerodromes. It must have been a hell of a trip.

We found out later that all the squadrons on each aerodrome, even those who were unfit for operations, managed to get their aeroplanes in the air and fly past the Anson on its trip north. Thus he had already seen some dozens of fighter squadrons in the air by the time he arrived. He did not realise these interceptions had been specially arranged for him.

When he came into the crew room we were delighted. He looked exactly as a Spanish fighter ace should look. He was of medium height, slim, dark-haired with flashing eyes and teeth and looked as if he were made of Toledo steel. He would be a very useful ally in a dogfight, a bullfight or a pub fight and as he spoke excellent English we soon established very friendly relations with him.

I showed him over my Spitfire and we talked about various comparisons of performance. He had flown Me 109s and knew their speed, rate of climb and so on, but it was all in kilometres an hour and metres so we had to do some mathematical adjustments as we went along. He might have found out a bit of information; we only found out what we already knew, except that he said the Messerschmitt should not dive at the speed of sound or it came apart. We already suspected that it did.

At his 'suggestion' we took the squadron off and ran through our rehearsed routine – we tried to make him think that it was just something we did on the spur of the moment. The air was terribly rough as the wind had got up to near gale force and the cloud base was down to four thousand feet – lower in showers.

Somehow we managed all our changes without any collisions and after the squadron landed I took off and climbed to the cloud base to do some aerobatics. It was very rare to do low aerobatics with the Air Ministry's full blessing. By arrangement, MacPherson and Wigg took the colonel out on to the aerodrome where I could see him and I started by diving at full throttle at a point about four hundred yards between where he was and my position. At a thousand feet and with 475 mph on the clock I began a level out and had a glimpse of him in front of my nose as I hauled up into a vertical climb. As the speed began to drop I fitted in two quick vertical rolls then as I pulled over the top I went into cloud. Out again, I could see them below me so I did two aileron turns as I came into the vertical position and began a pullout at about two thousand, five hundred feet. A climbing roll and a half took me about a mile and a half away and I came down again for another dive.

The air was extremely rough and the Spitfire jerked and ducked in the turbulence as if the wings would come off. As the colonel and the group came at me with nearly 500 mph on the clock, I pulled out as I saw the blades of grass. This time I kept the rolls at an angle of 45 degrees so as not to go into cloud. A stall turn brought me down on the dive again in the reverse direction and I hauled up into a 'rocket loop' and rolled off at the top of it. I was back in the cloud – no instruments – and the gyros were tumbling madly so I nosed down, half-rolled and went past at about three hundred feet in a slow roll, pulling up into another loop. This time I came down with the air speed needle flicking up near the 500 mph. With the assistance of the gale I was well over the 500 mark; after a stall turn I flew back into the wind with wheels and flaps down, scarcely making 40 mph over the ground. Just to show off I came in doing a prolonged side-slipping turn to within a few feet of the ground, then levelled out at the last moment to land and run up to the 'official party'.

The colonel seemed quite impressed. MacPherson and Wigg knew that I intended to make him lie down during the aerobatics. Afterwards they told me I had not succeeded but he had bowed pretty low each time I went over them. It was hard work and I was soaked in sweat. No doubt he would know all about that too!

We returned to the crew room and drank coffee. We talked some more about flying and he wanted to know what speeds I used for the various manoeuvres, what speed the Spitfire stalled at and so on. He seemed very surprised that we could fly so slowly. The Spitfire had almost half the wing loading of a 109; this was what gave it such an amazing performance, especially in turning competitions.

I think he would dearly have liked to fly one, but he would have to borrow one from his German friends. They had some we left behind on the Dunkirk beaches. After we had finished with him he spent some time with the Duke, then returned to the south.

A week later the Duke called me into his office again. A further letter in a 'MOST SECRET' envelope advised us that the exercise had been most successful. The colonel's message to his German friends had been intercepted. He said that any ideas they had that there were no fighter reserves left in Britain were quite wrong. He had personally interviewed a squadron resting in Scotland, and their standard of flying was first class and their morale excellent. He had seen many squadrons of Spitfires and Hurricanes on his way to and from Scotland, which indicated that there were a great many more in the area.

As the message was what the counter-intelligence boys had hoped for, it was allowed to go on unaltered in any way. They congratulated us on our performance and I came in for a special mention as my aerobatics had apparently clinched the deal. A few days later and the great massed raids were a thing of the past. This, I believe, was due to the end of clear-sky conditions rather than any discouragement by the colonel's report. We did not realise that the massed raids were over at the time, as we had to wait, day by day, to see what the weather and the enemy would do. However, after a month without the large bomber formations showing up it became clear that the crisis was over.

The confusion in the German high command over our reserves was partly due to the extravagant claims by their own fighter pilots. The top ten had claimed more destroyed than we possessed. If the claims of the lesser aces and the new boys all anxious to be aces overnight were added on, we had been destroyed at least five or six times. The Germans had a fairly accurate idea of our aircraft production and this left a huge discrepancy. In all their previous campaigns, the fighter pilots' claims to have destroyed the enemy air force had proved correct. This time the Luftwaffe's top command had no reason to doubt their figures until it became clear that the 'destroyed' Fighter Command was still actually killing more of their pilots than ever. Something was obviously wrong. The colonel's job was to be the referee.

We liked him very much. He was a very good spy – for us.

*

Of the few Australians who were in the battle, several had lost their lives. My old squadron friend Jack Kennedy had been shot down and killed. He had made an attempt at a forced landing, but high-tension wires in the way at the last minute caused his fatal crash. Poor Jack was one of the two pilots in our group rated as exceptional before the war. The other was Bob Stanford Tuck, who by this time was challenging South Africa's Malan for top-scoring pilot. With better luck Jack would have been up with them.

Stuart Walch, from Tasmania, was killed off Portland Bill. True to his nature, he had gone back to try to extricate two new boys out of trouble when they lagged behind and were caught up by a large force of German fighters. He saved his new boys, but lost his own life in the process. If any of the boys were mourned by their fellows, Stuart was.

Another tragedy was the loss of Pat Hughes. Those who knew Pat well were all agreed that he typified the best of the Air Force pilots. Virtually without fear, he had a sense of humour which never deserted him in the worst moments. After being credited with six kills by his fellow pilots (and sixteen by his commanding officer), he was killed one day as the wing of a bomber broke off because of his determined and excellent shooting. Unfortunately Pat was so close up behind the bomber that he flew into the wing, and it wrecked his plane and no doubt killed him instantly.

Pat died at the height of his prowess and in the full bloom of his manhood. There was no more typical Australian in the fight than Pat. His end was a personal loss to all who knew him.

15

Winter Patrols

We had succeeded in training most of our new boys to a stage where they could keep in formation, shoot and, with reasonable luck, hope to survive for a few weeks if the pressure came on again.

Towards the end of November we flew south once more, this time to Tangmere. An hour after we arrived we were in the air and half-frozen at thirty thousand feet looking for enemy fighters supposed to be in our vicinity. The sensation was not a pleasant one. After the relative safety of Scotland my system rebelled at the thought of returning to the hazards and dangers of daily air combat.

We soon discovered that the fighting was by no means as intense as had been the case in the summer months. Bad weather conditions made it hard for the enemy to operate. On the other hand, if we had to intercept, the difficulties involved in finding our way back to base with safety were often very real. Frequently the cloud was extremely low, reducing visibility to about half a mile, and with high hills in the vicinity there was quite an element of danger in the flying alone.

High-altitude fighting in summer was very cold and uncomfortable. One entered the plane a little too warm for comfort due to sitting around in hot weather with too many clothes on. Inside fifteen minutes the temperature would drop to 40 degrees below zero or 72 degrees of frost. The cold at altitude was just plain hell. In winter the stratosphere temperature was no lower, but one started out on the ground half-frozen even before the engine kicked into life!

On landing, after an hour of intense cold and misery, during the last minute or two at warmer altitudes all the ice crystals melted and dripped off everywhere. Inside the cockpit was a mass of dripping water as if a small rainstorm had occurred. The only part which stayed frozen was the very thick armoured glass in the front, which took much longer to warm up and so retained its frost usually until we landed.

Winter was well established now, and for the first time I found myself watching the weather with a sense of pleasure. Bad weather meant no flying, and that meant rest. I was still very tired. A thoroughly wet and filthy day meant that I could sit over the little fire in my office and doze or read and not have to steel myself for battle, death or destruction that day. How I relished those bad days that winter.

Only young Dave Glaser and Wigg, the New Zealander, were left in my flight from the old squadron faces. Glaser had only a short, if intense, burst of experience in the summer fighting, and Wigg was now my number two although his eyesight was still in doubt.

MacPherson was sent to another squadron for a rest, but a few days later he turned up and complained that he wasn't happy so he had managed to wangle a posting back to us. I was overjoyed to see his long, angular body and smiling face again and, as the local doctor assured me that the new, relaxed regulations permitted aircrew to have imperfect vision correctable by glasses, I was at last able to persuade him to go for a commission.

While this was going on, the fact that Mac was still a warrant officer did not detract from the enjoyment we had of being back together again. The evenings we spent together with the rest of the boys, usually having a few drinks and perhaps singing some of the disreputable songs popular among the aircrew.

During the day we sat out in the little wooden hut on the aerodrome trying to keep out of the draughts and to get some heat out of the little stove. We read, chatted or played cards according to the mood and now and again we would fly. Operational sorties were down to once a day or less, and frequently even that was against a single intruder or a small formation of enemy planes. Still, it seemed impossible that the great clouds of bombers and fighters were a thing of the past. In their day they had seemed so permanent.

One lunch time (we were back on regular meals now), a slightly swaggering, jaunty individual strode into our mess with the air of a conquering hero. He had a scar down his otherwise handsome face and his sleek black hair looked sleeker than ever. He had a maroon and white polka-dot scarf tucked into his tunic with the top button undone. His flying boots were immaculate and a pair of overlong stockings, which were pulled up the legs at high altitudes, were rolled down over the boots in a way which was reminiscent of the boots of buccaneers of two hundred years ago. Except for the Air Force blue uniform he could have stepped out of the past as a pirate king. It was old Tucky, or Stanford Tuck as he was now known, number two ace of Fighter Command with over thirty kills to his credit. We had a most enjoyable lunch, after which the squadron was to stand by at readiness.

Just after Tucky flew back to his aerodrome, Control rang to say that they were expecting a German reconnaissance machine over to photograph Portsmouth prior to an impending attack that night. They wanted the reconnaissance machine destroyed if at all possible, as it was most important that shipping in the area should not be known to the enemy.

The phone went and the controller spoke. 'We think he's coming up now, patrol over the east of the Isle of Wight and keep radio silence as much as possible so as not to let him know we are after him. The guns will try to locate him for you.' I took off with two new boys on either side of me and climbed to seventeen thousand feet in silence. The controller then called up and advised that the guns were firing at a 'bandit' at twenty thousand feet above Portsmouth.

I looked in the direction and saw three white anti-aircraft shell bursts bracket either side of an aeroplane which otherwise would have remained invisible in the clear blue sky. He was flying inland about five thousand feet above me. Shortly afterwards he turned about and I turned quickly and chased after him. He had been flying fast and I was still moving slowly from the climb so I could not catch him at first, but slowly the distance closed and I could tell from the crude rangefinder on the gunsight that he was about eight hundred yards away.

By this time I was clocking nearly 500 mph, and as the machine was a Messerschmitt 110 it was just about as fast as the Spitfire. I still had to close in to about 200 yards before it was worthwhile opening fire at that speed, but I was already in range for his backward-firing gun.

For the next two or three minutes I sat on his tail, closing at about 5 mph, which was the difference in our speeds. His tracer bullets were streaking either side of me, so I steepened the dive slightly to come just below his tail. As he didn't have a belly gun he could only hit me by shooting off his own tail. Still, some of the tracer seemed terribly close.

After what seemed an eternity, his wings filled the gunsight and slightly overlapped. I pressed the trigger as the red bead of the reflector sight sat on his cockpit. Immediately I came into his zone of fire again and tracer streamed all around me.

I could see the bullets from the eight machine guns of the Spitfire hewing holes in his wing roots and corrected my sight to hit one engine, which at once threw out black smoke. With the guns still going I moved the bead along to the other engine and as I did the twin tail fell off and sailed past. I thought of Pat Hughes, who was killed when he cut the wing off a bomber and then crashed into it.

With its tail off, the Me 110 dived more steeply. A huge yellow flame like a blowtorch streaked out from the body of the machine and I pulled away to watch it plunge vertically towards the blue-black water of the Channel five thousand feet below. I felt no elation whatever at this incident. After the fighting of the summer it seemed unsporting, like shooting a lame duck. Admittedly he had eight guns firing forward the same as I had, but he did not attempt to use them. He tried to make a break for it with his reconnaissance information and had been unable to make it. I had done my part of the job and the two new boys were quite impressed.

About a week later, Tubby Franklin, our squadron ace, who claimed some twenty German aeroplanes to his credit, was flying with a flight on a similar job. This time the reconnaissance plane was a Ju 88 and more heavily armed. He had two boys with him and another section in his rear.

As Tubby dived to attack, his Perspex hood was shot away and no doubt Tubby's head with it and he went straight on down into the sea. His number two suffered a similar fate, while his third man was so shaken by escaping that, instead of flying home, he went the wrong way and landed in France, where he was imprisoned for the rest of the war.

Two days later, I was sent after another Ju 88. A number of huge storm clouds were moving up the Channel. With Tubby's sticky end in mind I was not quite so bothered about the sporting angle, and when I located my quarry I did a certain amount of plain and fancy weaving as I closed in to get into range. The Ju 88 was almost as fast as a Spitfire and again it took a long time to get into range. All the time he was sniping at me with a pair of half-inch guns that fired off tracer bullets, which seemed as big as golf balls.

At last he came in for the treatment, but apart from chipping off a lot of skin I did not get his tail to fall off and his engines seemed still to be functioning. I broke off at about fifty feet expecting to see my number two a couple of hundred yards behind, but to my surprise he was about thirty yards behind the bomber giving it everything he had. A second later and they both entered a huge storm cloud.

After our return, an unsolicited Army report came in from a coastal battery that a twin-engined aircraft had crashed in the sea a few miles from our encounter. For some reason they never substantiated it, so although there was a good chance that we got it there was no wreckage. We forgot about it. We had done our best.

At Tangmere I found my friend Bob Bungey, a fellow Australian who had been a cadet at Point Cook with me. It was good to see him as I always had a great admiration for him. It was quite a surprise to see him on fighters, as before the war Bob had been one of the Bomber Command boys and it was seldom that a pilot turned from bombers to fighters.

I knew that Bob had flown Fairey Battles in France and had been one of the few survivors of the Maastricht Bridge attacks, which had seen some of the most heroic and desperate air fighting of the French campaign. Having had a terrible time in that tragic phase, including being shot down a couple of times, Bungey's spirit was such that he applied for service in Fighter Command when we were so hopelessly short of pilots. He could fly and he knew all about the Merlin engine, which powered the Hurricanes as well as the Fairey Battles.

So he came in to fight in the last desperate days of the Battle of Britain, where he gave a very effective account of himself and in the process was shot down again trying to outfight too many of the enemy. On this occasion he damaged his knee and was as a result very lame. This did not seem to discourage him, nor did it stop him from flying at every opportunity. His dual performances in France and in the Battle of Britain alone must rate Bob Bungey as one of Australia's truly great airmen. His heroism had gone unheralded at the time as his COs never seemed to survive long enough to put him up for the gallantry awards he merited so often. Later he formed the Australian No. 452 Squadron with Paddy Finucane from our squadron and Bluey Truscott, and the success of this unit and the wing at Kenley that he subsequently led were a tribute to his outstanding ability as a fighter commander.

I am sure that no man ever gave greater service to his country and it was a terrible disgrace to the high command of the Australian Air Force that they treated him so shabbily on his return to his homeland. Instead of a welcome reserved for their greatest hero, he was treated as a disgraced officer, reduced in rank twice and in seniority by several years.

It was a double tragedy that at this time his beautiful young wife died of a malignant disease. This, with the enormous strains he had endured almost continuously since the outbreak of war, broke his great heart and caused his death – one of the greatest blots on Australia's record of neglect of its national heroes.

As our squadrons took it in turns to stand by at readiness, I saw Bob only at meal times and when we were off in the evenings.

*

Early in 1941, I was advised by Fighter Command that my presence was required at a conference of all the aircraft manufacturing companies' design engineers, who were getting together to hear the pilots' point of view of aeroplane performance.

All the leading aeronautical designers were at the conference, about sixty in all, and four fighter pilots had been nominated by Fighter Command. Sailor Malan, the leading fighter ace; Adrian Boyd, who was close up behind him; John Kent, the Canadian; and myself.

How I rated for this conference was a complete mystery to me, as all the others were top-ranking aces. I could only explain it as a whimsical desire for some comic relief, or perhaps they realised that the Air Force was not composed entirely of aces. However, I felt very conscious of the honour, as we were supposed to be representative of the fighter pilots who had the most experience of daylight fighting. Three days were spent locked up with these long-haired gentlemen who fired questions at us such as, 'What happens when a Spitfire gets into a steep dive above 450 mph?' When I answered that the lateral control became unmanageably stiff, they all started gabbling in a foreign language, flattening one another with 'tangents', 'coefficients', 'functions' and technical phrases I vaguely remembered from my university days.

Then when they had thrashed that simple answer of mine into shreds they would fire another one at Malan or Boyd or Kent, with the same results.

We had been puzzled during the Battle that the Germans had such refinements in their engines as fuel injection, which made it possible for them to dive very abruptly without causing their engines to miss a few beats by flooding the carburettor, as happened with us. We all, at some stage, complained bitterly to the designers about this, and to our surprise there was a very good reason, as indeed there was for most of our complaints. It seemed that although the German fighters had this refinement, it involved a very complex pump unit with approximately 1,200 components, all precision made. Naturally all these components could, and did, wear, and occasionally broke, and the maintenance and serviceability problems for aeroplanes fitted with these devices were most complex. It was doubtful whether they were much of an advantage in the long run, as unserviceability due to this cause alone kept hundreds of aeroplanes out of the air every day. At least so the 'boffins' assured us.

These 'boffins', as we called the scientists and engineers, hit on an ingenious device to solve this one. They decided to give us petrol injection, but to inject it into the intake manifold and not into each cylinder, and thereby to cut the number of components to a twelfth of the German figure.

We all had our pet idea of just what the ideal fighter of the future should be able to do.

We all agreed that we should have heavier-calibre guns and more of them, if possible. The other three were very keen on what could best be termed a medium- to low-altitude fighter, very fast, and with overwhelming firepower. While I agreed with this in part, it became apparent that whereas the others had been primarily involved in attacking the bombers due to their location around London, I had been more or less exclusively involved in the fighter-*versus*-fighter role, which was necessary as a first step in an engagement to let the others do their work without undue interference from overwhelming numbers of unmolested enemy fighters.

For my part, I held out for any fighter force to include a small number of very high-altitude fighters which would have a better ceiling than the enemy. I argued that at whatever height the enemy flew he should never be safe from attack. Obviously, if the enemy pilot feared attack from above he would spend at least half his time searching for a possible attacker, and thus could not search as efficiently for his quarry below him. As the tactical advantage in such warfare is always with the high-altitude aeroplane, I felt very strongly that we should always keep that bit of initiative if at all possible.

One feature of this conference was my surprise at the way the engineers of rival companies, in competition with each other for the manufacture of the world's best aeroplanes, got together and pooled their ideas with apparently no reservations. In the war years that followed, it was most interesting to see the thoughts we had expressed translated into aeroplanes designed to achieve our dreams of the ideal fighter. To my personal satisfaction there were always a number of very high-altitude fighters, and they maintained throughout the war a technical superiority over the best the enemy could produce.

*

As the rugged storms of March imperceptibly eased, and the ice became less brittle and turned into slush, our squadron approached the end of its third tour in the front line. It was obvious by now that the Battle of Britain would not be renewed in the spring and summer of 1941. Perhaps, after all, the German high command had taken such punishment that they felt they could not afford another try. They had, after all, conceded a moral victory in 1940 even if they denied outright defeat in the air. What we did not know was that Hitler had already turned his eyes east to grasp for the satisfaction of vast territorial conquests in Russia.

After the Battle of Britain, Sir Hugh Dowding had been pensioned off as Commander-in-Chief and Sir Keith Park was taken off for a rest too. Sholto-Douglas and Leigh-Mallory were now enthroned in the seats of the mighty at Command and Group Headquarters, and many new changes were being made.

Air Vice-Marshal Leigh-Mallory came down one lunchtime and gave us a pep talk. He explained that the Battle of Britain had been fought on a wrong principle. We should have massed our fighters into huge multiple formations then attacked the bombers in strength. To show that this was the way, he proposed to send huge formations of many wings of fighters over France to tackle the Germans on terms favourable to ourselves. This time, Leigh-Mallory promised, we would have the superior numbers and the Germans would have a taste of the Battle of Britain in reverse.

I did not like this idea. Had Leigh-Mallory implied less criticism of Park and Dowding, I still would not have liked it.

I had learned that large formations of fighters had big disadvantages and small ones big advantages. Large formations could be seen too easily and from too far away; they could be stalked and taken advantage of tactically. They were also very unwieldy, and as all the pilots were busy keeping station in their formations only the leaders had any time or

opportunity for effective search. This made the big formation a liability rather than an asset.

From the start I felt that the only result would be that we would fly over enemy territory and meet not the great massed formations of 1940 but small elements of twos and fours which would dive out of the sun or other positions of advantage and destroy our large formations aeroplane by aeroplane just as we had done the summer before. I had the privilege of leading the squadron and on occasions the wing during the early experiments with this new type of manoeuvre, but I was not happy with the reversal of roles. We formed up huge masses of seventy or more fighters and ground our way over the familiar fields of northern France.

We were so large and cumbersome that we were unable to climb to our best altitudes and had to stooge along at heights which could be ten and even fifteen thousand feet below the enemy fighters' ceiling. The enemy did not, as anticipated by our armchair tacticians, rise in a grand armada to offer us battle, but sniped at our clumsy outfit with small but telling hit-and-run attacks mostly by pairs of fighters.

After several attempts to rouse the enemy in accordance with the theorist's ideas, we adopted a method which the 'experts' were convinced would force the issue. A formation of bombers was to go over with us and, by bombing their aerodromes, force them to defend themselves. We formed up in even greater formations and flew even slower and lower to protect the bombers. The enemy still failed to put in an appearance except in piecemeal attacks in pairs or at the most in elements of four.

Because of their futility, I hated these sweeps – one in particular. It was April 1941. I was leading our squadron, Sam being off for his forty-eight hours' leave. As I took off, the engine began to throw out little puffs of white smoke at intervals and inside the cockpit was the smell of baking bread. It was the glycol system leaking slightly. If it got no worse there was a chance that I would get away with it, but if the leak increased the engine would develop a hot spot, and probably blow up – not a pleasant thought with two hours of flying ahead of me over water and over enemy territory.

I knew I should turn back, but on my previous trip I had damaged a propeller and had to abandon the flight so I knew that if I did not make this trip it would look a bit peculiar, especially in the eyes of the new boys. The leak was only slight, but so were they all to begin with.

Accordingly, for the next two hours I nursed the engine around northern France, watching the bombers we were escorting drop their loads on enemy hangars while we were tied to their sides by invisible shackles of stupidity. We were tied by inexpert and deluded tacticians who insisted on doing to the enemy what they had done to us to their infinite cost. We lost two more pilots from our team and I didn't even see what hit them. Eventually, we returned but by then my machine was trailing a steady stream of white glycol vapour.

I was more than delighted to learn on our return that it was our last mission of that tour. We were being relieved in the morning. Douglas Bader, the great exponent of these new tactics which I disliked so much, was coming down and he would show us how it was done. We felt that we had not done so badly. During this time our squadron had lost some twenty-two pilots killed due to enemy action and our claim of kills, though conservative in the extreme, stood at about seventy-five. We were all very angry and not at all in the mood to offer ourselves at that stage as sacrificial lambs to the whims of unsound tacticians.

Further news angered us more. Not only was it to be the end of our third tour in the front line, the squadron was to be completely broken up. Perhaps the 'new order' had reason to think that we were too critical of their magnificent new tactics. Perhaps they felt we were too tired to appreciate brilliance when we saw it, or perhaps we were too set in our ways. Sam was to go to an operational training unit. MacPherson was to go to another. Wigg was to go for a rest too, as were all the others who had completed the last tour. I was to be promoted to squadron leader and stay on at Tangmere as a controller in the operations room for three months. At the end of the rest I was to take over command of another squadron.

It was all very sad. Our old unit, which had battled on through some of the toughest fighting ever experienced in the air, which had survived the worst the enemy could do to smash it up, was now broken up completely by officialdom.

MacPherson and Wigg were morose, and Sam was even more remote than ever. Paddy Finucane and Dave Glaser were the only ones not visibly affected; nothing ever worried them.

There was little chance for farewell parties. The prospect of a rest seemed to have no appeal for any of us. The let-down was not worth it. We all preferred being in the front line and I felt MacPherson and Wigg disliked the idea of breaking up the old flight as much as I did. True, I was not a born fighter pilot, but I had learned the trade the hard way, and we all knew that it was much better to keep on flying in the thick of the fighting than to go away to a safe area and then have to shock the nervous system into a return to the hot area. We were not tired this time; we felt we could go on indefinitely at the present tempo. We were getting plenty of sleep and the operations were nothing like as hazardous as the previous summer.

However, that was it.

We had a somewhat sad series of farewells and the squadron flew off to its rest area, leaving me at Tangmere. I never saw Wigg again. Sam Saunders I was to see twice, but that is trespassing on the future. Mac, my dear friend Mac, I would see only once more. It would have been a very lonely time for me but for Bob Bungey. His unit, 145 Squadron, stayed on for a few more weeks.

Our squadron's place in the line was taken by Bader's 242 Squadron, and Bader took over command of the wing. Prior to his appointment we'd had no formal wing leader. The senior pilot in the formation led the wing, and when Sam had been away I had frequently led it myself. Now a formal wing leader was appointed.

In due course, Bader arrived to lead the wing and he had immense confidence in the whole scheme. With some interest I took up my ringside seat in the control room to watch the great exponent of the massed formations demonstrate his technique. However, I was not unhappy that I was relieved of any obligation to support his ideas as one of his squadron commanders, and such was Bader's infectious enthusiasm that all his pilots were supremely confident that they were revolutionising air tactics and blazing a trail of unprecedented success.

It was with a certain amount of secret satisfaction that after a few weeks, when even the most optimistic apologist could not produce a profitable balance sheet of losses in our favour, I noticed that under the heading 'Intention in the Operation Order' the words 'on terms favourable to our own fighters' were quietly deleted.

However much I deplored the loss of life involved in such a form of war, there can be little doubt that the prodigality with which we expended pilots and aeroplanes over northern France on near-futile missions must have impressed the German command with the thought that we had more fighters than we knew what to do with and possibly contributed to a decision on their part not to have another crack at smashing Fighter Command. To this end, which no doubt was well to the fore in the thinking under the hats of the top brass, these sacrifices were not in vain.

It was still an unnecessary waste of life and valuable equipment. If Sholto-Douglas had been as zealous in conserving his Spitfires, and if Leigh-Mallory had been less carried away with enthusiasm for proving his theories right, we could have saved some two hundred pilots and their Spitfires. Had these been available for such points as Singapore and the Far East, the history of the Pacific theatre may have been vastly different from the tragedy that engulfed them and dragged the reputation of the British Empire into the Oriental dust. Perhaps, with more genuine insight, we may have averted this tragedy which has had such far-reaching repercussions for our prestige in the eastern hemisphere.

16

Fighter Controller

Over the next three months, while I worked as a controller in the operations room at Tangmere, for the first time I would become something of a spectator of the war, with no items of operational interest for me personally in the air. At first I felt appallingly out of it all. I had imagined, as a pilot, that the life of a controller was insufferably boring, but I soon found this to be far from the case.

My duties introduced me into some of the mysteries of night fighting. Whether I liked it or not, I had to do my share of duty on the night shifts. I soon discovered that, contrary to my opinion, the night fighter was not just an official gesture of defiance at the elusive night bomber.

No. 219 Squadron, one of the first radar-equipped Beaufighter squadrons, was coming into operation against the Germans with their new equipment. Immediately, the losses of the German night raiders began to mount up and our interest in the new device became intense. I was very fortunate to go on to controlling duties at this time as it gave me a box seat to watch the latest developments of science playing their part in modern warfare. A significant number of kills were mounting up and John Cunningham, the pioneer of the art, was already claiming a score of some twenty-odd, about which there was not a suspicion of a doubt.

I threw myself into this new phase with enthusiasm and intense interest. The enemy raided nightly and it was easy to get practice at the technique of controlled interception.

First, the fighter was ordered into the air when the radio intelligence service advised that messages intercepted from France and Germany indicated a raid on its way. The fighter was given a convenient spot to 'orbit', where he just sat and flew around in circles waiting for a 'vector'.

When the radar chain detected the first plot, he was sent off in the general direction and every effort was made to estimate the raider's altitude and speed. This was all phoned through on the radio telephone, which, now that frequency modulation was being used, was far superior to any land telephone in clarity and strength. As he approached the raider he was handed over to a much more accurate intercepting machine, which showed both raider and interceptor on the same tube, in most respects a modified TV tube.

This special radar-control station, known as GCI, then brought the fighter to within a mile or so of the raider, on an identical course and, as far as was practicable, immediately behind. Then the night fighter went over to his own radar set and 'homed' in on the radio echo from the bomber. On most nights either exhaust flames or a silhouette could be established and these were at once shot at.

On my first attempt we intercepted a large, fat bomber in a stream of two hundred or so raiding London. It was shot down but to my dismay it turned out to be one of ours. It seemed that somehow, by sheer bad luck, this bomber had run into trouble over Cherbourg and, unknown to the pilot, had returned in the middle of a German bomber stream. By a two hundred-to-one mischance he was chosen for interception. By another mischance the interception was a complete success (probably only 10 per cent were) and by further mischance he had no means of identifying his friendly nature as his electrical and radio equipment was all out of action. His crew all bailed out successfully, though one died of wounds from the attack.

Another night shortly after this, all the aerodromes in England were fogbound except Tangmere. I was on duty and fifty of our bombers were stuck up above the fog. I had to get them into Tangmere or they would all run out of fuel and crash. Time was the critical factor and some two hundred lives depended on speed. Enemy bombers were in our vicinity and I had to decide whether to turn on the aerodrome lights to speed up the landings and thus risk a bombing of our aerodrome or whether to get them down on the unlit aerodrome, which was much slower and harder and which would mean some would be unable to get in.

It was a nasty decision to have to make. I turned on a portion of the lights and a stick of bombs came down. Then I turned on the lot. I held my breath for about five minutes. The radar was completely jammed by all our own bombers and it was impossible to judge if more enemies were in the area. No more bombs fell and after a frantic hour we brought every single bomber in. It was one of the most exacting jobs in which I had ever been involved.

The following morning I met some of the bomber crews. One was a lad I had known well at Point Cook. He was Duncan Good, a wing commander at twenty-two, probably the youngest in the RAF. Duncan had lived in the room next to mine as a cadet and I had always been amused by his almost childish complexion and delicate good looks. Now I could hardly believe my eyes. His skin looked like that of a man of forty-five, his giving him a hawk-like appearance, and he had the restrained manner of a man twice his age. The change seemed quite impossible, but was no doubt brought about by severe wounds suffered in the Norwegian campaign. We talked for a couple of hours and then he took off and returned to his base in Yorkshire. I never saw him again. He was killed a few months later laying mines off the French coast.

When there was no activity it could be rather dull, but for most of the time there was some action. There were convoys to be protected, various sweeps and raids to be attended to and, last but by no means least, practice with 219 Beaufighter Squadron in the new art of radar interception by means of radar in the aeroplane and a special new precision radar set for ground-to-air control.

In this respect we were years ahead of every nation. The work was of the most secret nature and the results most satisfactory. Throughout the day we carried out exercises using these new devices and at night did the real thing in action against the enemy bombers. This was an excellent and obvious example of the dependence of aircrew on ground crew for results. Without capable and accurate controlling, working to split-second timing, the night fighter could not hope to make his all-important radar contact in order to bring the interception to a successful conclusion.

Wing Commander Tom Pike, who had been on staff work for years, took over command of 219 Squadron when the night raids were at their height. Popular fighter pilot opinion gave him three weeks, which was about the length of life left to staff officers who returned to flying. Pike, however, fooled the experts and after spending a phenomenal time on link trainer exercises, and exercises aimed to perfect his blind flying and radar interception, he took the air and on his first operational trip destroyed two aircraft, which crashed in the vicinity of the aerodrome. Pike went from success to success and was soon challenging John Cunningham and Peter Townsend as a top night-fighter ace.

During this period I learned to fly Beaufighters. I had been an operationally trained night pilot for years, but now that the threat to England was coming over under the cover of darkness I felt that I would like to go on to night fighters or at least be able to fly them.

The technique of flying twin-engined aeroplanes was new to me and handling them at night presented many difficulties. Unlike day fighting, it did not place the pilot in any great danger from enemy action. The night fighter had the initiative. When he opened fire his firepower was usually overwhelming, and return fire was seldom effective if it occurred at all.

On the other hand, the risks involved in flying a somewhat unstable high-speed aeroplane in all kinds of weather, and trying to return to an aerodrome under completely blacked-out conditions were great enough in themselves. The real enemy, from the pilot's point of view, was the problem of night flight, not the enemy aeroplane. Weather and the poor navigational facilities of those days claimed hundreds of deaths from the few squadrons employed in night defence work.

There were several reasons for this unsatisfactory state of affairs. The first was the primitive and unreliable radio facilities, which were unserviceable half the time or at best functioned only indifferently. The weather, especially in winter, was appalling, with the ever-present threat of deteriorating while the plane was in the air and reducing visibility to nil. Becoming lost without radio, and unable to find where to land was, in general, the pilot's greatest dread. As most of the night-fighter aerodromes were on the vulnerable coastline opposite the French coast, full landing lights were seldom, if ever, turned on. Hooded runway lights were used, which could only be seen from one angle and were very difficult to locate in an emergency. A new scheme of lighting, which had been devised by Group Captain Atcherley, was being introduced. When finally installed, and properly operated, it was a great help, but in those days little or no light installations had been made and to find the way back to base after a sortie was similar in most respects akin to the problem of the blind man in the dark room looking for the black cat which wasn't there.

When the radio functioned without a hitch, however, the task was much easier. Provided one's instrument flying was good, it was only necessary to follow instructions and keep on instruments to eventually find the way back to the base. Here the pilot was very much, if not entirely, in the hands of the ground staff, who literally had to 'fly' him around to a position where he suddenly found that he could see the hooded runway lights and was in a perfect position for executing a landing.

The night-fighter techniques were pointing the way to a new conception of fighter tactics. Gone were the days of the standing patrols which had been the order of the day in the First World War and even in France and at the Battle of Dunkirk in this one.

The first steps in guided interception were employed in the somewhat crude but effective methods used in the daylight battles of the Battle of Britain. These were too inaccurate for night fighting. Now the idea was to control the pilot from the ground to the target then back to the ground again by means of the information shown on the table in the operations room.

The pilot, as soon as he left the ground, especially on a dark and cloudy night, could see virtually nothing. While climbing, he entered cloud and after an interval came out above it or perhaps between two layers in a hopelessly black and featureless world. He had to continue to fly by the little fluorescent instruments a few inches in front of him. The only reality was the voice of the controller, which came over to him as clear as a voice on a good telephone line (providing the radio continued to function).

The pilot's range of vision was effectively two feet, and he had to concentrate on that instrument panel because he had no automatic pilot to help him. Any failure to keep the aeroplane in the correct attitude and on the right course at the indicated altitude would not only result in a wasted mission but possibly in an aircraft out of control and, in a few seconds, a fatal crash.

By contrast, the controller was in a brilliantly lit room with all the relevant information at his fingertips. He could not only see everything in the room, but the information shown on his map gave his vision a range of hundreds of miles.

For the final stages of the interception, the controller handed the pilot over to the ground radar controller, who, operating in a darkened room, concentrated on the precise information displayed on a television tube that showed him the position of both the defending aircraft and the target aircraft. The radar controller could speak to the pilot, who was perhaps a hundred miles away, at twenty-five thousand feet in complete blackness, and juggling a ten-ton aeroplane at 300 mph as if he were sitting on a chair beside him. Operating as a mutually confident team, they had to work to position the interceptor about three miles behind and at the same height as the target, where the pilot and his own radar observer could switch on the aircraft's radar set and close the distance down to a few hundred feet.

Even on the blackest night, it was usually possible to see something of the target aeroplane. If it was so dark that his silhouette could not be seen, then the flames of the exhaust pipe would show enough light to give him away. The pilot then turned on his little electric reflector sight, lined up on the target indications ahead and pressed the gun button, thus normally terminating the performance.

After raiding continuously for about two months, one night the Germans had a setback which stopped night bombing for some weeks. Possibly they felt we had a new weapon. The facts were never released to the public, as their suppression kept the enemy in a state of nervous doubt.

I was on duty as the controller at about 8 p.m. when the meteorologist came in with a strange, triumphant look about him. This particular weather prophet had been a pilot in the first war and was an exceptionally accurate forecaster. He explained that a warm front was moving in from the Atlantic. This, of course, meant that the change would pass over Britain before the Germans would be aware of it. For some weeks the air had been freezing both by day and night and now a great wave of warm air was moving in from the west at about twenty miles an hour along a front over a thousand miles long. It was as if a huge tidal wave of warm air was rushing across the country. As it came, it pushed the cold air ahead of it, but in the process a wedge-shaped formation developed across the front, with the cold air dragging behind and the warm, moist air banking up on this wedge of cold.

As the warm air rose up on this thousand-mile-long wedge, it condensed into warm rain which fell through the cold air and became super-cooled rain. It is a scientific fact that pure water can be reduced in temperature several degrees below freezing point and remain as water, but if it is disturbed or a drop of impurity introduced into it it will freeze instantaneously. This is what was happening to the frozen rain. If it fell on to the ground it formed ice immediately, yet it was falling as rain, not hail or snow.

These factors make the most dangerous flying conditions it is possible to meet, and when the rain is heavy an aeroplane has only one or two minutes of grace before it is iced up and unable to fly. In daylight it is essential, as soon as this type of ice accretion is met, to turn about immediately and get out of it within a couple of minutes or the aeroplane will become uncontrollable and will certainly crash. At night, as such conditions are accompanied by thick cloud, the chances of seeing the ice building up in time are very slim and accordingly disaster is almost inevitable.

Raids commenced to move across the operations room table. The coastal radar stations showed the customary number of some seventy to a hundred raiders at their usual heights ranging from ten to fifteen thousand feet. They advanced as relentlessly as usual and their target appeared to be Portsmouth. I had ordered the first Beaufighter to take off when the first plot showed up, but now he called me up from the runway and advised that his engines were throwing ice everywhere and his windscreen was so iced up that he could not see out. I spoke to Group and it was decided that we should not send him out. It would be murder on such a night.

The raiders came on unopposed. None of our aerodromes could operate. Rain was falling and some inches of ice were forming on the runways.

The weather man drew the position of the front on the map and then sat up on the dais and watched. He explained the situation as the raiders came on towards the invisible wall of icy death.

Suddenly a WAAF plotting the leading raider took the counter off the table and altered the height from fifteen thousand to ten thousand. She looked at the weatherman and he nodded as we looked back at the board. Another plot was taken off and the height reduced from ten thousand down to five.

Now the half-dozen WAAFs moving the counters became very busy, acting on instructions from the radar station to reduce the heights of every raider approaching the fatal line. The first plot was reduced to two thousand feet and the plotter advised that radar had reported the plot had vanished completely. It seemed the forces of nature were retaliating on these men who were carrying out the will of that evil genius Hitler in a way which was terribly complete. One by one they followed the same mysterious pattern. Two-thirds of the way across the Channel and the plots lost height and disappeared. Only three crossed the coast and they all crashed on the hills. The Army immediately claimed to have shot them down. (They hadn't had a kill for weeks).

At the end of an hour it was all over. Obviously, the enemy pilots had little idea of what was happening until they crashed, for none of the later raiders turned back. They just came on to their nemesis.

No more raids were experienced for some two or three weeks and we said nothing. No doubt for some time the Germans must have puzzled over whether the weather conditions had caused their disaster or whether it was a new secret weapon which the British had up their sleeves.

It was not surprising that when the next raids started they paid some attention to our aerodrome just in case we had a finger in the pie. One of the night-fighting boys, Tony Dottridge, came in one evening with the disturbing news that he had traced the German beam to our aerodrome. This did not sound too promising, and as darkness fell the sirens blew. Shortly afterwards, a series of explosions shook the anteroom in which the Catholic padre and I were playing shove-halfpenny. Instinctively, we dived for cover.

We collected our wits, looking at each other and the room from under the card table on which stood the shove-halfpenny board, and laughed at the ridiculous sight we must have made. The other inmate of the anteroom had turned up the upholstered chairs and crawled under them for cover.

As the clatter died down, we went outside to see a dense fog of dust from the explosions and went in search of the trouble. Some more bombs fell, but we ignored them, having surmounted the initial confusion. At last we caught up with victims being brought into the sick bay. Their faces were a ghastly blue colour and they had been blinded by an explosion in their faces. It was the first time I had seen such a horrible spectacle up close, and I was very upset at their obvious distress.

The padre then showed me where his role came in. Gently he spoke to each man in a reassuring way and in a matter of seconds soothed their poor, tortured minds in a way nobody else could possibly have done.

There was nothing else I could do and so I went off to bed as I was on duty at midnight and it promised to be a busy time. I made for my room and when I got there found that all the windows had been blown in by the blast from one of the bombs. I asked my batman, Murphy, to put up the gas curtain as the room was bitterly cold and the gas curtain would keep out the keen east wind. While he was doing that I went back to the bar to buy some toothpaste.

At the bar I found the padre again. He invited me to join him in a beer before turning in. I declined, but for some reason he was most insistent. I relented and accepted the drink and we adjourned to the anteroom to enjoy it in comfort. Without warning a bomb scream interrupted our conversation. It mounted to a fiendish crescendo then a terrific explosion rocked the place. This time we pulled the upholstered chairs over and dived under them, and as we did so a huge shattered rafter came through the ceiling like a giant javelin. A great piece of concrete crashed into the bar and smaller pieces came smashing through the roof. Plastered ceiling crashed down, taking all the electric lights and plunging us into blackness.

After the crash and roar of the descending debris ended, we groped our way out through an evil-smelling fog of brick dust and explosive fumes.

We located the point of the explosion – my bedroom. But for the padre and his glass of beer, I would have been found next morning with my bed, a tangled mass of iron and blankets, a hundred yards away in the parade ground. Murphy was dead.

We hurried around to the outside and started clearing debris. Lights from torches flashed briefly, trying to locate some poor devils who were trapped, including a fellow officer due to go on duty with me at midnight. As we laboured to reduce the heap of rubble and remove the concrete from those entombed, the bombers returned to the attack. Guided by the light of our torches, which we had to use from time to time, they strafed us with cannon shells and lobbed stick after stick of bombs around us.

I have never seen such an inspiring man under such conditions of concentrated air attack as that red-haired Catholic priest. He was a magnificent leader born for such emergencies. In no time he had a gang of some twenty volunteers, working with his own inspired disregard for danger. Mud from exploding bombs and the work he was doing covered him from head to foot and all the time he exhorted everybody to greater and greater efforts. He wore no tin hat on his carrot-coloured head and his dog collar was black, the colour of his face. The padre's name was Father Christopher Ulliott.

At last we relieved those trapped and the padre went off to hospital to console the wounded. I went down to the operations room to start the night's work.

In addition to working as a controller, when my turn came around I spent my spare time with the night-fighter boys in an endeavour to perfect our flying techniques. There was an elaborate code-word system to master, and to thoroughly understand the procedures it was necessary to visit the radar stations and watch them at work as well as to go through the motions in flight.

As my rest from operational flying came to an end late in June, I managed to persuade the powers that be that I should go back to operational flying. At first it seemed that I would be given command of a day-fighter squadron based at Manston, back on the tip of Kent. My hair stood on end every time I thought of Manston and the numerous narrow escapes of less than a year ago.

A day before I was due to pack my bags, a signal arrived from Command posting me to start a new night-fighter squadron to be formed by the Australian Air Force in England. It was to be No. 456 Squadron. I subsequently learned that I was the only Australian qualified at that time to form a night-fighter unit. My posting to the Spitfire squadron was cancelled.

My new posting came through a day or two after the stunning news that Russia had been attacked by Germany, and I knew then that there would not be another Battle of Britain. The worst threat was from the night bomber, and John Cunningham, Peter Townsend, Tom Pike and others had already shown that it could be broken. It was in high spirits and confidence that I set off on my next adventure.

17

Night Fighter

The new squadron had not begun to form when I arrived at Valley. Some Defiants were on the aerodrome and a handful of men, but nothing else.

Valley was a new aerodrome on the north coast of Wales, on the island of Anglesey to be exact. Our job was to become operational as soon as possible and to generally protect the western approaches to Liverpool, Manchester and the West Midlands from night raiders, which had a habit of sneaking up the Irish Sea or over Ireland and coming in from the west. In this way they avoided flying across England, which by this time was a very risky business for an enemy aeroplane either by day or night.

Defiants, with which we were at first equipped, were slow and relatively useless aeroplanes. They were the product of some self-appointed genius who believed that the expert was always better than the amateur. Thus the theory was that an aeroplane with an expert pilot at the controls and an expert gunner at the guns was a far superior combination to an aeroplane with a pilot who had to combine the arts of both and who was restricted to firing his guns in one direction only.

The only snag with this faultless piece of logic was that it *did not work*! Enemy aircraft found the Defiant terribly easy to knock out of the sky. They were accordingly relegated to night-fighting duties, but as they were not designed for the job and had no radar in them they were not much use in that role either.

Australian ground staff for the new squadron were on the sea, but they would not be arriving until September, and this was the first week of July. Temporary ground staff were coming in, having been recruited from Fighter Command by a series of directives to various squadrons to post two fitters or two riggers, signallers or whatever was necessary to No. 456 Squadron. When the Australians arrived these would be sent off to form some other unit – perhaps going overseas.

Needless to say, I thus found myself with quite a few discards from other squadrons as, under such conditions, the unit commanders did not send their best men, nor even their second best. Pilots arrived and we set up a headquarters and started forming.

The struggle to get the squadron operational was a big one, and after working for a full day on organising and scrounging to accelerate progress and short-circuit officialdom, I would sit out on the aerodrome every night to watch over the terrifying antics of my fledglings.

The aerodrome had been a few square miles of sand dunes on the coast off the Irish Sea. It was wild and desolate country, reminding me quite strongly of some of the dune country on the Pacific coast back in my homeland, but there was no surf of course, only minor imitation waves when a strong wind was blowing.

Runways had been set down in the sand after the dunes had been levelled out, but it was too bad for a pilot if he landed on the runway and veered off it for any reason, such as a crosswind. As soon as a wheel ran over the soft sand it dug in and ripped the plane around in a ground loop, usually completely snapping the wheels off. This type of accident became a regular occurrence with raw pilots trying to land in such conditions at night.

Denys Gillam was the other squadron commander on the station, and as we knew each other quite well the whole set-up was most enjoyable, if tiring. He commanded the day-fighter squadron.

My senior flight commander was a man worthy of more than passing mention. By name John Stuart Hamilton, he was a tall, lean product of Scotland by blood, but English by adoption. He had been in the Air Force for five years when he crashed and broke his neck in a nasty accident. Paralysis and tetanus nearly finished him, but although that had happened ten years before he had only managed to get back on to flying and then only by seizing on the desperate shortage of pilots after the battles of the previous summer. Somehow, he had persuaded the RAF doctors (who seemed to have far more flexible minds than most) that he could and would fly if he were given half a chance.

The only trace left of his infirmity was his insistence of always swimming on his back when we went for a cooler in the sea, which was so inviting on the hot summer days. It seemed that his neck muscles were so weak that he could not keep his head out of water if he swam in the conventional attitude, so he swam on his back to avoid drowning.

Naturally a man of such a history and with the maturity which goes with much suffering was one in a million, and once again I found a guide, philosopher and friend to help me in my youth and ignorance. Hamilton had learned to fly fifteen years earlier and whether some of his techniques had been current practice in those days or whether he had worked it out for himself I never found out, but one afternoon he shook me to the core when he insisted on taking off in a sea fog with visibility down to about two hundred yards or less. Flying in such conditions was suicidal, but there were other aerodromes at which he could land so I took no notice of his claim that he could land back on our base in such conditions.

An hour later he was overhead trying to get down. The fog was not very high, perhaps a hundred feet, and he could be seen as he passed directly overhead. As I raced for the nearest telephone to ring Control to tell him not to be such an idiot as to attempt a landing, I heard his wheels hit the runway. To my astonishment he made a perfect landing.

When I subsequently had words with him for being so crazy, he merely laughed and offered to show me how it was done. It was not until I saw him do the same thing on three other occasions that I was convinced that it was not just luck. He obviously had something and I asked to be initiated into the Hamilton approach.

It consisted of a surprisingly simple exercise in precision flying that could be applied to situations of low-lying mist when it was possible to see the flare path while flying directly overhead, and for situations of very low cloud with rain when visibility could be down to 200 yards and it was possible to see and identify a runway or flare path into wind and fly over it. Usually under these conditions the ground could be seen, but the difficulty was to arrive back at the runway at a height and direction from which a landing could be made without dangerously steep or slow turns.

First, by radio aid or other methods, the aerodrome was located and the pilot flew directly up the flare path into wind and set his gyro compass to 0° degrees and his speed to, say, 150 mph. As soon as he passed the last flare he had to turn left at 'rate one' onto a course of 180 degrees and thus downwind, maintaining constant speed. He then timed himself on a stopwatch for two minutes, by which time he should be about two to three miles beyond the leeward boundary of the aerodrome. A further

180-degree turn left at 'rate one' took him back on to the alignment of the runway and he was then in a position to put down his undercarriage, his flaps and reduce height to about one hundred feet. The ground ahead should then be visible for about two hundred yards or so, and after a few seconds the runway should appear almost immediately ahead or at least in a position where a shallow 'S' turn would put the aeroplane on it with complete safety.

Once I mastered this simple procedure, many of the worries of flying in bad weather were a thing of the past. It was incredible how easy it was to locate the runway this way, even though the aerodrome and the runway were completely out of sight for seven out of the eight minutes involved in this approach. This technique saved my life on several occasions subsequently when things went wrong at night and it was essential to make a landing in conditions of very poor visibility.

By this time I was just twenty-five years old and I had four hundred tough characters to deal with as well as the problems of training twenty-two green boys to become night-fighter pilots. At the same time we had to take over the operational commitment for the defence of the area.

The neighbouring night-fighter squadron was commanded by Max Aitken, the son of Lord Beaverbrook, and he used to send two or three of his boys over to defend the area until we became operational. Sometimes, he would come down himself and do a stretch of duty. Max had fought in the day battles in the previous summer and had now been bitten with the importance of breaking the night bomber. He was one of the original Auxiliaries!

Denys Gillam was on the aerodrome in command of his old squadron, No. 615, one of the Auxiliary units. He had some very notable characters with him, two of the most outstanding being Pete Hugo of South Africa and Rene Mouchette, the indomitable Free Frenchman mentioned in Closterman's famous books. They were all on their third rest here, as this was considered a quiet area for day fighters, and they were starting to fuss about going south again.

Denys rang Winston Churchill one night – Churchill was the squadron's honorary air commodore – and asked for a posting to an operational area. Next day he and his men were at Manston with a special mission to attack and sink German flak ships. These were small vessels designed for the sole purpose of shooting down our aeroplanes. Flying Hurricanes armed with 20 mm cannons, they threw themselves into the fray with such abandon that inside a month they had practically eliminated flak ships in the area. But before they sank the flak ships they eliminated most of the squadron too. Denys, so report had it, eliminated part of one foot and a portion of his backside. He came out of it with a DSO.

Gillam deserves a book written about him as he was, in my opinion, the most outstanding fighter pilot in the world and he was the most typically English of them all. Of very slight build, he had a boyish, freckled face and a most infectious grin. This went with a mischievous chuckle which often had an almost insane quality, and was somewhat misleading to those who did not know him. His capacity for self-effacement was enormous, which made him so typically English, but he was much more sociable, at least towards Australians, than the average Englishman. He was awarded an Air Force Cross (AFC) for a tour of duty as a meteorological research pilot and for an act of heroism in a full-blooded cyclone (he really earned it twice). He subsequently led his Auxiliary squadron throughout the Dunkirk battle, for which he should have received a decoration. He then led them again in the thickest of the Battle of Britain, which should have given him further awards. He received a belated DFC.

He then went flak-ship sinking and subsequently led innumerable raids against the leading enemy squadrons and wings with tireless enthusiasm. His capacity for understatement stayed with him throughout, but he still received three DSOs and two DFCs to go with his AFC. Probably the most decorated airman in the world, yet I believe the most under-decorated for the effort he made.

Having digressed to mention England's unsung hero, I must return to the lesser mortals – we who were burning the candle at both ends preparing to ward off the night bombers which did not arrive.

When the pilots arrived, Hamilton and I found ourselves with some twenty completely inexperienced aviators. They soon found out about our sand-surrounded runways which snapped landing wheels off like carrots if they slipped over the outside edges – some of them the hard way.

We worked like slaves, averaging about three hours' sleep per night if we were lucky. All day we trained the worst of the new pilots in elementary experience on this type of aeroplane and all night struggled to teach the better ones the art of night flying. At last we managed to produce six operational pilots, including Hamilton and myself. Then we worked all day, training more green pilots, and spent every night standing by for operations while we continued to supervise and organise night flying. After six weeks we were reasonably 'operational'. This was in half the time we had been allowed and we were very proud of ourselves. We had both been existing on so little sleep, kept going by our frantic enthusiasm for the project.

Just when the pressure eased up, it started again when Command decided to re-equip us with Beaufighters Mark IIs!

Six weeks of intense effort, night and day, by Hamilton and myself had put the squadron on an operational footing but the other flight commander had not been prepared to put in the same effort. He insisted on his eight hours' sleep, and I became very fed up with his lack of keenness. As a result I flew down to Tangmere to see if Tom Pike would let me have Tony Dotteridge as a flight commander.

At Tangmere I saw Ron MacPherson again. He was a flight commander and looking very fit and happy. We were both overjoyed to see each other, and I asked him if he would like to join my outfit as a flight commander. We had been re-equipped with Beaufighters and it meant immediate promotion to squadron leader. Mac was obviously very tempted, but he eventually decided that his boys needed him and he just felt he could not walk out on them. I knew how he felt, and the new boys were terribly green in our eyes and such delightfully eager youngsters.

Tom Pike, however, agreed to parting with Tony Dotteridge, so I flew off back to Valley, hating to leave Mac behind. Two weeks later Tony turned up. The posting had been arranged. We now set to work to convert every pilot to Beaufighters. Only Dotteridge and I could fly them, so we had to carefully put every boy through his paces. Hamilton was the first to make it. It was no trouble to him. He was easily the most natural and able pilot I had ever seen.

The training pandemonium broke out again, and this time lasted for three months before we had six pilots operational. Then, as fast as we trained crews they were removed from the squadron and sent to the Middle East! Hamilton and I continued to work frantically as we both felt that England would have another season of nocturnal bombardment come winter, so we did not spare ourselves. With Tony Dotteridge helping, we looked like building a first-class squadron up in record time.

Our round-the-clock programme started again, only this time it was more exacting. Five of the first Beaufighters delivered to us were wrecked on landing. The ferry pilots edged off the runway for a second and the soft sand did the rest. The aerodrome was dotted with wrecks all close enough to the runways to constitute a hazard to flying both by day and night.

Oddly enough, we had very few accidents in the squadron at this stage – perhaps the derelict wrecks in the centre of the field had a salutary effect – but there were two worthy of mention.

The first was manipulated by a Sgt Kirkman, a red-headed product of Australia who slammed his throttles open too violently when he was overshooting the aerodrome on landing. Only one engine responded and he was going so slowly that it caused the plane to bank violently at about five feet altitude. The port wing dug into the sand and in a second or so the plane had wrecked itself in a series of spectacular 'Catherine wheels' along the runway. The engines were ripped out and rolled along the runway like a couple of huge smoking sausages.

I was sure no one could survive the violence of the shocks, so I did not hurry over to the fuselage, which had finished the right side up, stripped of wings, engines, tail and wheels. Imagine my amazement to see a gory head climb out of the front cockpit. Another emerged from the rear cockpit and oblivious of my presence conferred about number three occupant. A Beaufighter was built to carry only two people, so the third, who was one of the ground staff, had been free to rattle up and down the fuselage during all the drama.

In the midst of the discussion the third party appeared – a bit dopey for sure, but not even scratched as far as could be seen. Apparently it was no good unless your number was up – you just could not get killed, or so it seemed to me as I surveyed the scene.

The second crash was by another red-haired Australian sergeant, one David Spring. He developed a bad swing on take-off, but as he had a fair bit of speed up by then he decided to try to get into the air. With better luck he may have succeeded. As it was he hit the windsock, which was mounted on a twenty-foot length of railway line embedded in concrete. This neatly removed the wing inboard of the engine. The separate pieces came to rest in flames. Spring fortunately scrambled clear, but not before he received burns sufficiently severe to put him out of action for some months.

Winter descended on us before we had more than half a dozen pilots operational. Neighbouring squadrons were having a bad time from accidents. One squadron had lost fifteen crews in under six months. So far we had been lucky.

Words cannot describe how we slaved and exhorted and drove our men in order to be ready in time. Then the winter set in, and just as we were over the worst of it a nasty series of events shook us.

The first instance was a Beaufighter with Tony Parker, an Australian, as pilot and with two crew members, one an American officer attached to us to learn about radar. They were coming in to land in broad daylight, approaching from over the Irish Sea when, without warning, they suddenly fell out of the sky in a spin and crashed in some ten fathoms of water. All were killed. At first we thought that it was just an error of judgment, and as we could not get at the wreck we decided that Parker had relaxed too soon. However, he was a very experienced pilot, which made it strange.

Then Meredith, an Englishman, took off one night and found, as he reached the end of the runway and left the ground, that all his trimming tabs had been jammed and the aeroplane was almost impossible to fly. In the hands of an average pilot it would have crashed. As it was, by superhuman strength and skill he made an emergency landing.

Sabotage! A cold sweat still breaks out at the thought. Before we could organise any prevention, a sergeant pilot crashed in a bog east of the aerodrome. This time it was not a write-off, by some miracle, and we soon saw what had caused this and the earlier crash of Parker's. One flap jack had been partially sawn through, and when the flaps were put down for the last part of the landing one collapsed, causing the aeroplane to spin as it was so close to its stalling speed when the failure occurred.

Tony Dotteridge had been in a squadron which had suffered at the hands of a saboteur, so he knew the drill. We took all precautions, posted guards on all aeroplanes and notified headquarters of our predicament. It says a lot for British counter-espionage that they had the squadron de-sabotaged in a couple of days, but not before two more nasty – but fortunately not fatal – incidents took place.

I thought most of my administrative worries were over when five hundred Australian ground troops arrived from sunny Australia. The sight of these lean, bronzed men in their slouch hats gave me quite a thrill of pride, but how wrong I was about my administrative worries. In a way, what followed was a first-class example of the force of a single personality on a community. The chain of events or misadventures was all directly or indirectly due to the impact of a wild Australian of Irish extraction on an unsuspecting and otherwise hospitable people.

By this time we had been joined by our Australian ground troops, but quite a few of the British troops remained with us as the handing-over process was somewhat protracted. I had been very thrilled at their arrival, and they certainly looked bronzed and fit after nearly three months at sea.

Prior to their arrival, the only other Australian had been an air gunner named Gallaher. In a burst of patriotic enthusiasm I appointed him my own air gunner. This was an error of judgement, for Gallaher was a very unreliable customer, with no sense of time and little sense of discipline. No doubt today he would rate as a delinquent and even the rigours of RAF discipline made little impression on him. At first I remonstrated with him when he neglected to turn up on time for flying duty. Later I had to get tougher but it was all the same to Gallaher. He was quite good for five days of the week until payday, then he got blind drunk for two days. After that he had no money so he was a useful member of the unit once more. Unfortunately war did not recognise a five day week, so Gallaher had to be sorted out. It turned out to be an endless task.

Not only had Gallaher been a nuisance on the stations, he had gone into the local villages and towns where he had energetically lived up to his self-styled reputation of being a 'one-man wave of destruction'. His distinctive dark-blue Australian Air Force uniform made him conspicuous, and his behaviour did the rest. He was short, stocky and red-haired, and very aggressive indeed.

A few days after the Australian troops arrived, they had their first leave passes to go to the local towns. The main cities were Bangor and Holyhead. Bangor was the more popular, so the boys all went to Bangor. The next day I had a call from the local inspector of police. He wanted to arrange for an identity parade as the Australian troops had practically wrecked Bangor and the whole countryside was in an uproar of indignation, or so it seemed. This was a new one for me, as I was not sure whether the police had the right to insist on such a parade.

The local legal officer sorted it out, and it was decided in the interests of getting reasonable relationships with the locals that we would accede. The aggrieved parties turned out to be a couple of publicans and the proprietress of one of the local houses of ill repute.

An inquiry which lasted days, and wasted an enormous amount of time and money, revealed that the first place the boys had visited was a hotel. On being rudely told to get out, they wrecked the place. Another hotel suffered a similar fate, but they got some grog at a third.

After celebrating a little, a group set off to the local bawdy house. Here, too, the first to arrive were thrown out by a group of BBC announcers who were apparently self-appointed 'chuckers-out'. Reinforcements arrived simultaneously and a first-class battle raged, the upshot of which was that the BBC announcers were heaved out before the place was systematically wrecked. Souvenirs were brought back covering a fairly considerable range of property. This was the object of the identification parade.

Establishing the original cause of the Welsh hostility was easy. It all went back to Gallaher. He had been there before. He had established a reputation. Everything else was a logical result of Gallaher's depredation. This was the first of a long list of deputations, complaints and threats of civil action I had to endure. Almost daily the police inspector turned up with a farmer or a publican in tow with a long schedule of complaints. Even the police officer himself arrived one day complaining that he had run into a barricade of bitumen drums placed across the main road in the blackout. He had wrecked the police car as a result, and he blamed the Australians. In fact, in no time the entire crime sheet of north Wales was daily put on to the Australians.

For the most part we just denied the charges, leaving it to the police to produce proof before we would agree to searches of the camp. This was a bit tough for them to do every time. However, with John Pike, the Australian adjutant, I made some checks around the barracks after a series of complaints about stolen chickens. We found plenty of poultry, all right. We also found impressive supplies of ducks, turkeys, geese and even sucking pigs. It seemed I had a squadron of bushrangers to cope with.

It was no time before the next barrage of accusations descended. This time it was angry farmers who had been relieved of their double-barrelled shotgun by the guards as they passed the guardroom. Their daughters were all in trouble, and of course the boys were getting the blame. It seemed as if nothing like this had ever happened until the bushrangers arrived in the district.

I had no doubt that these charges were as well founded as the chicken-thieving ones, but my job was somehow to organise a night-fighter squadron to defend the cities of Liverpool, Manchester, Birmingham, Blackpool, Glasgow and so on from night raiders sneaking up the Irish Sea or coming in over Ireland itself. I was not cut out to be a super Sherlock Holmes, although there was plenty of raw material on the camp for a series of first rate whodunnit mysteries.

One of the most difficult jobs I had was to keep a straight face when some of the excesses of the brigands came officially to my notice. Almost daily a new list of crimes had to be formally dealt with, as the overloaded Welsh civil constabulary clamped down on some of the more or less elusive of my countrymen. Typical was the case of two huge, virile bucks who were paraded before me one afternoon with all the solemnity of a military court.

The sergeant major bawled out, 'Prisoners and escort quick march, lep-right-lep-right-lep-right. Prisoners and escort 'alt! Left turn, LAC Flannigan and A/C Kloppenhouser, sir.'

At twenty-five years of age I had to sit in judgement on men twice my age, frequently more. This time the accused were about my own vintage, but about twice my size – Irish and German extraction. It was usually one or the other. Those of Scottish extraction were too ambitious to get into trouble, while those of Welsh extraction were too cunning to be caught. The boys of English extraction usually ran a poor third to the former categories.

The Welsh constable began giving his evidence in his singsong dialect, reading from a prepared manuscript: 'On proceeding to the public 'ouse known as the Golden Bull at 6.30 pm on the — day of October, I entered the premises and proceeded to the bar where I saw the accused, who I now recognise as LAC Flannigan, sir, shouting to the customers in the bar. "Come and get it. It's on the 'ouse. We're running this flogging pub now."'

Sniggers from the accused. The constable continued solemnly, 'I approached the accused and said in a loud voice, "Come out from behind that bar, you have no business in there." The other, who I now recognise as A/C Kloppenhouser shouted out, "Don't take any [unprintable] notice of the bastard Paddy, he's only a [unprintable] rookie."'

Hoots of mirth from the prisoners, strangled explosive noises from the escort. A badly suppressed guffaw from my adjutant standing behind me all but shattered the dignity of the court, and I could see full well the humour of it. The policeman being so obviously incensed about it all made it somehow even funnier. I had to bite my tongue literally to keep control myself, or I would have joined in the general mirth.

Eventually I felt sufficiently in control of my voice to say as sternly as I could, 'Sergeant major, are you unable to control the behaviour of the prisoners?' Obviously he could not.

The constable proceeded with his evidence and I was more prepared for the unconscious humour of the alleged backchat from the bushrangers.

At last it came to my turn to pronounce sentence on the culprits. I felt I could not, with decency, inflict punishment on them, as I realised they intended no real mischief though it must have been very galling to the owner of the hotel and to the police officer. Equally, if I let them off there would be innumerable repeat performances on the next visit, as it would be inferred that I was sympathetic to their high spirited nonsense.

I chose the easy way out. I remanded them to the station commander for sentence. He could take an impartial view. He was ten years older than I, which would be more satisfactory all round.

Unfortunately the station commander went to hospital that night, and I found myself, the next morning, acting station commander, and so I had a complete repeat matinee performance – there was no escape. They had to be sentenced to a short stretch in the local Army detention barracks. I hated doing it, but there was no other way. Fortunately, the second performance was a more dignified occasion than the unrehearsed premiere.

*

The resolving of these little excesses of my fellow countrymen made me long for the law-abiding cast-offs of the RAF. However, after weeks of hearing charges, confessions, accusations and denials, we settled down to a less exhausting way of life. Apart from the inevitable thieving of chickens and sucking pigs, which were all devoured before their loss was established, I was able to relax and give more attention to my primary role of aerial combat as distinct from a magistrate trying to suppress the bush-ranging instincts of the 'boys'.

Night fighting was a difficult business in winter, especially when the weather was bad, which in England was about nine nights out of ten. The risks of damage or death in combat were small even if interceptions were frequent, but the risks involved in attempting to fly in virtually impossible weather in blacked-out conditions were great, and both neighbouring night-fighter squadrons had lost an average of twelve crews in three months. Of course, this rate fell off later in the war as more experience was gained.

I am reasonably sure that much of this in the early days was due to the haphazard methods of bringing an aeroplane onto the runway as most of the accidents were due to attempts to turn too tightly at a low speed. A Beaufighter had a wing loading of some sixty pounds to a square foot.

Now, any substance which weighs sixty pounds and has an area of only a square foot is a very heavy one, and if it is going to fly it has to keep moving pretty fast. Steep turns which increase this loading by two or three times would cause the wing loading to go as high as 180 pounds to the square foot. Such a wing loading will not support itself in the air under speeds of 200 mph. It stands to reason that turns at low speeds would cause stalls and fatal crashes.

We had a drive and insisted on everybody adopting the 'Hamilton approach', and as a result almost entirely eliminated landing accidents simply because it eliminated the necessity to make tight turns at the last minute to get on to the runway.

Two occasions early in 1942 proved to me the value of this method. The first was due to a hydraulic failure which left me with no flaps. This meant that I had to make a low, long approach to the aerodrome if I were to get on to the runway and have enough room for a 'no-flap' landing. It was a dark night, with mist reducing visibility to 1,000 yards at 150 mph low down. There was no chance of seeing the runway lights until I was almost over them. By using the Hamilton technique, I managed to hit the end of the runway on the second try and no damage was done.

On the second occasion an engine cut out just after take-off. This was a prolific cause of fatal accidents, as a Beaufighter Mk II was almost impossible to fly on one engine. I managed to get back on to the runway by the same method, even though visibility was again reduced to 1,000 yards by mist. Altogether, it was a very 'twitch-making' business and just about the most frightening trip I have ever had as pilot of an aeroplane except when bullets were crashing around the cockpit.

After this I think everybody in the squadron was sold on the idea and used it religiously. As a result I believe we had only one serious flying accident in twelve months, which must have been a record for any night-fighter squadron. Although I was not with the squadron throughout the period, it was very gratifying to me, as I always deplored the loss of valuable life in war, and while it was reasonable to risk death in combat I always felt that death due to a flying accident was a tragic waste and a win for the enemy.

18

Breaking Point

Christmas 1941 came and went. I flew over to High Ercall and had dinner with Max Aitken, Lord Beaverbrook's son and CO of the neighbouring night fighter squadron.

Early in the new year of 1942 we had a few attempted interceptions of stray German bombers coming in over the Irish Sea, but without success. It seemed a little unrealistic as we waited over that sea at twenty thousand feet to see Dublin and various other Irish cities a blaze of lights, giving the enemy navigators every chance to make an accurate check on their position as they set course for the last leg of their run in to Manchester, Liverpool or Birmingham.

Of course there was no reason why the Irish should turn off their lights; they were not at war. However, they must have been thereby instrumental in assisting many a German bomber land his load of bombs on an English city. In their absence, the bombs could have fallen on the open countryside. No doubt many innocent people thus paid for Ireland's neutrality. Perhaps their blood may have atoned for the bloodshed of another age which still rankled in many Irish hearts.

Then, on the night of 10 January, about six enemy aircraft rounded Land's End and continued inland via St George's Channel and the Irish Sea. At eleven o'clock, my friend John Hamilton and his radar operator, P/O Dan Norris-Smith, were scrambled. They lost their first contact because of radio failure on the part of Ground Control. Eventually they were handed over to another controller and a second contact was made. Visual was obtained and the target identified as a Do 217. Hamilton fired two bursts and the Dornier went down in flames. It was 456 Squadron's first success and it showed what could be done.

There was great excitement. The Australian press went to town and to the intense disgust of the squadron and Dan, they only mentioned Norris-Smith. They did not even mention Hamilton's name. As Hamilton was by this time a household name in the squadron, this was very poorly received, and indeed it was a fair indication of the parochial nature of the Australian press at the time.

*

On 28 January 1942, I woke with a feeling of disaster and sadness hanging over me. It was not something I could shake off, and as the day went on I felt progressively more distressed at its persistence. I had frequently felt worried over some job I had to do, and fear was no stranger to me, but this was different. It persisted all day.

That evening I had a try at dispelling it with a few drinks with the boys, but it would not go. I returned to my flat. There Helen told me that a cable had arrived from Australia, telling me that my brother, Tony, had been killed in a crash in Australia.

At first I could not believe it. Tony was eighteen months younger than I, and we had been great friends as well as brothers. He had joined the RAAF and had graduated as a pilot only a few days earlier. I had been greatly excited at the news; I had even written to him suggesting he tried to get over to England, where we could see each other again. Now he was gone. That strange feeling of disaster – I had never known it before – I knew now what had caused it.

For several days I was almost unable to realise what had happened. I had seen so many of my friends killed, or perhaps it would be more correct to say they failed to return, but Tony was almost part of me. I had always had Tony for a friend and playmate since I could remember.

As was so often the case with those who died young, Tony was one of those rare characters completely devoid of vice or hardness of any kind. I doubt if he had an enemy in the world, and he found life just one great big bit of fun. He had grown into an outstandingly good-looking lad with a personality and a nature to match it. 'Those whom the Gods love die young.' Part of me died with Tony.

I pressed on with even greater bursts of effort, for I had always found that activity was better than brooding on a sadness, but the vacuum remained.

For nine months I had been living on a minimum of sleep. In fact, since the bombing of Tangmere a year before, when I first went on to shift work in the Tangmere control room, I had been averaging little more than three or four hours sleep a night. I always found it most difficult to sleep in the daytime.

Since the formation of 456 Squadron, with the problem of combining an adequate training programme by day with the provision of operational crews on 'Standby' at nights, I had been cutting regularly into my daily quota of sleep. Frequently I had to manage on two or three hours.

Combined with these tiring hours were the very real strains of night operations. In this field of war there was little danger from the enemy. The technique was to stalk him by radar. If he were detected then usually his destruction was swift and certain. I never heard of any effective return fire damaging a night fighter.

Nevertheless, the casualty rate in night fighters was at least as high as day fighters on account of the hazardous weather conditions which had to be faced. Enemy bombers frequently took off from Continental aerodromes enjoying clear weather to bomb Britain, which was being subjected to the most severe storms or entirely blanketed in fog. Frequently, when no other aeroplanes were operating, the night fighter had to take to the air. On such occasions he had only a slim chance of a safe return, and that was where the deaths occurred. Flying under such conditions was a continuous strain. Sleep was the only remedy for tired or exhausted nerves, and I had been depriving myself of sleep for over a year.

Without realising it, I had been imposing an impossible strain on my weary system. I had lost two stone in weight, and when Helen or the squadron medical officer suggested I needed more rest I simply laughed at them – me, need sleep? Never. I did not realise a man could go on so long and feel so fit without sleep.

The squadron had become an obsession with me. I frequently did not get home at all, instead following a night on duty by going straight to the office to attend to the day's administration after breakfast.

One afternoon, toward the end of February, I was flying at about twelve thousand feet over the Welsh mountains. It was a clear blue sky, and there was quite a lot of snow on Snowdon and the adjacent peaks. I was relaxed and at peace in the air and thoroughly enjoying myself. I thought how good life was and how much better it would be if there were no Hitlers to curse us with wars.

Gradually the scene in front of me grew darker, yet the sun was still shining. I suddenly realised with a flash of alarm that I was on the point of passing out. I grabbed the oxygen-control tap and turned it on full, then, as best I could with the parachute harness and other gear around me and the control column in the way, tried to put my head between my knees.

The oxygen, the exertion or the fright stopped the trouble and I returned to normal with my heart beating madly. I throttled back, returned to the aerodrome and landed. When I got out I felt very shaky. It was the first time in my life I had gone so close to fainting except for that one occasion at thirty-five thousand feet when the oxygen pipe had slipped off my mask. There had been a good reason for it that time, but this time there was none as far as I could see. For the first time I realised how vulnerable a pilot in a single-seater aeroplane was to disaster if he passed out. There was no way to prevent a crash unless he came round in time, which of course would be very unlikely.

The next time I flew all was well, and the following day I flew again. I was just reassuring myself that all was well and that the fright over the Welsh hills was just a figment of the imagination when it struck me again. This time I was much more frightened, and I was feeling very washed out by the time I landed.

I made no mention of it to anybody. I had a couple days' leave due, so I went off home for a rest. That night I awoke with severe cramps in the stomach. Helen got some hot milk and they subsided, but I could not sleep. The next night I had more cramps in the stomach and thought I must have developed appendicitis, so I reported to the medical officer.

Tom Burfitt was a friend of mine and he sometimes came up with me at night when we went flying. He sounded me over pretty thoroughly and decided there could be something wrong, but he wanted me to go into hospital for tests. He had warned me frequently that I was working too hard and he thought maybe I had overdone it. I assured him that no one had ever died of overwork. He shook his head at me and refused to argue.

I reported to the nearest RAF hospital in Chester. There they investigated me and asked me hundreds of questions. Most of them meant nothing to me. None of them gave me the slightest clue as to what was my trouble. The stomach pains had subsided due to various drugs I had been fed on, but I just could not sleep.

At first this did not worry me, as I had accustomed myself to two or three hours a night. I would be awake until 3 a.m. or 4 a.m., when I would begin to doze off. Almost immediately the hospital routine took over and I was woken up to have a bath. Sleep left me, but just in case I did doze off the scrubbers and polishers arrived and turned everything upside down and inside out, including my bed.

After a fortnight of this relentless technique, during which my three or so hours was systematically reduced to one or less, I was solemnly advised by the senior medical officer that there was nothing the matter with me physically, I was just tired and needed a rest. I entirely agreed with him about the latter, but I felt doubtful that such severe pains as I had experienced could be just nothing. However, as there was nothing the matter with me I asked to go back to my squadron.

'Oh no,' he replied. 'You need a few weeks' complete rest. We are sending you down to Torquay to the convalescent hospital.'

'But I want to get back to my squadron,' I persisted. The squadron was my pride and joy, and even while I was away it occupied most of my thinking.

'I am afraid that is impossible,' he replied. 'You see, you will not be fit to return for some weeks, and as you know two weeks absence with sickness is the maximum. After that a new commander is posted in.'

I knew that too well. It was a sickening blow to have it confirmed. The bottom suddenly fell out of my world. The tremendous interest I had developed in the squadron, which was the cause of the relentless way I had driven myself and the others who were with me, now had no object on which to focus its attention.

I packed my bags and set off for Torquay, a dreary journey from Chester, travelling via a number of minor railway back alleys until I reached Torquay. Then I found my way to the hospital.

This was a first-class holiday hotel which had been converted into a convalescent centre. It had everything for an enjoyable holiday. After the arrival formalities I was shown to my room, a small but luxurious one with a bathroom attached. I felt this would soon put me back on my feet and back in the squadron – perhaps another squadron, but no doubt I could soon adjust myself.

A gong announced the evening meal, and I found my way to the sumptuous dining room. I was quite hungry when I sat down but my appetite left me as one bunch of officers walked in and sat at a nearby table. Their faces were all shapeless and scarred. They were the victims of fires in aircraft and had lost much of the skin and flesh off their faces and hands. They were undergoing plastic surgery and were convalescing after various stages of the treatment. They were all very cheerful and jovial, but the effect on me was devastating. I was unable to finish my meal.

That night I did not sleep a wink. Whenever I shut my eyes I saw those hideously burned faces and the clawed hands. No horror film or description of disaster had ever had such a shattering effect on my imagination. It was like some ghastly nightmare, only it was real.

The next day they were still there, and again I felt ill when I tried to eat any food. There were many others in the hospital, men with legs missing, hands and arms missing, broken limbs by the dozens, in effect the human wreckage of war in the air.

In the squadrons it was possible to dismiss from the mind much of the inevitable suffering of war. As the victims of crashes and bullets were taken away to indefinite hospitalisation and suffering, they were soon almost forgotten in the fast and furious business of war. Here in the hospitals it was not possible to dismiss that aspect by a mad burst of work or even drinking. It was a reality which had to be faced daily.

A week of complete sleeplessness on top of the rest of my history of weariness with nothing constructive to get my mind on to had a very alarming effect on me. I began to fear I was going crazy. My head and eyes ached as if they would burst, and I could not eat.

In the middle of the night I would develop an uncontrollable feeling of panic, as if I was being haunted by some unknowable horror. My room seemed to be a hideous little tomb and I wanted to rush out into the open air to breathe.

The medical officers had scarcely noticed my arrival and it was several days before I saw one. I think they thought there was little wrong with me that a couple of weeks' rest would not cure. Initially no doubt that was true, but by the time I was able to discuss my troubles with them I was a nervous wreck and I spent most of each day in considerable physical pain.

This, I was assured, was pure imagination. There was nothing organically wrong, but there would be if I did not 'snap out of it'.

'All that's the matter with you is a complete breakdown both nervous and physical. You know a medical practitioner could make a fortune out of your case', said the fat, sleek doctor, and I felt he was mentally calculating how I would have swelled his bank account if there were no war. For my part I felt he would not have had me as a patient had it not been for the war.

'That's all right for you to be so nonchalant about it, but this place gives me the horrors. If you keep me here I feel I will go completely crazy,' I replied.

'Well I suppose it is a mistake to expose a person as tired as you are to the nervous shocks which are part and parcel of this business, especially the boys with the burnt faces,' he announced, 'but I don't see what else I can do. By the way, is your wife down here?'

'No.'

'Well I suggest you get her down at once. In the meantime you must snap out of it, you know. It's only a psychological problem really.'

'It's a bloody funny sort of philosophy that can't do much for me. I'm too exhausted mentally to think straight for five minutes on end, especially when I've been so long without sleep.'

'Well you'll have to snap out of it – that's all I can say.' That was his last instruction for several days.

Helen dropped everything and came down to Torquay. I was in no mood for making friends and had become very lonely as well as melancholy. Indeed, what few new friends I had made seemed determined to itemise in detail their symptoms and tell me ghastly stories of fellows who had developed melancholy and committed suicide.

Helen arrived to find me a sorry remnant. She found some accommodation and set about trying to salvage some of the wreckage.

She planned walks and little trips and gradually dragged me out of the abject depths of my despair – the walks were enjoyable, I liked the physical action, but for days on end I could not shake off a feeling of impending disaster and I was quite sure I was cursed with an incurable disease which would kill me.

The abdominal pains persisted and restricted my walks on some days. I could not believe the doctor's claim that they were imagination. There were quite a variety of pains and they corresponded with all the symptoms of ulcers (duodenal and gastric), appendicitis, gallstones, coronary occlusions, angina and numerous more deadly diseases, at least so my various hypochondriac acquaintances convinced me. It was very exhausting to suffer from such a schedule of dangerous diseases and I rapidly became a hypochondriac myself, as I had nothing better to do with my time. I found I excelled at collecting symptoms. I had more symptoms than anyone I knew.

A medical officer joined the ranks of the patients. He was a friendly soul and Helen and I saw quite a lot of him. He went out of his way to help me.

'How many operational trips have you done, old man?' he asked me shortly after we met.

'I don't exactly know, but I suppose it would run into at least a couple of hundred,' I ventured.

'Well look at it this way,' he said. 'For some two hundred occasions when you should have been badly frightened, you pushed fear to one side and managed to concentrate on doing some physical action associated with flying and using the aeroplane as a weapon of war. That's no mean achievement, but it does not mean that you have conquered fear. You haven't. Now you are terribly tired both physically and mentally and that part of your system which reacts to danger by developing fear – which is quite a natural reaction – is now allowed an uncontrolled run because you are too worn out to control it. You will experience the sensations of fear without any cause. It will seem quite crazy and you may even feel that you must be mad because it is happening.'

'You've put your finger right on it,' I agreed, 'but how long will it go on? This fear and panic business frightens the hell out of me while it is on.'

'Oh, not very long. It will become less and less. I think you ought to get away from this environment though, on to a farm or something, and then you would be right in no time. The spectacle of all the suffering and disfigurement triggers off all your pent-up negative emotions of fear and anxiety. As you have nothing positive to do, it is becoming an obsession with you.'

'I'm sure you're right', I agreed, 'but this place is like a prison.'

Two days later I saw the hospital medico.

'I've been giving some thought to your case, and I think a few weeks on a farm would be the shot,' he announced.

'I entirely agree, when can I go?'

'Oh, not so fast. We haven't got a farm, and it's only a thought,' he replied, 'but I do think this place is no good for you. We have had many cases similar to yours and it has puzzled us why you don't respond to rest in this atmosphere. Yes, I think perhaps a farm. But it may be a month or so before we can arrange something.'

'Look here,' I replied. 'This place will kill me in a month. I can get on to a farm in twenty-four hours or less if you will agree to it. I know people in London who fix just that sort of a holiday and I could be there tomorrow.'

'All right, see what you can do, and I'll see if I can arrange for a month's leave for you.'

I contacted my friends in London who looked after homeless colonials and explained my plight. Two hours later a phone call told me I could go and spend a month at the home of a family in Cornwall who would be delighted for me to work on their place as long as I liked.

The details were sorted out and Helen and I set off for Cornwall and the life of a clodhopping yokel. The very idea made me feel vastly better.

19

Unwanted Prodigals

After my time in the countryside I visited the Australian Air Force Overseas Headquarters, who seemed very keen to avail themselves of my experience before transferring me back to the RAAF. This experience, to date, was eighteen months' operational experience on Spitfires almost entirely in the south-east corner of England, in addition to almost a year's operations on night fighters, a few months in the control room and nine months on training fighter pilots. This meant I'd had experience that only a few men in the RAF at this stage of the war could claim.

There was only one difficulty, and that was a personal one. I had been a wing commander for nearly eighteen months in the RAF, and there was doubt that I could transfer with that rank to the RAAF as my rank was acting. However, I was assured that as I had received my acting rank on operations I would be entitled to retain it until I was re-employed in Australia. Later, I found this to be mere sales talk.

My transfer to the RAAF turned out to be a fairly simple affair, and almost before I knew what was happening I found myself issued with the dark-blue Australian uniform and all the trimmings. A certain amount of correspondence had gone back and forth to Australia concerning my transfer, and it was said that the RAAF in Australia was very much in need of somebody with wide experience both on operations and on control of operations for staff duties.

Before I was sent back, I suggested that as my experience had been confined to the British Isles it might be a good idea if I spent a few months with the Second Tactical Air Force, which was forming up with great secrecy in the south of England.

The Second TAF was modelled on Arthur Tedder's First TAF in North Africa and was designed for a fast-moving war of attack, whereas the fighter operations over Britain were almost exclusively static defence with short-range nuisance raids for diversion when the role was at a standstill. I felt that a few months working with the men who were planning and training this new force (which was destined to go with Montgomery to Berlin) would be of the greatest importance as the men had learned their methods in the brilliantly victorious campaign which started with El Alamein.

After a few cables had been exchanged, I was duly sent to the Tactical Air Force and supplied with a staff car. I spent the next four months wandering around the south of England on practice operations aimed at developing the highest possible mobility.

The months went by very quickly, and I was kept very busy making notes for future reference and nosing out all the latest developments in radar and the control of fighters. Almost daily I would come across some old face I knew well – a friend who had been in the desert for years and whom I thought dead, or another I had lost trace of for years. It was most gratifying to discover that I had many old friends in this particular organisation.

Most of them, by this time, were group captains and were appointed to quite responsible positions. This was fortunate for me as they took more trouble to explain points to a friend than they would to a stranger, and Englishmen can be very reserved, especially on hush-hush work and when they are working against time.

I think I was looked upon by many of them as a bit of a fool, as my transfer into the RAAF turned out to involve a considerable drop in rank. I was reduced to squadron leader, without any seniority, which effectively put me about four years behind my contemporaries who stayed in Australia. There was not much I could do about it, though my friends often asked guarded questions as to whether I had 'boobed' or been court-martialled for some crime.

At that stage I was too busy to be worried about the matter. In any case, I knew that when one meets such treatment in the service, kicking up a fuss does not usually worry anyone except the fusser.

October came and almost had gone when I received frantic messages from Helen and from the Australian headquarters that I had to return and get on a ship. Passage had been arranged so that my wife and I could travel out on the same ship.

I returned and packed, and in two days was on board a ship in Liverpool bound for somewhere in Australia.

The trip out was very interesting. Our ship was a 'meat freezer' which before the war had been used to make fast trips between Australia and the UK or Argentina and the UK. Since the war it had been very much on active service, and its most famous voyage had been the relief of Malta, when it was one of a handful of ships to succeed in running the gauntlet to bring help to the gallant defenders of that famous island. The ship had not escaped unscarred and had been hit in the bows with a torpedo. This had blown a huge hole in the bow, and a temporary repair had been affected by filling the hole with seventy tons of concrete.

Out in the North Atlantic we struck some heavy weather, and I was amazed to see that when the bows were lifted out by huge waves the concrete patch made the bows look like a huge turnip. Yet so powerful were the engines that we made the trip averaging about seventeen knots.

Helen and I had five weeks together on that ship, and although I knew that there was plenty of risk in those green waters of the Atlantic, and even more risk in the blue waters of the Caribbean (an old friend of mine and his wife were reported lost at sea in the Caribbean just before we left), I had the best rest and the best food since the war began.

Our only port of call was at Panama, where we got ashore for a few hours. Helen longed to buy all the pretties in the shops, but the prices were high, and our puny supply of dollars was quickly exhausted. We visited nightclubs and danced in the evening, but we had to be back on board before 10 p.m. so our revelry was short-lived.

The remainder of the trip was uneventful, except for the sighting of a periscope about two days out from New Zealand. The ship did some violent turns and all hands went to action stations. The crew had learnt their stuff in the Mediterranean, so there was no alarm, but nothing further happened. I had overheard the first mate tell the customs in Panama that our freight was mines and explosives so any torpedoes would have made a job of us and there would not have been any swimming to do.

One bright morning, about 11 a.m., we saw a long, flat line of land ahead and in a few hours we had our first glimpse of Sydney Heads. Helen was very miserable, as were the other six British wives on the ship, because until one sees one's destination the sea gives one no indication that one has moved from one's place of departure. The temperature changes, but the sea and the sky remain the same; it is only when one can see the solid land that one realises that one has arrived.

To me it was home, or nearly home; to Helen it was a new and strange land, and poor Helen was not too sure that she liked leaving her beloved England.

It was evening before we had tied up in Pyrmont and received clearances to go ashore. At last I set foot on solid earth and we all made a dash for Sydney proper to eat fruit and see how ice cream tasted. The girls had a marvellous time and could not believe their eyes when they saw all that was for sale in the shops. I think it cheered them up considerably.

The next morning I left Helen to arrange for the movement of our luggage when it came off the ship and I reported to the local air force authorities. I was told that all arrangements for dispatch of the luggage would be undertaken by the RAAF. It all sounded fine, but it seemed I could not take it with me on leave to Brisbane because the dockworkers were having one of their usual little strikes and the luggage could not be moved.

I tried every avenue I could but to no avail, and after spending two days of my fortnight's repatriation leave in Sydney waiting for the strike to clear I left the luggage to be sent on. I was very loath to leave it, as there was one steel trunk with all our wedding presents in it, but there was nothing for it.

Some of those trunks eventually arrived home four months later. All had been bashed open by being dropped from a great height, and all my wife's and my own treasures had been pilfered. One trunk, the most prized of the lot, with the few treasures salvaged after my belongings had been bombed by the Huns at Tangmere, was thieved in its entirety. It was the one with all our wedding presents.

After a somewhat exhausting train journey, Helen and I arrived in Brisbane on a Friday afternoon, a week before Christmas. Although we had tried to keep our arrival a secret, the news had leaked out as the Department of Air had made an announcement of our arrival in Australia and accordingly there was quite a gathering of aunts and uncles in addition to my parents to greet us on our arrival.

I hate crowds of people at farewells, and I'm not sure that I like a crowd on one's return home after many years. One cannot do justice to responding to everyone's welcome and one feels somewhat exhausted on both occasions. Besides, twenty-four hours in an Australian train at the height of summer makes one rather weak for such emotional strain. However, it was very flattering to one's vanity to see so many friends.

I found my home town, Brisbane, much smaller and much dirtier than I had ever imagined it could be. After seven years' absence I had imagined it to be much more glamorous and far more stable than it appeared in the hard light of a summer afternoon. The houses were ugly and up on stilts – I had grown so used to houses on the ground that I had almost forgotten Brisbane's idiosyncrasy in this regard. The weatherboard houses had not been painted for years, and, with the men mostly absent in the forces or in hard-worked war industries, gardens were just tropical jungles.

My own home brought me back to earth. It was much smaller than I could have imagined, and the allotment of land on which it was built seemed to have shrunk too. It was with relief that the following morning we all left for the surf and ten days of sunshine and leisure.

The beach and the surf had not changed. They were exactly as I had left them, and it was here that I felt that I was at home at last. How my wife felt about it all I'm at a loss to know. If she was disappointed, she gallantly kept it to herself. When we settled in at the little hut on the beach, I believe she began to feel life was not at all bad in Australia.

The next week went like a flash of lightning. I could not believe I was really home, and felt it was all a dream for a few days. The black days in England had seemed so very black and I think I must have almost given up all hope, deep in my heart, of ever seeing my homeland again. Everything seemed quite unreal at first.

My mother and father were much older – they'd had anxious and sad days. One of my brothers was dead and the other, still only nineteen, was an air gunner in the RAAF somewhere in New Guinea or the islands. I began thus to realise the passage of the years. Cousins who had seemed babes in arms were fully grown, or perhaps I should say the ten- and twelve-year-old small fries had become the seventeen- and nineteen-year-olds of wartime society and were very much men and women of the world. In these I found little of the personalities of the original children, and it was like meeting new people.

At the end of the ten-day spell I reported to the local air force personnel depot – here I had to take a sheet of paper around in order that twenty or so officers could sign it. It seemed quite unnecessary to me. However, there were several dozen other rankers all doing likewise. I felt quite sure that, assuming each officer took two minutes to check whether or not the man had a pair of overalls he was not entitled to or if he had his correct number on his sheets of documents, there was a full day's work for at least twenty-five officers who devoted their time to signing a piece of paper which became useless upon entering the gate. It seemed a remarkable if novel method of wasting manpower. Everybody, including the Chief of Air Staff, seemed to know about these depots, so I felt it useless to protest.

After a morning of waiting in queues miles long in the boiling sun (officers had almost no privileges in the RAAF), a medical officer suddenly discovered that my documents had not arrived and as far as he knew they would be unlikely to arrive for a month. He told me that he had tried to persuade the Air Board to send medical documents out by airmail or special delivery but the Air Board declined on the grounds of the unnecessary expense.

However, it seemed somewhat penny wise and pound foolish when I worked out that because of late documents I would probably be paid approximately £2 a day for thirty days for doing nothing as the policy of the Air Board also ruled that no one could be posted to a job until checked medically and found fit for it. I found it impossible to believe that my medical and other papers would cost £60 to bring out via airmail. By making casual inquiries, I established that my case was by no means a unique one; in fact, I was already just one of three senior officers in the same situation.

Perhaps that last statement is incorrect, for I had been reduced to squadron leader. Empire Air Trainees who had gone through a much abbreviated training to pre-war officers were permitted to retain acting rank which had been granted on operations. This was largely because of political pressure brought to bear after the first Spitfire squadrons returned to defend Darwin. The officers' ranks were smartly reduced, which was grossly unfair, and as these same officers made an embarrassing fuss to the newspapers the government made the rule that they could retain their rank on return to Australia from overseas until re-employed by the RAAF. However, as there were only three or four of the old pre-war hands in our category, we were bluntly reduced and had no redress. The law did not apply to us as we had no political strings we could pull.

Our type of prodigal was not wanted.

20

Australia's Pacific War

Being back in Australia delighted me at first. It seemed incredibly good to be back home and I wallowed in the Christmas sunshine and the surf. I wondered whether it had all changed as much as it seemed to me or whether I had changed. At last I concluded that probably it was a bit of both. No doubt I had changed a lot, but I am sure the war changed the Australia I knew.

Very few Australians had the slightest idea of what war meant. Those who had lost relatives knew a little of the hell of war but these people had lived a life of plenty. Their stomachs had been well filled (alas far too well in some cases) for the whole period. They knew not the fear that churns up the stomach as a bomb screeches into the ground. They had no such unpleasantness to snap them out of their snug complacency. They did not sleep with the fear of waking with their house burying them alive or freezing cold all day for months on end, hungry into the bargain.

They'd had one nasty shock when the Japanese were within two thousand miles of their populated areas, but they did not know the menace of eighty million Huns twenty miles away, just across the water where they could be seen through binoculars on a clear day. Nor did they have them menacing them for a whole year while they stood alone frantically straining every sinew to make a few guns and tanks to stave off an imminent invasion. These people did not know hunger or fear or hard work and most of them could not have cared less.

Where was the British sense of honour which made the black market virtually unknown in Britain? It was gone, and all struggled with each other to grab the coveted luxuries which alone were absent from the shops.

There were exceptions, of course, but they were almost pathetic – sincere folk in civilian life who had been precluded from joining the services and old soldiers from the last war who were conscientiously working themselves to death. The majority were just apathetic.

One feature I could not accustom myself to was the somewhat uninspiring little tune which preceded the news whenever it was broadcast. I was informed it was called 'Advance Australia Fair'. However, I never felt happy about it; it used to remind me of the National Socialists' theme song played before the German news in English as presented by Lord Haw-Haw. Probably my impressions were due to the BBC in London, which presented its news regularly without fanfare or ostentation. Of course, 'The King' was played before the news on Sunday night.

Another RAAF officer perhaps completed my antipathy with a touch of ridicule. 'Oh,' he said, 'Australia won't be there; we'll have the news soon. You know the stuff – America has advanced one more island and destroyed thousands of Japanese – the Americans are winning the European war – the Russians are magnificent and are super-heroically smashing their way towards the Reich – Britain's Air Force has been over Germany in great strength and we're winning in Asia and Italy and so on. Then, of course, there's the Australian news. Mr Curtin has had further discussions with trade union leaders over the prolonged waterside strike in Sydney and is confident of an early settlement.'

I thought this was a little uncharitable and said so as I could not get used to the Australian habit of everlastingly howling down the government. I said so, too, on more than one occasion as I believed that Australians should show the same united war effort as their British brothers and forget political squabbles in the common effort. Unfortunately, it was not long before I realised how exact a formula my cynical friend had evolved and I had to admit that it gave a very fair precis of any news session.

It was not long before I was back at work and the pleasant summer holiday fading into a memory. One of the staff of Air Vice-Marshal Bostock, Air Officer Commanding RAAF Command, noticed a press item mentioning my return to Australia, and the next thing I knew I was recalled and given a job as Staff Officer Operations on the AOC's staff. This was my first experience of Staff work, and the first office job I'd had during the war, and I could not settle down to the indoor routine. However, I struggled with it for nearly a year and on looking back I am very glad indeed to have had the opportunity.

To begin with, I took over from an RAF group captain whom I had known very well in England before the war. In fact, he had commanded No. 74 Squadron at Hornchurch pre-war and so was more or less one of the boys. He gave me as complete a picture as possible, and as we both had served in RAF Fighter Command, where we had learned the principles of air defence, we spoke the same language in the technical sense.

After the seven years I had spent in the RAF, I found the RAAF very disappointing. As a cadet I had vastly enjoyed my year at Point Cook, and no one was more predisposed to like the RAAF than I. I had sacrificed several years' seniority in coming back to the service of my own country, so naturally I was not ill disposed towards it. Unfortunately, a change had come over the Air Force I knew, and it did not require the group captain's diagnosis to show it up; it was patently obvious to all who had served in a well-organised service such as the RAF.

The Australian Air Force was effectively split into two halves. One half, RAAF Command, was supposed to do the fighting, and the other half was responsible for organising the supplies – food, aeroplanes, etc. – to the fighting units. There was no supreme commander to coordinate these two sections. The Chief of Air Staff tried to establish himself as the overlord of RAAF Command, but that was impossible because General MacArthur gave his orders direct to the commander of RAAF Command. This created the ridiculous situation whereby a man (the commander of RAAF Command) had to try to serve two bosses (the Chief of Air Staff on one hand and MacArthur on the other). Impossible! Never was there a truer saying than the one that 'a man cannot serve two masters', and that applies to all men – great and small, singly and collectively.

The squabbles with RAAF Headquarters (or 'hindquarters' as they were irreverently called by most people who sampled their 'organisation') were of considerable moment to all who served with the RAAF in the south-west Pacific area, especially as the unfortunate victims of the system were sacked almost to a man as soon as the war was over, Air Vice-Marshal Bostock being one of the first to go.

Over the next year I had abundant opportunity to watch the feud from a front seat – and a sorry spectacle it presented. I was particularly interested in the employment of our fighter pilots and their aeroplanes, and as far as the squabbles affected them – it was my business to know as much as possible about the situation.

In conferences with American staff officers regarding the employment of our fighter forces, it became very clear to me that we were not wanted. We were given a few second-line jobs but they were unworthy of the men who were manning our squadrons and who had acquitted themselves so magnificently in Britain and the Middle East. It was no wonder that, after a few months, when the employment these men desired was not forthcoming, they would become restive.

A handful of our squadrons were up with the US front line as far as Noomfor, but after that we were left well behind. The only explanation the Americans would give was that our organisation was not good enough. That was no news to us; the surprising feature to me was that they had suffered our slow-moving administration as long as they had.

Together with other staff officers, I worked on plans for most of the operations from Cape Gloucester to Morotai, and when the opportunity came those of us who had the chance would fly up to the battle areas to see just what happened to our plans after they left our headquarters. It was commonplace to find the movement of vital machinery, on which the Americans had rightly insisted, as much as six months behind schedule.

Our protests to RAAF Headquarters were to no avail. On two occasions I was detailed by the AOC of RAAF Command to go to Melbourne to try to explain to the Chief of Staff that we really needed the alterations in plans and procedures for which we were so insistently crying out. After the second trip I realised how hopeless the position was. I had worked so hard that the medical officer ordered me to take a month's sick leave and so my activities as a staff officer came to an end.

After a month's leave, I felt more like myself. I had somewhat conditioned myself regarding my disappointment at things in Australia, and, relieved of the endless office work, I was able to sit back and take stock of the whole situation.

It was clear that we were not wanted in the Pacific theatre. To help the war effort I had wasted my time returning to Australia when I should have stayed in Britain. The Americans did not want us because our administration was hopeless. Their objections were well founded.

The government would not, or could not, take any steps to decrease the inefficiencies of its armed forces administrators. This I attributed to two complementary reasons. The first was that they did not realise how poor their administration really was, and as their favourites were appointed to high offices they did not care to remove them in any case. The second was that, realising the war was going very favourably in spite of Australia's absence from the fray, they resolved that they would take no real further part in the struggle.

This was very opportune as the Labor Cabinet was, with one minor exception, a team of non-combatants led by conscientious objectors, an unlikely combination in all events. These same men, being adept at least in animal cunning, knew how the fires of battle and the hardship of war weld men into a resolute and unified body. It was just as well for men of such fortitude as those in our government that the returned men from the First World War were a small minority of the population, and they knew it; they had no desire whatever to finish the 1939–45 war with such a spirit abroad in the land. It would have proved too great an embarrassment to their own pet union organisations. Politically they were shrewd and very cunning.

The Army was split into two mutually hostile camps – the 2nd AIF and the militia – and every effort was made to keep them from uniting in effort and spirit. If possible, there would be no strong Returned Sailor's Soldier's Airmen's Imperial League of Australia after this war. To assist in the mischief, the men were kept out of action for years, with ample time to get thoroughly fed up and to experience to the full the inefficiencies of administration of the government's appointed service chiefs. The Air Force was split into two similar and likewise hostile camps and the same fate swamped them.

The result was a million men who were sick to death of the service and who blamed the Army in their blindness for the lamentable way they were muddled about. They would return to their homes rightly fed up with the services and never consider that it was Mr Curtin's war effort, Mr Forde's Army and Mr Drakeford's Air Force.

For the next six months I enjoyed a 'rest area' job in Sydney. As there was a regular flow of time-expired personnel returning from the islands to the mainland, it was desirable to retain units at central points on the mainland, where these people could have a base job, become acquainted with the latest developments and then be held in readiness for a posting back to the islands.

The headquarters I commanded was responsible for checking all aeroplane movements over New South Wales and had units scattered throughout the state; some were on the coast and some inland. A staff car was at my disposal and the routine visits to these units gave me an excellent opportunity to see something of the country. I became very conscientious in the discharge of my duties and shortly found myself feeling amazingly fit and ready for a more active part in the fray.

Sundays I usually reserved for a visit to one of Sydney's beautiful beaches. It was shortly after Easter that Helen and I, while walking along the beach one afternoon after a swim in the surf, found a baby fairy penguin which had been washed up in an exhausted condition. Its feathers had been covered with oil and it was very wet and cold. I rescued the little fellow from a crowd of urchins anxious to dispatch him with a stick and took him home on the electric train to the camp. Helen and I had several good laughs at people's reactions to the little bird, which I had securely tied up in an Air Force shoulder bag with his head sticking out for air.

I smuggled him past the railway ticket collectors only to be disconcerted by a series of penetrating squawks as we stood at Wynyard station. Perhaps the funniest, almost classic, response came from an elderly lady who remarked, as she passed with her friend, 'Oh, look at the penguin,' and then, after moving on a dozen yards, suddenly stopped – mouth open, staring dumbfounded – and repeated, 'A PENGUIN!'

The bird was named Percy, and as he was automatically a member of the officers' mess he was given the honorary rank of pilot officer. A rush visit to the keeper of the Sydney Zoo and a conference with the local fishmonger and Percy's diet was organised. He proved a little expensive, as he could eat two shillings' worth of fish in one meal and had to be fed at least once a day. A small travelling box was expertly made by the camp carpenter so that Percy could accompany us wherever we went, while at the camp he lived more or less an unrestricted life.

A visit by the Duke of Gloucester to the unit resulted in a formal presentation of Percy to the duke, who was obviously very taken with the quaint ways of the little chap. He must have left a deep impression as the duke's ADC rang two days later to inquire concerning the bird's progress.

He became amazingly tame and would follow me around the camp wherever I went. When I went to Brisbane for pre-embarkation leave, a certain amount of difficulty was experienced with railway officials who had never heard of such a thing. Diplomacy to the tune of a ten-shilling note was sufficient to establish a precedent.

The day before I left for the islands, Percy vanished. Helen and I were staying at the seaside, and we followed his tracks to the water's edge. There was no doubt that the call of the surf had claimed him and we saw him no more. We were both very sad.

A little leisure in Sydney early in 1945 gave me ample opportunity to observe my fellow countrymen and to speculate on what was in the air. Coal strikes and wharf strikes were everyday occurrences. The workers were very restive and seemed to be on the point of demanding a utopia 'or else'. There seemed to be no realisation of the fact that we had all narrowly missed a most horrible fate. The days of panic which preceded the Coral Sea Battle were forgotten and the great fight was on; the fight for material advantages by the union bosses on the one hand and a struggle to preserve the status quo or as much of it as remained by the employers on the other.

The government remained sublimely aloof, though the Prime Minister, on whom much of the stigma of inaction fell, succumbed to the strain. The country was more rotten than ever, with black markets and rampant racketeering, while morals seemed to be degenerating into chaos.

In England, the socialists, anxious for power, clamoured for elections and the country became a wordy battlefield shortly after the cessation of hostilities in Europe. It was too much to expect them to carry on the work which had contributed so much towards winning the war into the difficult days of peace. I was amazed to hear Mr Attlee presenting his case for socialism, proclaiming to the world that socialism had been such an unmixed blessing to Australia and New Zealand. Australia I could answer for, but New Zealand was beyond my scope and I sincerely hoped that, for the future peace of Mr Attlee's soul, there was at least an element of truth in that portion of his claim.

Before the British elections developed I was posted to the islands, and late June found me packing my tropical kit. July found me established in command of a headquarters, at least nominally responsible for the air defences from Biak to Borneo.

July and August were busy months concerned mainly with getting to know my job. Towards the middle of August I was instructed to fly to Brisbane for a two-day conference. Rumours were everywhere that peace was in the air, and I had the good fortune to be at home with Helen when we heard the confirmation a couple of days later. Nevertheless, I

had to return to Morotai next day, and it was four more months before
I returned to Australia with my discharge in my pocket.

*

On the train back to Brisbane I had time to look back on it all. So much
had happened. A first-class book could be written about most of the
forty-five boys who had gathered at RAAF Point Cook ten years ago.
Another could be written on the twenty-five of our number who had
gone to the United Kingdom. Perhaps later. What a deal that had turned
out to be!

As we made our farewells that summer, none of us had doubted that
we would all get together in a few years and reminisce on that rather
remarkable and altogether enjoyable year we had just spent together at
Point Cook. It was not to be. Lew Johnston was still in the RAF, but
fate had not been kind to so many of the others. Carl Kelaher had been
shot down over Berlin in his Lancaster one night in September 1943; Cec
Mace had been killed in action at the end of March 1940; they said that
Pat Hughes had taken his Spitfire too close to an exploding Dornier and
collided with the wreckage, but there was a rumour that he had flown in
front of an attacking Spitfire and been accidentally shot down; and Bob
Cosgrove's Hampden had gone missing while searching for the dinghy
of another Australian who had ditched south of Norway.

What had at first been just an adventure had changed our lives forever.

Epilogue

Gordon Olive was discharged from the RAAF on 7 March 1946 and he transferred to the RAAF Reserve. In civilian life, he returned to Brisbane and joined Rheem Australia Pty Ltd in an executive position. In 1948 he became state commandant of the Air Training Corps.

Gordon had married London girl Helen Thomas on 22 June 1940 at the parish church of Kensington in London, and she was one of the first English brides to arrive in Australia in 1943. After reaching Brisbane, she formed the British Brides Club and became its first president. She also worked with the Red Cross.

In 1946 tragedy struck the couple when Helen became ill at a function for Gordon, who was then standing as Service Party candidate for the Brisbane electorate. She collapsed and was admitted to hospital for an operation but she died shortly afterwards.

The engagement of Gordon to Beryl Gwendoline North of Cannon Hill, Brisbane, was announced on New Year's Eve 1947/8, and the couple were married in St John's Cathedral, Brisbane, on 17 April 1948. It would be a blessed and lifelong union.

Gordon was a notable member of Brisbane's United Service Club, serving on the committee from 1947, and as president in 1970–71. He also became president of the Australian Division of the Battle of Britain Fighter Association.

He stood for the seat of Petrie as a Country Party candidate in 1972 but was unsuccessful.

Gordon retired from Rheem that year, but after a spell of farming he joined Boral Ltd, staying with this company until he retired again in 1981.

Always involved in community service, Gordon was recognised with his appointment to MBE in 1967, in particular for his work in organising the Empire Youth Movement, and promotion followed to CBE in 1978. He was aide-de-camp to HM The Queen 1961–63, chairman of the Commonwealth Youth Council, Queensland, 1950–72, and chairman of the Brisbane Metropolitan Fire Brigade 1979–87.

After courageously, and characteristically, fighting off a long-term illness for several years, Gordon Olive died at Boonah, Queensland, on 20 October 1987. He was survived by his wife, Beryl, and their two sons, Richard (Rick) and Denys, and Maria, one of their two daughters.

The Mayfield State School in Queensland named each of its houses to honour a famous Second World War pilot. They are Olive (Australian), Bader (British) and Malan (South African). More recently, an award-winning Defence Housing Estate at McDowall, Brisbane, was named the 'Gordon Olive Estate' in his honour and as a permanent reminder of his significant contribution to his community and Australia.

Notes

Introduction

1. The 'Messerschmitt Me 109 and Me 110' aircraft the Allies referred to during the war years were actually the Messerschmitt Bf 109 and Bf 110 respectively. The company manufacturing these aircraft was *Bayerische Flugzeugwerke* and the prefix 'Bf' was used in official German handbooks and documents. Professor Willi Messerschmitt had joined the company in 1927 and was head of the design team. He later took over the company, at which time it was renamed Messerschmitt AG. From then on the prefix 'Me' was used. Gordon in his narrative used 'Me 109' and 'Me 110'.

9 Channel Duels

1. The Heinkel He 113 (He 100) was an enigma. Much publicized by the German Propaganda Ministry, it was generally believed that it had entered service with the Luftwaffe but it was actually never accepted for service use. Only twelve production He 100D1 fighters were built. In a successful ploy to mislead Allied intelligence, these were painted and repainted with different insignia and many propaganda photographs distributed. This led to the erroneous belief that the He 100 was in widespread use. Despite the superior performance of the He 100D over the standard Bf 109E fighter, the official attitude was that the war would be won with the Messerschmitt and that production capacity could not be afforded for the high-quantity production of the Heinkel fighter.

Glossary & Abbreviations

AFC	Air Force Cross
AIF	Australian Imperial Force
AOC	Air Officer Commanding
AVM	Air Vice-Marshal
CO	Commanding Officer
DFC	Distinguished Flying Cross
DSO	Distinguished Service Order
F/Lt	Flight Lieutenant
F/O	Flying Officer
F/Sgt	Flight Sergeant
LAC	Leading Aircraftman
Lt	Lieutenant
MBE	Member of the Order of the British Empire
OC	Officer Commanding
OTU	Operational Training Unit
P/O	Pilot Officer
RAAF	Royal Australian Air Force
RAF	Royal Air Force
RN	Royal Navy
S/Ldr	Squadron Leader
Sgt	Sergeant
Stooging	flying in random or non specific patterns.
USAAF	United States Army Air Force
WAAF	Women's Auxiliary Air Force
W/Cdr	Wing Commander
W/O	Warrant Officer

Glossary & Abbreviations

AFC — Air Force Cross
AIF — Australian Imperial Force
AOC — Air Officer Commanding
ASR — Air Sea Rescue
CO — Commanding Officer
DFC — Distinguished Flying Cross
DSO — Distinguished Service Order
HQ — Flight Lieutenant
FLT — Flight Officer
Cpl — Flight Sergeant
SL/AC — Leading Aircraftsman
Lac — Seaman
MBE — Member of the Order of the British Empire
OC — Officer Commanding
OTU — Operational Training Unit
PO — Pilot Officer
RAAF — Royal Australian Air Force
RAF — Royal Air Force
RN — Royal Navy
SL/Ldr — Squadron Leader
Sgt — Sergeant
medium — things in numbers of men and the planes
u/s — Unserviceable, unserviceable Air Force
WAAF — Women's Auxiliary Air Force
W/Cdr — Wing Commander
WO — Warrant Officer

APPENDIX 1

Australian Cadets Who Sailed to Join the RAF in January 1937

At the Imperial Conference of 1923 the UK proposed offering four-year Short Service Commissions in the RAF to RAAF officers. By this method it was reasoned that a reserve of trained aircrew would be built up which could be used to reinforce RAF squadrons in an emergency and Australia would benefit when the men returned after four years' operational training at British expense. The scheme was accepted by the Australian government and it began in 1927 when the first graduates from RAAF Point Cook took up their commissions.

The scheme was officially suspended in Australia in July 1938 but the Australian press continued to run advertisements offering Short Service Commissions in the RAF to 'Gentlemen of the Dominions, Colonies and Territories under the Crown', who could apply to RAAF HQ, Melbourne. Those accepted at these later dates, although they were selected by a board of RAAF officers in each state, did not have the benefit of initial flying training at Point Cook and some did not have any flying training at all. Intakes continued until mid-1939, terminating with the outbreak of war.

The largest contingent to depart for the UK was drawn from the Point Cook cadet class of 1936, and they departed aboard P&O's elderly liner the *Narkunda* in January 1937.

Allsop, J. W.   Killed
Boehm, D. C.

Brough, J. F. T.	DFC
Campbell, D.	
Cosgrove, R. J.	Missing
Fowler, H. N.	POW Colditz, escaped, killed in air crash 26/3/44
Gilbert, C. L.	Injured in air operations 21/10/40
Good, D. C. F.	Seriously wounded in air operations 5/6/40, missing 29/4/41
Grey-Smith, G. E.	Missing 12/5/40, POW
Hughes, P. C.	KIA 7/9/40, DFC
Johnston, L. L.	MID
Kaufman, K. W.	DFC
Kelaher, C. R.	
Kinane, W.	Killed in crash ?/8/39
Mace, C. R.	Killed 31/3/40 DFC
Olive, C. G. C.	DFC
Power, R.	
Robinson, A. E.	Exchange duty in Australia
Rogers, K. R.	Killed 14/5/40
Sheen, D. F. B.	DFC
Wight, W. B.	
Yate, E. W.	Killed in crash 1/8/39

APPENDIX 2

Combat Claims of F/Lt Charles Gordon Chaloner Olive DFC, 65 Squadron RAF

Date	Claim	Area	Aircraft
1940			
26 May	1 Me 109E unconfirmed	Calais	Spitfire I K9903
27 May	1 Do 17 unconfirmed	E of Dunkirk	Spitfire I K9903
28 May	1 Me 109E unconfirmed	Dunkirk	Spitfire I K9903*
20 July	1 Me 109E	mid-Channel Folkestone	Spitfire IR6617**
12 Aug	1 Me 109E probable	off Deal	Spitfire I R6883
13 Aug	2 Me 109Es	off Dover	Spitfire I R6883
13 Aug	1 Me 109E possible***	off Dover	Spitfire I R6883
13 Aug	1 Me 109E probable	off Dover	Spitfire I R6883
14 Aug	1 Me 109E probable	off Dover	Spitfire I R6883
16 Aug	1 Ju 88 damaged	Deal/Dover	Spitfire I R6883
24 Aug	1 Me 109E probable	Thames Estuary Clacton	Spitfire I R6883
26 Aug	1 Me 110	Manston	Spitfire I R6883
8 Dec	1 Me 110****	Portsmouth area	Spitfire I R6883
1941			
15 Feb	1 Ju 88 damaged*****	S of St Catherine's Point	Spitfire II P7827

Total: 5 destroyed, 3 unconfirmed destroyed, 1 possible, 3 probables, 1 and 1 shared damaged.

* Spitfire K9903 damaged in combat, force landed at Mansion 28 May 1940.

** Spitfire R6617 burst into flames and crashed 7 August 1940.

*** Logbook entry. Not included in combat report.

**** Me 110C5, 2266 (5F+DM), of 4(F)/14, Fw Otto Mercier and gunner posted missing

***** Logbook entry notes it as a 'probable' and it seems likely to have been Ju 88A5, 6166, of K.Gr806 that crashed (30 per cent damage) at Caen after combat.

APPENDIX 3

Distinguished Flying Cross Citation

Flight Lieutenant Olive has led his flight and on occasions his squadron both on operations in France and later throughout the intensive fighting in defence of this country. He has personally destroyed at least five enemy aircraft. His fearlessness and cool courage in action have been a splendid example to other pilots he has led, and have contributed largely to their successes against greatly superior numbers of the enemy.

London Gazette, 24 September 1940

Distinguished Flying Cross Citation

BBC Broadcast Script for F/Lt Saunders and F/Lt Olive, 4 October 1940

Announcer: We have in the studio tonight two young fighter pilots who are straight from the battle front. They are going to tell you something of this air battle of Britain as they see it from behind their own guns. They are the flight commanders of a squadron which did fine work at Dunkirk, and which has fought the Luftwaffe almost continuously during the past few weeks. Perhaps they can answer some of the questions most of us have been wanting to ask. How do our pilots find the Germans, as adversaries? What is it like to fight such large numbers of the enemy? What are the pilots themselves thinking and feeling? Do you think you can tell us?

F/Lt Saunders: Well, the Squadron has seen a good deal of fighting since Dunkirk, when we brought down Junkers, Dorniers and Messerschmitts in our very first fight. Our 'bag' has risen to over 60 German aircraft whose destruction has been confirmed, and some 40 probables.

But we ourselves have not got away unscathed. I wouldn't say, either, that we still have that first elation for we know now, with absent faces in the mess, something of the tragedy of war. But I can say we are still full of fight. Fact is, we are far happier fighting than in ruminating over it. I know that I, personally, always find the period of waiting rather trying. There is, of course, something of the natural apprehension which the infantryman feels, waiting to 'go over the top'. But more than that, one begins to imagine all kinds of things not quite right with the aircraft, with the armament, or with oneself, and to be afraid of bungling something.

Once I am up, I find the machine and myself OK and I have too much to do to be apprehensive of anything. If a pilot comes out of an action with a kill or two to his credit he feels an insatiable desire to go on shooting down Germans. If he foozles an opportunity for a kill, and comes home with nothing to show for it, he usually looks a bit depressed. You can always tell, in the mess, who has had a successful day, and who hasn't.

I always tell my pilots that they can't expect to 'bag' a German every time they go up. But actually I like to see them peeved if they've been unsuccessful. I know then they are still full of fight.

They always will be. More so now, perhaps, than when we first went into action. For we've been at grips with the Luftwaffe in so many circumstances that we've come to know their measure. It's the measure of a bully, and everyone likes to paste a bully.

When the Germans are overwhelmingly stronger in numbers they will attack, but when the challenge is accepted, and the British Brownings begin to take toll, they go into a tight ring of mutual protection – like a boxer going into a huddle behind his fists. That is not the right spirit for bold aggressors sent to destroy the RAF.

On one occasion I got separated from the squadron and found myself running into a layer of Messerschmitt fighters, who were protecting a convoy of German bombers below them. It was my job to attack, and I flew straight towards them. I put in a long burst at the nearest Me's and then shot upwards to make another attack, the fighters – there must have been seventy of them – went into a protective circle, looking like a cat chasing its own tail, and they remained like that, all on account of one Spitfire. They were deserting the bombers they had been sent to escort; a British squadron met the bombers who paid the price for their fighters' timidity.

I must not give you the impression that all German pilots are chicken-hearted. We have all met exceptions to the rule who were both spoiling for a fair fight and quite capable of giving as good as they got.

But speaking of the Luftwaffe at large, I know that, whatever their strength in numbers, they will never succeed in effectively damaging this country's war effort. Not while the British pilots retain their present morale, and fighting spirit.

The day will come, soon I hope, when there will be a British fighter in the air for every German aircraft on the job. I don't believe the visitors will stay to fight. If they do stay there will be few who'll live to fight another day.

Announcer: The flight commander you have just heard has five German aircraft to his credit, as well as many 'probables'. His fellow flight commander in the same squadron has also shot down five of the enemy. He is a Flight Lieutenant in the Royal Australian Air Force, hailing from Brisbane, Australia. Here he is.

F/Lt Olive: I agree entirely that if the British squadrons can keep up the present punch – and they will – it'll be a sad day for Germany when we get anything approaching equality of numbers.

For instance, one day I got separated from the squadron and, high up over the coast, came upon six of the enemy. I approached, and shot one down. The rest dived for all they were worth and raced back towards France. I pulled up to a good height again and flew out to sea. Another six enemy aircraft met me, and again, after shooting one down, the rest raced for home. I turned back towards my patrol and while still near the French coast ran into 15 Messerschmitt 109s. They thought I was their 'meat', and swept in to attack. I replied by picking off one Me on the flank. He dived vertically out of the contact and I turned to attack another when he, too put his nose down and fled. Immediately the whole bunch dived after him, and then, flattening out a long way below me, turned towards France. Nearing England I met a single Me. We came out of a cloud together, and I think I saw him first when we were only 250 yards apart. I had my guns on him at once, and pressed the button. Five seconds' firing and the Me went spinning into the 'drink' leaving a column of black smoke behind him.

Some days the fighting provides what, in such grim circumstances, might be described as comic relief. I was up with my flight when we came through a bank of high cloud to find 20 Me 109s just below us. We picked off a couple before the full attack of the Nazi formation could develop and then dodged back into the cloud. The Germans knew the risks of entering the cloud, and left us alone. A couple of minutes later we popped out again, shot up another Me and dashed back to cover.

For several minutes we had wonderful fun at this hide-and-seek game. The Germans never knew from what direction we would jump on them from the cloud, and generally we managed to get in a few good bursts at one or other of them before slipping back to cover.

It puzzled us why they did not go lower. The answer was a patrol of British fighters far below. They hadn't spotted the Jerries, but seeing three Mes falling past them one after another, in smoke and flames, they came up to investigate; when they reached us the skies were innocent of enemy planes.

Some days, as a change from driving German planes to earth we were driven by German planes into the air. That is to say, they came over and bombed our base. On one occasion we were lined up ready to take off when the Jerries came into view behind us, diving to the attack. Our only chance lay in getting into the air quickly. Instead of each section taking off in turn, we all opened our throttles and raced across the aerodrome, in a terrific scramble. I don't know how we managed to get off without a mishap. A hundred and thirty bombs were dropped behind and round us during that furious rush across the ground. But we did get off, and once in the air we turned and stung the raiders plenty for disturbing a beehive. At least one of the enemy was shot down near the aerodrome, but the squadron suffered no harm.

Incidentally, we were able to check up on Lord Haw Haw's little inaccuracies. He broadcast that day the news that the Nazis had destroyed five of us on the ground, and six more in the air.

APPENDIX 5

BBC Broadcast Script for S/Ldr Gordon Olive DFC, 24 September 1943

Speaker: Squadron Leader Gordon Olive DFC, RAAF 39469, Kensington
Title: Battle of Britain.
Recorded: 24.9.43.
Length: 4'3".
Censor: Air Ministry and F.S.T.A. Mr. Hewlett

Cue: He's one of the comparatively few Battle of Britain pilots left. He's an Australian who at the time of the B. of B. was serving in the RAF (has now transferred to the RAAF). Comes from Brisbane, Queensland.

(Note: Since his recording is not good enough you find a reading recorded by air P/O H. H. Stewart, PR Officer at RAAF HQ, but please be careful not to suggest that it is Olive speaking – for his family's sake.)

We knew pretty well what was at stake. We had seen from the air the way the Germans had smashed through in the north of France; we had experienced the force of their air power over Dunkirk. We'd watched them building up their forces for what was obviously designed to be the invasion of Britain. And we had a fair idea what equipment was left for our Navy and Army. We realised that the Air Force was just about the last card in our hands.

I remember in those early days, before the major attack developed, watching the Germans trying out their tactics on our convoys in the Channel. We'd seen more German aircraft than we ever imagined could get into one formation, going for little strings of ships. And when the battle did come over Britain itself, we realised that the Hun had started in earnest.

I remember how we used to be bombed when we were taking off from our aerodrome on the tip of Kent – a hundred or more bombers doing their best to finish us off. From then on it was a daily experience to engage formations up to ten and twenty times our number – two, three and even four times a day.

It was only in those battles that we came to know the full characters of the men with whom we were fighting. I remember Sammy Saunders. Socially, he was very quiet and unassuming; in many ways he represented the typical Englishman. We didn't know him; we didn't even like him particularly then. But from the outset of the fighting his ruling principle was that the job and the results of their efforts were all that mattered – individual glory was a secondary consideration, if it had any value at all. That was why he deliberately refrained from making personal claims. He was responsible for our squadron. Incidentally, Paddy Finucane was in his flight and I think he learned most of his stuff from him. I've seen Sammy lead us into a Hun formation of 200 or more – outwardly with the utmost calm and determination. I doubt whether we'd have carried on with the fight if it hadn't been for his quiet, magnificent leadership. He received no decoration at the time; most of us in the squadron felt that his character and example were beyond the reward of medals.

And he was typical of most of the British boys who fought in that period, at least 80 per cent of them were British. The other 20 per cent came from every conceivable corner of the Dominions and Colonies – and from Poland.

Two of the Australians who were outstanding in that battle were Pat Hughes and Stuart Walch. Stuart was completely careless of his own welfare or success, and whenever inexperienced pilots had to go into battle, he personally shepherded them, and supervised their work. It was while he was trying to rescue two new boys from a hopeless position that he was killed. Pat Hughes was credited by his squadron with sixteen aircraft destroyed; he was rewarded for six. And of the New Zealanders, there was Alan Deere and Colin Grey. Both of them fought magnificently and most successfully, Alan Deere particularly putting up an all-time record for descents by parachute as a result of persistently attacking against impossible odds.

But the Battle of Britain was three years ago. Since then I've done more day fighting – and night fighting. Then, last December, I took over an Operational Training Unit. I wondered what those new boys would be like. I must admit, at first, I thought Britain could never contain many more pilots of the calibre of those who'd been decimated in the early fighting. But I was wrong. Those youngsters coming straight from school, and some of the older pilots who'd been side-tracked onto ground duties and training jobs, had just the same qualities of courage, moral strength and sense of responsibility. Their capacity to learn their profession and become first-class pilots left nothing to be desired. British quality has not gone down.

APPENDIX 6

Gordon Olive's No. 456 RAAF Squadron

On 20 June 1941, Gordon Olive was appointed to command and form No. 456 RAAF Squadron at RAF Station Valley, Isle of Anglesey, Wales. This was the first, and would be the only, Australian night-fighter squadron of the Second World War.

Its initial equipment consisted of sixteen Boulton Paul Defiants. The new unit came into existence officially on the 30th with a complement of twenty-eight officers and 155 airmen.

During this early period in the squadron's history much of the time was spent training to master night-fighting techniques. It suffered its first casualty on 21 July when Sgt A. F. Brooks RAF was killed while flying alone in Defiant T3933 which crashed at Llanerchymedd, Anglesey. By the time the squadron was officially declared operational on 5 September, it was already known that the Defiants were to be replaced and the unit would be converting to Beaufighter Mk IIs. Meanwhile, two of its Defiants had already flown the squadron's first sorties, a convoy patrol, on the 4th.

The first six Beaufighters arrived towards the end of September, the first, R2474, on the 26th. These machines were equipped with AI Mk IV radar. A training programme to become proficient with the new device was implemented under F/O G. Barker, an expert attached to the squadron. Former Defiant gunners were posted away or underwent a conversion course. The last operation using Defiants was on 20 October.

While at Valley the squadron was out of the main action as most of the Luftwaffe's attacks were concentrated against cities outside its area. However, it was during this period that it received its first decoration, though not for an action in the air. During August, a Blackburn Botha ditched into heavy sea off Valley and many people on shore tried to swim out to rescue the three-man crew. One of 456's air gunners, Sgt John Plunkett, a former Cairns lifesaver, swam out 300 yards through turbulent water and brought back an unconscious gunner. Several other would-be rescuers floundered and some drowned but Plunkett managed to recover three of them, undoubtedly saving their lives. For his heroism, the Queenslander was awarded the British Empire Medal.

John Plunkett was later posted to 458 RAAF (Wellington) Squadron and transferred with it to the Middle East. He then flew with 104 Squadron RAF. During an attack on Tobruk on 7 August 1942, his Wellington force-landed in the desert and he and his crew were captured. He was a POW for the remainder of the war.

1942

The long months of training at Valley proved invaluable for what was to come, but minor accidents due to the Beaufighter II's 'deadly swing' were a persistent problem. Reduced drag resulting from the cleaner engine nacelles housing the Beaufighter II's Rolls-Royce Merlin engines improved performance slightly over the earlier Beaufighter I, but also reduced its side area ahead of the centre of gravity, making it more unstable.

No. 456 was not fully operational after conversion when, on the night of 10/11 January 1942, S/Ldr John Hamilton and P/O Dan Norris-Smith in Beaufighter T3014 shot down a minelaying Do 217 (F8+IN of 5/KG40) for its first victory. Several weeks later, Gordon Olive was overcome by illness and, sadly, he had to leave the squadron he had created.

W/Cdr E. C. Wolfe assumed command on 27 March 1942. The Valley sector continued to be quiet at night so the Beaufighters were called on to carry out convoy patrols. The equipment in the Beaufighters made them suitable to be all-weather day fighters too and they were used extensively in this capacity as part of the squadron's secondary role.

On 18 May, P/O Bernie Wills RAF and Sgt Ron Lowther, flying Beaufighter T3022, damaged a Ju 88 (4U+FL of 3(F)/123) after a twenty-minute chase over Convoy Topaz. When the German crew was rescued in their dinghy, the claim was changed to 'destroyed'.

In July, 456 Squadron began switching to Beaufighter VIs powered by Bristol Hercules VI radial engines. Another night victory came on 30 July, when W/Cdr Ted Wolfe and P/O A. Ashcroft RAF, in Beaufighter VI X8251, shot down a He 111 (F8+LW of *12/KG40*) that crashed onto the beach at Pwllheli, Wales.

1942 ended with the welcome news that 456 would be re-equipped with de Havilland Mosquitoes.

1943

By mid-January over a dozen new Mk II Mosquito fighters had arrived. These aircraft were armed with four 20 mm cannons and four .303 inch machine guns and equipped with Mk V AI.

A new CO, W/Cdr Micky Dwyer, arrived on 1 February. Dwyer had a lasting effect on 456 Squadron, lifting its *esprit de corps* to a previously unmatched level. A move to Middle Wallop in Hampshire came on 30 March, bringing the squadron into the front line of the air defences. From its new location, it could patrol over the English Channel and perform offensive operations over enemy-occupied northern and western France.

All available aircraft were employed on Ranger and Intruder missions. Ranger sorties were conducted against the enemy's transport system and other special targets. Intruder sorties involved the night fighters in patrolling over enemy airfields waiting to intercept returning bombers. Ranger operations were particularly successful. The first triumphant attack on a rail target occurred on 16 April when W/O V. 'Red' Ratcliffe and F/Sgt Ron Lowther immobilised a French locomotive. Unfortunately, Ratcliffe and Lowther failed to return from another Ranger sortie on 2 June, giving them the dubious honour of being 456 Squadron's first crew lost on operations.

More success against rail targets followed, but none was as impressive as that of on 6 May when, during a daylight raid, F/O Gordon 'Peter' Panitz and his observer, P/O Richard 'Dickie' Williams, destroyed six trains in six minutes. This feat marked the beginning of Panitz's reputation as a 'train buster'. While with 456 Squadron, Panitz reached the rank of squadron leader and by the time of his departure on 11 December, he commanded 'B' Flight. Both he and Dickie Williams received DFCs while with the squadron.

On 5 June, three Mosquitoes with crews and ground staff were detached from 456 Squadron to RAF Predannack for Operation Instep, long-range fighter sweeps over the Bay of Biscay to protect Coastal Command aircraft. They formed a temporary composite unit with detachments from various other night-fighter squadrons. The crews were Panitz and Williams; F/O Johnny Newell and F/Sgt Allan Keating; and F/Sgt Robert Richardson and Sgt Tom Landy. On the 11th, the Predannack detachment with three Mosquitoes from 25 Squadron RAF bounced five Ju 88s over the Bay of Biscay. One Ju 88 crashed into the sea and Newell damaged two others. Later in the year, on 21 September, four 456 Squadron Mosquitoes engaged eight Ju 88s. S/Ldr Panitz and F/Sgt C. 'Tony' Samson (observer) destroyed one while W/O Gordon 'Gate' Gatenby was credited with a probable.

Amid an exceptionally busy month, W/Cdr George Howden DFC, a highly experienced night fighter pilot, assumed command on 12 June.

Air-sea rescue patrols were an integral part of the work. On 23 June, F/O George Houston and P/O Lars 'Gus' Engberg spotted a Spitfire pilot in the sea. They dropped him the observer's dinghy and a Walrus amphibian later picked him up.

Three nights later, guided by flares dropped by other aircraft, F/Sgt Bob Richardson and Sgt Tom Landy searched for the pilot of another Spitfire who had parachuted into the English Channel. They saw a torch flashing on the sea. The position was pinpointed and the downed pilot rescued by launch. The Group commander sent the squadron a letter of commendation for achieving the most flying hours for the month in the Group, 830.5 hours, free from accidents.

Ranger sorties continued. On 12 July, two Mosquitoes (F/Lt Panitz and F/O Williams, F/Lt Bas Howard and F/O Jack Ross) heavily damaged the transformer station at Guerledan. On the way home, Panitz strafed two goods trains on the Guingamp–Chateaulerun railway line for good measure.

On the 26th, Panitz and Williams, accompanied by F/Os Ron Pratt and Stewy Smith, attacked a power station near Marais de St Miche. There was an explosion and the station was left in flames.

On 7 August, P/O 'Tony' Samson, Ron Pratt and W/O Arthur McEvoy, with their usual observers, attacked two armed trawlers off La Rochelle, south-west France. An explosion blew away part of the bridge of one vessel that was left smoking. On the night of 13/14 August, F/O Ern Griffith and F/O Jimmy Thomson heavily damaged a train near Caulines.

Panitz led four Mosquitoes to attack the German flying boat base at

Lake Biscarosse on 3 October. A refuelling launch was left sinking and a tender damaged. On the way home, a minesweeper south of Biscarosse was set alight. Panitz and Dickie Williams then found and exploded a Ju 88.

Fighter Command was now carrying out a new type of operation to support bomber operations over Europe. Codenamed Mahmoud, Mosquitoes equipped with AI Mk IV radar were despatched to specific areas to try to surprise German night fighters. No. 456 Squadron flew two Mahmoud sorties on the night of 3/4 December when Leipzig was the target for 527 bombers. P/Os Gordon Gatenby and John Fraser returned because of engine trouble but P/O 'Tommy' May and F/O Les Parnell were killed when they crashed in Germany from unknown causes.

On 14 December the squadron received a new Commanding Officer, W/Cdr Keith Hampshire DSO. The squadron was about to attain a level of efficiency that would earn it the reputation of being one of the most successful night fighter squadrons of the war.

1944

On 29 January, 456 Squadron took delivery of its first new Mosquito Mk XVIIs equipped with the latest AI Mk X radar. February saw strenuous activity as crews became operational on their new equipment. During the night of 25/26 February, F/Os Tony Samson and Alec Abbey destroyed a Ju 88 while patrolling Rennes airfield. At the end of the month, the squadron moved to Ford in Sussex, a good location for intercepting raiders attempting to attack London or the Portsmouth and Southampton areas.

Success came almost immediately. When the Luftwaffe launched several raids over south-east England on the night of 1/2 March, P/Os Robert Richardson and Tom Landy in Mosquito HK282/L damaged a Do 217. Some 140 German aircraft attacked London on 21/22 March and for 456 Squadron, F/Os Keith Roediger and Robert Dobson shot down a Ju 88 and Lt Dennis Thornley RNVR and S/Lt Derrick Phillips in Mosquito HK359 probably destroyed an Fw 190.

Three nights later, approximately 120 enemy aircraft crossed the south coast to attack the capital again and 456 Squadron's CO, Keith Hampshire, with F/O Tom Condon shot down a Ju 88. They destroyed two more Ju 88s on 27/28 March. Debris from the second victim damaged their starboard wing, preventing further engagements, but Bas Howard and Jack Ross downed another Ju 88 off the French Coast.

After three quiet weeks in April, seven 456 Squadron Mosquitoes scrambled on the 20th/21st despite terrible weather. F/Lt C. Brooks and W/O F. Forbes in Mosquito HK253/F sent a Me 410 down vertically to crash near Horsham, Sussex. One blade of the airscrew, perforated by a cannon shell, was recovered and hung as a trophy in 'A' Flight's dispersal.

At the time of its arrival at Ford, the squadron's record stood at six destroyed, one probable and five damaged, but this improved dramatically at the new location. For the three months of operations out of Ford, the squadron claimed eleven destroyed, one probable and one damaged.

With the launch of the D-Day offensive on 6 June 1944, the squadron gained a new role – protection of the Allied invasion fleet at night. Early in the morning of the 7th, F/O Ron Pratt and F/Lt Stew Smith in Mosquito HK303/H destroyed an He 177; F/Os Fred Stevens and Andrew Kellett in HK290/J two He 177s north of the Cherbourg peninsula; and W/Cdr Keith Hampshire and F/O Tom Condon in HK286/A an He 177 into the sea. There were more successes over the landings that night: S/Ldr B. Howard and F/O J. R. Ross in Mosquito HK323 claimed the destruction of two more He 177s; and P/O R. Hodgen and F/Sgt A. McCormick in HK302/Z4 another He 177.

Two nights later, F/Lt R. 'Bob' Cowper and F/O W. Watson of 456 Squadron in Mosquito HK353/M destroyed an He 177 and a Do 217 over the beaches. The Heinkel had an Hs293 glider bomb slung underneath each wing, outboard of the engines. On 12/13 June, W/Cdr Keith Hampshire and F/O Tom Condon of 456 Squadron in Mosquito HK286/A bagged yet another Ju 88. By the end of June the squadron had added fourteen destroyed and two probables to its tally, all without loss.

The activity continued into July and on 4/5 July, 456 Squadron Mosquitoes had a fruitful night: P/O S. Williams and F/O K. Havord in Mosquito HK282/L destroyed a Do 217, and He 177s were destroyed by F/Lt Bob Cowper DFC and F/O W. Watson in HK356/D; F/O E. Radford and F/Sgt W. Atkinson in HK312/G, and P/Os I. Sanderson and G. Nicholas in HK249/B.

It was during June that the Germans began their flying-bomb assault. The first attack on 12/13 June was a flop because of lack of equipment and special fuel. Out of ten bombs launched, only four crossed the English coast. Three of these fell in open country and the fourth demolished a railway bridge in the East End of London, killing six people. However, the threat posed by these vengeance weapons was dire. Rings of anti-aircraft batteries were deployed in the flight paths of these incoming 'malignant robots', and 'AntiDiver' patrols by fighters – Tempests, Spitfires, Mustangs, Meteors and Mosquitoes – were set up to intercept. F/Lts K. Roediger and J. Dobson made 456 Squadron's first definite V-1 kill on 9/10 July and by the end of the month ten had been destroyed. By the end of August, the squadron tally stood at twenty-four, F/Lt Roediger accounting for nine of them.

A lull in flying-bomb attacks saw the squadron training for cross-country navigation in preparation for new work. Prior to this, squadron aircraft were not permitted to penetrate deep into enemy territory because of the highly secret apparatus carried. This was no longer a concern and eight aircraft were deployed to Manston, a forward base, for patrols over the Holland and Belgium fronts. On 6/7 October, W/O J. Mulhall and F/O J. Jones in HK317/Y destroyed a Ju 188. Hopes for more successes were dashed when bad weather restricted flying for most of the rest of the month. On 5 November, W/Cdr Hampshire was promoted to Group captain and succeeded by S/Ldr B. Howard (later promoted to wing commander).

Once more the squadron's role was changed from Continental patrols to new anti-diver work. This latest role had it searching for and destroying He 111s that were launching flying bombs from over the North Sea. Although successes were achieved, losses were high. On 7 November, an unusual crew was posted missing, Lt E. Woodward and Ensign W. Madden, two of four US Marine fliers attached to 456 Squadron for operational experience. They were to have returned to the USA to instruct on RAF night-fighting techniques.

An extended period of poor weather followed and by 18/19 November it had been so bad that No. 2 Group, of which 456 Squadron was part, had been unable to operate for eleven consecutive days and twelve nights. The following day, F/Os D. Arnold and J. Stickley in Mosquito HK246/U destroyed a Heinkel that dropped burning into the sea.

W/O J. Mulhall and F/O J. Jones failed to return from an antidiver patrol on 23/24 November but the following night, F/Os F Stevens and F/O W Kellett in Mosquito HK290/J destroyed a He 111 after a twenty-five-minute chase. It blew up on the sea close to the Dutch coast.

On 30 December, 456 Squadron was re-located to Church Fenton and re-equipped with Mk XXX Mosquitoes.

1945

The squadron was held in reserve for much of the first quarter of 1945. With its new aircraft, training now centred on another fresh role – that of night fighters for bomber support. Unfortunately, by the time it was ready for operations there were few opportunities left as the Luftwaffe was now a spent force and the battlefronts were almost beyond the range of home-based fighters. The squadron was ordered to Bradwell Bay on 3 March but the move was delayed until the 17th. From there it did provide support for raids by Bomber Command over south Germany and Czechoslovakia under the direction of 100 Group. There were also low-level raids over Germany, which were basically Ranger sorties attacking ground targets.

On 3 April, 456 Squadron Mosquitoes flew four early-morning Ranger sorties. F/O J. Darling destroyed one locomotive and F/O D. Hewson claimed two locomotives probably destroyed. The next night, Bomber Command launched three major raids against Leuna, Harburg and Lutzkendorf. Thirty-three Mosquitoes were sent off on high- and low-level bomber support patrols, 456 Squadron providing seven aircraft. F/Lt McLennan and F/O K. Munro obtained two radar contacts but could not convert them. F/O D. Hewson strafed the runway at Luneburg in the vicinity of a landing aircraft, but without obvious results.

On the night of 22/23 April, thirty-six RAF Mosquitoes patrolled over airfields in Germany and Czechoslovakia on Ranger operations. 456 Squadron flew six sorties. Flak hit F/O D. Hewson's Mosquito in the fuselage, both propellers and tail, but he returned to base without difficulty. W/O W. McWhinney and F/O J. Costigan caused an explosion in the north-west corner of Bad Aibling airfield after strafing an unidentified aircraft.

Four nights later, four Mosquitoes of 456 Squadron flew low-level Ranger patrols to the Munich area. F/Os R. Richardson and T. Landy claimed an unidentified aircraft as damaged on the ground at Schleissheim airfield.

The last operational sortie flown by 456 Squadron occurred on 2 May, when S/Ldr C. S. Sampson and F/Lt C. R. Houston took off to fly an intruder operation over Denmark only to be recalled soon after. Germany surrendered unconditionally a few days later.

Under the direction of S/Ldr Bob Cowper, plans for the squadron's dissolution were pushed forward and it was officially disbanded on 15 June 1945, just a fortnight short of four years of service.

No. 456 Squadron's personnel received no less than sixteen awards, including one DSO and ten DFCs. It was the RAAF's only night-fighter unit, and its air-to-air tally alone included forty-one enemy aircraft destroyed (thirty-eight by Mosquitoes, three by Beaufighters), four probables and seven damaged plus twenty-four flying bombs destroyed. To achieve this, the squadron flew 6,226.5 operational hours and it also enjoyed great success against shipping, road transport, power stations and, in particular, trains, with thirty-eight damaged.

Logbook Entries, July–December 1940

YEAR 1940		AIRCRAFT		PILOT, OR 1ST PILOT	2ND PILOT, PUPIL OR PASSENGER	DUTY (INCLUDING RESULTS AND REMARKS)	SINGLE-ENGINE AIRCRAFT				MULTI-ENGINE AIRCRAFT						PASS-ENGER	INSTR/CLOUD FLYING (Cols. (1) to (10))	
							DAY		NIGHT		DAY			NIGHT					
Month	Date	Type	No.				Dual	Pilot	Dual	Pilot	Dual	1st Pilot	2nd Pilot	Dual	1st Pilot	2nd Pilot		Dual	Pilot
—	—	—	—	—	—	TOTALS BROUGHT FORWARD	50.40	615.40	2.05	30.50		.30					2.55		
	1	SPITFIRE	R.6617	SELF	SOLO	DEFENSIVE PATROL		1.15											
	2	"	R.6617	"	"	RECCO "		1.40											
	3	"	L.1045	"	"	PATROL		1.30											
	4	"	R.6617	"	"	RECCO PATROL		1.30											
	5	"	K.9906	"	"	AIR TEST		.45											
	6	"	R.6607	"	"	TO MANSTON		.25											
	6	"	R.6606	"	"	PATROL MANSTON		.55											
	6	"	R.6606	"	"	" "		.20											
	6	"	R.6606	"	"	" "		.10											
	6	"	R.6606	"	"	" "		.20											
	7	"	N.3091	"	"	MARSTON – HORNCHURCH		.35											
	8	"	R.6617	"	"	E + A TEST AND RECOVERY		.15											
	8	"	R.6617	"	"	PATROL		.35											
	11	"	K.9911	"	"			1.05											
	12	"	K.9911	"	"	TO MANSTON.		.30											
	12	"	K.9911	"	"	PATROL.		1.15											
	14	"	K.9911	"	"	TO HORNCHURCH.		.30											
	14	"	K.9911	"	"	TA HUNTER + PATROL		1.35											
	14	"	N.3091	"	"	CONVOY PATROL		1.00											
	14	"	L.1045	"	"	" "		1.25											
	14	"	L.1045	"	"	TO HORNCHURCH		.30											
	15	"	R.6617	"	"	CONVOY PATROL		1.35											
								18.55											
						TOTALS CARRIED FORWARD	50.40	617.50	2.05	39.50		.30					2.55		

GRAND TOTAL [Cols. (1) to (10)] ....731.... Hrs. ....50.... Mins.

YEAR 1940		AIRCRAFT		PILOT, OR	2ND PILOT, PUPIL	DUTY	SINGLE-ENGINE AIRCRAFT				MULTI-ENGINE AIRCRAFT							PASSENGER	INSTR/CLOUD FLYING [Cols. (1) to (10)]	
							DAY		NIGHT		DAY			NIGHT						
MONTH	DATE	Type	No.	1ST PILOT	OR PASSENGER	(INCLUDING RESULTS AND REMARKS)	Dual	Pilot	Dual	Pilot	Dual	1st Pilot	2nd Pilot	Dual	1st Pilot	2nd Pilot		(11)	Dual	Pilot
						TOTALS BROUGHT FORWARD	59·40	617·30	2·05	39·50		·30						2·55		
—	15	S.PITFIRE	R6854	SELF	—	E.A. TEST.		·15												
	15	"	RL777	"	SELF	SOLO		·10												
	15	"	A.1775	"	"			·10												
	16	"	R6886	"	"	FLY PAST FOR EAST INDIA FUND.		1·00												
	17	"	RL777	"	"	TO MANSTON.		·30												
	17	"	R6617	"	"	CONVOY PATROL		1·15												
	17	"	R6617	"	"			·50												
	17	"	R6617	"	"	TO SQUADRON. (base)				·30										
	17	"	R6617	"	"	PATROL. LAIRED MANSTON		·45												
	18	"	R6617	"	"	TO REDCAMBE		·35												
	18	"	R6886	"	"	E.A.v AIRCREW TEST.		·10												
	19	"	R6619	"	"	TO MANSTON.		·40												
	20	"	R6617	"	"	PATROL.		1·20												
	20	"	R6617	"	"			1·25												
	20	"	R6617	"	"	LONDON.		·40												
	20	"	R6617	"	"	" RETURN MANCHESTER		·50												
	21	"	R6617	"	"			1·15												
	21	"	R6407	"	"	TO ROCHFORD		·55												
	21	"	R6887	"	"	CONVOY PATROL		1·05												
	26	"	R6887	"	"	TO MANSTON.		·40												
	26	"	R6887	"	"	PATROL.		·15												
	26	"	R6887	"	"			·40												
								10·15												
						TOTALS CARRIED FORWARD	62·40	651·15	2·05	44·20		·30						2·55		

GRAND TOTAL [Cols. (1) to (10)]
745 Hrs. 45 Mins.

745 Hrs. 45 Mins.

YEAR 1940	AIRCRAFT		PILOT, OR 1ST PILOT	2ND PILOT, PUPIL OR PASSENGER	DUTY (INCLUDING RESULTS AND REMARKS)
Date	Type	No.			
					TOTALS BROUGHT FORWARD
16	SPITFIRE	R6613	SELF	SOLO	RETURN FROM MANSTON-REPAIRS
17	"	R6617	"	"	PATROL. CLIMBED MANSTON
17	"	R6617	"	"	PATROL
17	"	R6617	"	"	TO ROCHFORD
17	"	R6617	"	"	PATROL
17	"	R6617	"	"	DUSK PATROL
18	"	R6617	"	"	TO MANSTON DAWN
18	"	R6617	"	"	PATROL
18	"	K9906	"	"	TO REPICHURCH BROKEN TAIL WHEEL
18	"	N3164	"	"	TO ROCHFORD
19	MAGISTER	P2444	"	"	TO ROCHCHURCH
19	SPITFIRE	R2244	"	"	RUSHCHURCH-REPAIRS-MANSTON
29	"	R6617	"	"	PATROL
29	"	R6617	"	"	TO ROCHFORD DUSK
29	"	R6617	"	"	PATROL
30	"	R6677	"	"	WEATHER TEST
31	"	R12244	"	"	TO MANSTON
31	"	R6617	"	"	FROM MANSTON
31	"	R6617	"	"	PATROL
31	"	R6633	"	"	PATROL

Summary for JULY 19
Unit ___ 65 SQDN Aircraft
Date ___ 31. 7. 40 Types _____
Signature _____

1. SPITFIRE
2. MAGISTER
3. ---
4.

GRAND TOTAL [Cols. (1) to (10)]
7.59 Hrs. 05 Mins.

TOTALS CARRIED FORWARD

	SINGLE-ENGINE AIRCRAFT				MULTI-ENGINE AIRCRAFT					PASSENGER	INSTR/CLOUD FLYING [Incl. in cols. (1) to (10)]	
	DAY		NIGHT		DAY			NIGHT				
	Dual	Pilot	Dual	Pilot	1st Pilot	2nd Pilot	Dual	1st Pilot	2nd Pilot	(11)	Dual	Pilot
	50.40	67.15	2.05	44.25	-	.40	-	-	-	1.55		
				2.0								
		1.40										
		.30										
		2.0										
		.35										
				.45								
		.20										
		.30		2.0								
		1.0										
		.40										
		.45										
		.50										
		1.00		.45								
		1.10										
		.10										
		.20										
		1.0										
		1.50										
	50.40	66.15	2.05	42.30	-	2.40	-	-	-	2.55		
	-	41.50	-									
	-	.40	-									

Left page

YEAR 1940		AIRCRAFT		PILOT, OR 1ST PILOT	2ND PILOT, PUPIL OR PASSENGER	DUTY (INCLUDING RESULTS AND REMARKS)
MONTH	DATE	Type	No.			
—	—	—	—	—	—	TOTALS BROUGHT FORWARD
AUGUST	1	SPITFIRE	R6647	SELF	SELF	To Manston. PAT
	2	"	R6647	"	"	To Manston
	2	"	R6647	"	"	Interception "
	2	"	R6647	"	"	FADY Patrol "
	2	"	R6647	"	"	Convoy Patrol
	3	"	K9818	"	"	From Manchester to Rochford
	4	"	R6647	"	"	To Manston
	4	"	R6647	"	"	To Rochford
	4	"	R6647	"	"	To Manston + Return
	5	"	R6647	"	"	Patrol
	5	"	R6647	"	"	Fighting Patrol "
	5	"	R6647	"	"	Convoy Patrol
	5	"	R6647	"	"	Weather Test + Pat.
	6	"	R6647	"	"	To Manston
	6	"	R6647	"	"	From Manston
	7	"	R6647	"	* "	Scrambled per Man. A/F. Comst Pat. Comst Recall.
	7	"	P3606	Self	Self/Cyner	To Warmwell
	10	SPITFIRE	R6883	Self	Self	To Rochford
	10	"	R6883	"	"	To Manston
	10	"	R6881	"	"	Patrol
	10	"	R6881	"	"	Patrol
	10	"	A5812	"	"	From Manston.
						Total for Month
						TOTALS CARRIED FORWARD

GRAND TOTAL (Cols. (1) to (10)) ...768... Hrs ...5.5... Mins.

Right page

	SINGLE-ENGINE AIRCRAFT				MULTI-ENGINE AIRCRAFT				PASSENGER	INSTR./CLOUD FLYING [Incl. in cols. (1) to (10)]	
	DAY		NIGHT		DAY		NIGHT				
	Dual	Pilot	Dual	Pilot	1st Pilot	2nd Pilot	1st Pilot	2nd Pilot		Dual	Pilot
	(1)	(2)	(3)	(4)	(5)	(6)	(7)	(8)	(11)	(12)	(13)
Totals Brought Forward	50.40	641.25	2.05	42.34	—	.30	—	—	1.55		
		.30									
		.20									
		.20									
		.20									
		1.25									
		.15		2.0							
		.15									
		1.00									
		.15									
		.30									
		.30									
		.30									
		2.5									
		.15									
		.00									
		.30					.30				
		2.0									
		.20									
		1.20									
		.15									
		.10									
	50.40	671.58	2.05	42.50	—	.36	—	—	3.55		

YEAR 1940	AIRCRAFT		PILOT, OR 1st PILOT	2nd PILOT, PUPIL, OR PASSENGER	DUTY (INCLUDING RESULTS AND REMARKS)
	Type	No.			
			—	—	TOTALS BROUGHT FORWARD
11	SPITFIRE	R6805	SELF	SOLO	PATROL AND MANTOR
11	"	R6781	"	"	PATROL
11	"	R6809	"	"	PATROL
11	"	R6892	"	"	PATROL
11	"	R6883	"	"	TO ANSFORD
12	"	R6883	"	"	PATROL AND TO MANSTON —
12	"	R6881	"	"	FIGHTER PATROL
12	"	R6881	"	"	PATROL AND RETURN TO ROCHFORD
12	"	R6781	"	SO. DOBBY	FLY FAST FOR E.I.F.P.
12	MASTER	"	"	SOLO	LOCAL RECCO CONVOY PATROL
13	"	R6883	"	"	TO MANSTON
13	"	R6883	"	"	FIGHTER PATROL
13	"	R6883	"	"	PATROL
13	"	R6781	"	"	FROM MANSTON
14	"	R6881	"	"	TO MANSTON
14	"	R6889	"	"	FIGHTER PATROL RETURN TO MANSTON
15	"	R6881	"	"	PATROL AND TO MANSTON
15	"	R6881	"	"	FROM MANSTON TO EAST FAIR
16	"	A6881	"	"	PATROL
15	"	R6789	"	"	TO MANSTON
16	"	L6086	"	"	TO ROCHFORD
16	"	R6889	"	"	TO MANSTON
					TOTAL FOR MONTH
					TOTALS CARRIED FORWARD

GRAND TOTAL [Cols. (1) to (10)] 785 Hrs. 20 Mins.

Pilot's Flying Log Book — facing pages

Left page

YEAR 1944	AIRCRAFT Type	No.	PILOT, OR 1ST PILOT	2ND PILOT, PUPIL OR PASSENGER	DUTY (INCLUDING RESULTS AND REMARKS)
—	—	—	—	—	TOTALS BROUGHT FORWARD
1	SPITFIRE	R.6884	SELF	SOLO	TURNHOUSE - BASE.
1	"	R.6884	"	"	PATROL. NO INTERCEPTION.
1	"	R.6886	"	"	BASE - TURNHOUSE OPS.
2	"	R.6887	"	"	TURNHOUSE - BASE. OPS.
2	"	R.6883	"	"	DATA TURNHOUSE AFI.
2	"	R.6883	"	"	SECTOR RECCE AFI.
2	"	R.6881	"	"	FORMATIVE
4	"	R.6883	"	"	PREDATION ATTACKS
4	"	R.6883	"	"	TURNHOUSE SPECK - OPS.
4	"	R.6883	"	"	BASE - TURNHOUSE OP.
4	WELLINGTON		"	"	EXPERIENCE ON TYPE
11	SPITFIRE	R.6884	"	"	TO BASE. DREM.
11	"	R.6883	"	"	N.F. LYING DREM.
11	"	R.6883	"	"	FROM DREM TO TURNHOUSE.
12	"	K.4134	"	"	TURNHOUSE CHURCH FENTON.
12	"	K.4134	"	"	CHURCH FENTON - BICESTER
12	"	K.4136	"	"	BICESTER - BENSON
13	"	K.4136	"	"	BENSON - HALFMANBERG
13	"	K.4105	"	"	SQUADRON FORMATION
16	"	R.6883	"	"	PATROL. NO INTERCEPTION.
17	"		"	"	N.F. TEST.
17	"	R.6883	"	"	E.A. TEST
20	"	"	"	"	TOTALS CARRIED FORWARD

GRAND TOTAL. [Cols. (1) to (10)] 912 Hrs. .05 Mins.

Right page

	SINGLE-ENGINE AIRCRAFT				MULTI-ENGINE AIRCRAFT						PASS-ENGER	INSTRUMENT/CLOUD FLYING (incl.%) cols. (1) to (10)	
	DAY		NIGHT		DAY			NIGHT					
	Dual (1)	Pilot (2)	Dual (3)	Pilot (4)	Dual (5)	1st Pilot (6)	2nd Pilot (7)	Dual (8)	1st Pilot (9)	2nd Pilot (10)	(11)	Dual (12)	Pilot (13)
TOTALS BROUGHT FORWARD	50.40	763.05	3.75	42.50		.30	—				2.55	115	100
		.15											
		.50											
		.15											
		.15											
		1.10											
		.35											
		.45											
		.10											
		.10											
		.15											
			1.00			1.00							
		.15											
			1.00										
		.15											
		1.20											
		1.10											
		.30											
		.45											
		.55											
		1.00											
		.15											
		.35											
TOTALS CARRIED FORWARD	50.40	714.45	5.05	43.50		1.00	—				2.55	115	100

| YEAR | | AIRCRAFT | | PILOT, OR 1ST PILOT | 2ND PILOT, PUPIL OR PASSENGER | DUTY (INCLUDING RESULTS AND REMARKS) | SINGLE-ENGINE AIRCRAFT | | | | MULTI-ENGINE AIRCRAFT | | | | | | PASS-ENGER | INSTR/CLOUD FLYING | |
| | | | | | | | DAY | | NIGHT | | DAY | | | NIGHT | | | | | |
Month	Date	Type	No.				Dual	Pilot	Dual	Pilot	Dual	1st Pilot	2nd Pilot	Dual	1st Pilot	2nd Pilot		Dual	Pilot
						TOTALS BROUGHT FORWARD	50.40	744.45	2.55	43.50	—	30	—				2.57		
T	1D	SPITFIRE	R6883	SELF	Selo	E+A TEST		.15											
	24	"	R6883	"	"	N.F. TEST		.15											
	23	"	R6883	"	"	TO BAEN		.5											
	23	"	R6883	"	"	TO PRESTWICK		.45											
	23	"	R6883	"	"	TO TURNHOUSE		.30											
	24	"	R6883	"	"	FLIGHT FORMATION		.45											
	25	"	R6883	"	"	TO PRESTWICK		.30											
	25	"	R6883	"	"	PRESTWICK - DREM		.45											
	25	"	R6883	"	"	DREM TURNHOUSE		.15											
	26	"	R6883	"	"	N.F. TEST		.15	.45										
	25	"	R6823	"	"	N.F. PRACTICE, CIRCUITS & LANDING													
	24	"	R6803	"	"	N.F. TEST		.19											
	10	"	N3163	"	"	E+A TEST		.15											
	10	"	N3101	"	"	E+A TEST		.15											
						MONTH TOTAL		16.50	1.45		—	1.00							

Summary for... AUGUST 1940 ... 1.SPITFIRE
Unit. 65 SQDN. .... Aircraft 2.WHIRLWIND
Date. 30·8·40. .... Types ... 3. ....
Signature _____ 4. ....

G.K. Oakins O.C. 'A' Flt.
P/O. 65. Sqdn.

N. Holland Sq.Ldr. O.C.
65. Squadron

| | | | | | | TOTALS CARRIED FORWARD | 50.40 | 744.45 | 2.55 | 44.35 | — | 1.30 | — | | | | 2.55 | | |

GRAND TOTAL [Cols. (1) to (10)]
820 Hrs. 00 Mins.

E.&R.		AIRCRAFT		PILOT, OR	2ND PILOT, PUPIL	DUTY	SINGLE-ENGINE AIRCRAFT						MULTI-ENGINE AIRCRAFT							PASS-ENGER	INSTRUMENT FLYING	
				1ST PILOT	OR PASSENGER	(INCLUDING RESULTS AND REMARKS)	DAY			NIGHT			DAY			NIGHT						
4.C.		Type	No.				Dual	Pilot		Dual	Pilot		1st Pilot	2nd Pilot	Dual	1st Pilot	2nd Pilot	Dual		Decke	Pass.
		—	—	—	—	TOTALS BROUGHT FORWARD	50.40	712.55		2.05	24.35		1.30						2.00		
4		SPITFIRE	R6893	SELF	SOLO	I.A. TEST		.15													
7		"	R6893	"	"	SQUADRON FORMATION		.50													
7		"	R6893	"	"	I.A. TEST		.15													
7		"	R6883	"	"	N.E. TEST		.15													
8		"	X4583	"	"	TO DREM		1.00													
9		"	R6893	"	"	LOOP WITH WHIRLWINDS		.15													
8		"	R6893	"	"	DREM - TRAINING GS.															
11		"	X4583	"	"	DEFENSIVE A.I. PATROL					1.00										
13		HARVARD		"	CAPT. DAVDON	EXPERIENCE on TYPE		.20													
15		"		"	W.C. HAMILTON	TO ACKLINGTON		1.10													
15		"		"	"	ACKLINGTON— WITTS RING.		2.00													
15		"		"	"	WITTERING — HATFIELD		1.20													
14		"		"	"	HATFIELD — MONTROSE		4.0													
13		SPITFIRE	R6893 A	"	SOLO	TURNING WEATHER TEST		.10													
2.A		"	R6897.J	"	"	I.A. TEST . HOOD U.S.		.10													
1.A		"	X4110 X	"	"	I.A. TEST . OK.		2.0													
1.F		"	R386J.J	"	"	I.A. TEST.		2.0													
15		"	R6395.0	"	"	I.A. TEST		1.30													
15		"	R6883.A	"	"	TO DREM.		.20													
2.5		"	R6883	"	"	FROM DREM.		.20													
2.0		"	X4681	"	"	SCATCH ASSES		1.05													
3.0		"	R6883	"	"	WEATHER TEST.		.10													
						TOTALS CARRIED FORWARD	51.40	731.55		2.05	45.35		1.50						2.05		

GRAND TOTAL [Cols. (1) to (10)]
893 ....Hrs......0 .....Mins.

YEAR 1940	Aircraft Type	No.	Pilot, or 1st Pilot	2nd Pilot, Pupil or Passenger	DUTY (Including Results and Remarks)	Single-Engine Aircraft — Day Dual	Pilot	Night Dual	Pilot	Pass.	Multi-Engine Aircraft — Day Dual	1st Pilot	2nd Pilot	Night Dual	1st Pilot	2nd Pilot	PASSENGER	INSTR./CLOUD FLYING Dual	Pilot
	—	—	—	—	Totals Brought Forward	—	72·15	2·05	44·25	—	—	420	—				2·55		
					1. SPITFIRE	—	6·30	—	1·00										
					2. HARVARD	—	75·30	—	—										
					3.	—	—	—	—										
					4.	—	—	—	—										

Summary for ... Agent ... 18 m.

Unit ... 65 Squadron. Aircraft

Date ... 3 — 10 — 40 Types

Signature ... [signature]

[signature] Flt. Lt. O.C. "A" Flight
No. 65 East India Squadron.

[signature] Sq. Ldr. O.C.
No. 65 East India Sqdn.

| | | | | | Totals Carried Forward | 50·40 | 73·55 | 2·05 | 44·25 | — | — | 1·30 | — | | | | 2·55 | | |

GRAND TOTAL [Cols. (1) to (10)]
523 ... Hrs. ... 50 ... Mins.

YEAR 1940 Month	Date	AIRCRAFT Type	No.	PILOT OR 1ST PILOT	2ND PILOT, PUPIL OR PASSENGER	DUTY (INCLUDING RESULTS AND REMARKS)	SINGLE-ENGINE DAY Dual	Pilot	NIGHT Dual	Pilot	MULTI-ENGINE DAY Dual	1st Pilot	2nd Pilot	NIGHT Dual	1st Pilot	2nd Pilot	PASS-ENGER	INSTR/CLOUD FLYING Dual	Pilot
						TOTALS BROUGHT FORWARD	50.40	731.55	2.05	46.55	—	1.20	—				2.55		
	7	SPITFIRE	P9562	SELF	SOLO	TURNHOUSE LOCAL		.05											
	7	"	P9562	"	"	TO DREM		.20											
	7	"	N3101	"	"	TO TURNHOUSE		.20											
	8	"	R6603	"	"	TO LEUCHARS		.40											
	10	"	R6693	"	"	FORMATION PRACTICE		.35											
	11	"	R6691	"	"	LOCAL AEROBATIC		.40											
	11	"	R6693	"	"	WEATHER TEST		.15											
	12	"	R6693	"	"	AEROBATICS & DOG FIGHT		.45											
	12	"	R6603	"	"	TO TURNHOUSE		.40											
	12	"	R6603	"	"	TO LEUCHARS		.25											
	13	"	R6693	"	"	TO TURNHOUSE		.45											
	13	"	R6693	"	"	TO LEUCHARS FLUS		.20		.45									
	14	"	R6693	"	"	TO TURNHOUSE		.50											
	15	"	5G683	"	"	CLIMB TO 34000		.40											
	19	"	N3101	"	"	TURNHOUSE – LEUCHARS		.40											
	21	"	R6693	"	"	SQN. FORMATION LEADING		.20		1.00									
	21	"	S0637	"	"	LANDINGS		1.00											
	21	"	R6693	"	"	R.P. PRACTICE + LANDPRI		.15											
	22	"	R6682	"	"	AEROBATICS & LANDINGS		.25											
	22	"	R6693	"	"	WEATHER TEST													
	27	"	R6693	"	"	AEROBATICS		.25											
	3	"	R6603	"	"	AEROBATICS													
						TOTALS CARRIED FORWARD	50.40	742.10	2.05	48.20	—	1.84	—				2.55		

GRAND TOTAL [Cols. (1) to (10)]
8.45 Hrs. 10 Mins.

YEAR	AIRCRAFT		PILOT, OR 1ST PILOT	2ND PILOT, PUPIL OR PASSENGER	DUTY (INCLUDING RESULTS AND REMARKS)
DATE	Type	No.			
—	—	—	—	—	— Totals Brought Forward
28	SPITFIRE	R6883	SELF	SOLO	LEUCHARS — CHURCH FENTON
29	„	R6883	„	„	CHURCH FENTON — TANGMERE
30	„	R6883	„	„	SQUADRON PATROL
					TOTAL FOR MONTH

Summary for .... NOVEMBER. 19 .. 40 ....
Unit .. No.66 Squadron
Date .. 1 — 12 — 40
Signature ....

Aircraft   1. SPITFIRE
Types   2. ——
   3. ——
   4. ——

TOTALS CARRIED FORWARD

GRAND TOTAL (Cols. (1) to (10)) .... 847. Hrs. .. 55. Mins.

	SINGLE-ENGINE AIRCRAFT				MULTI-ENGINE AIRCRAFT						PASS. ENGER	INSTR/CLOUD FLYING (Incl. in cols. (1) to (10))	
	DAY		NIGHT		DAY			NIGHT					
	Dual	Pilot	Dual	Pilot	Dual	1st Pilot	2nd Pilot	Dual	1st Pilot	2nd Pilot		Dual	Pilot
	(1)	(2)	(3)	(4)	(5)	(6)	(7)	(8)	(9)	(10)	(11)	(12)	(13)
	50.40	742.10	2.05	48.40	—	1.30	—				2.55		
		1:20											
		1:05											
		.20											
		13.20		1.45									
	—	13.20	—	1.45	—	—							
	50.40	745.50	2.05	48.40	—	1.30					2.55		

F/Lt O.C. A FLIGHT.
Nᵒ 66 SQUADRON.

SQN. LDR. O.C.
Nᵒ 66 SQUADRON.

YEAR 19.42	AIRCRAFT		PILOT, OR	2ND PILOT, PUPIL	DUTY
MONTH	DATE	Type	No.	1ST PILOT	OR PASSENGER	(INCLUDING RESULTS AND REMARKS)
		—	—	—	—	TOTALS BROUGHT FORWARD
	2	SPITFIRE	R6593	SELF	SOLO	PATROL
	4	"	R6593	"	"	"
	5	"	R6593	"	"	"
	8	"	R6593	"	*	ONE MELYO
	10	"	R6593	"	"	MOST FLYING IN LANTENSE
	11	"	R6593	"	"	PATROL
	21	"	R6593	"	"	"
	22	"	R6593	"	"	"
	27	"	R6593	"	"	LOCAL FLYING STAND BY
	27	"	R6593	"	"	E.A. TEST
	28	"	99862	"	"	PATROL
						TOTAL FOR MONTH

SINGLE-ENGINE AIRCRAFT				MULTI-ENGINE AIRCRAFT						PASS-ENGER	INSTR/CLOUD FLYING
DAY		NIGHT		DAY			NIGHT				
Dual	Pilot	Dual	Pilot	Dual	1st Pilot	2nd Pilot	Dual	1st Pilot	2nd Pilot		
(1)	(2)	(3)	(4)	(5)	(6)	(7)	(8)	(9)	(10)	(11)	(12)
50·40	743·55	2·55	48·20	—	1·30	—				2·55	
	·20										
	1·10										
	·50										
	·55		·55								
	·55										
	·45										
	·35										
	·45										
	2·0										
	·20										
	6·55		·55								

Summary for DECEMBER 19.42 L.SEPTEMBER

Unit ... 65 SQUADRON ... Aircraft { 2. ...
Date ... 1 ... 42 ... Types { 3. ...
Signature .... F.LT. { 4. ...

| | — | 6·55 | — | ·55 | — | 1·30 | — | | | | — |

GRAND TOTAL (Cols. (1) to (10))
855 Hrs. 45 Mins.

| 50·40 | 750·50 | 2·55 | 49·05 | — | 1·30 | — | | | | 2·55 | |

TOTALS CARRIED FORWARD

[signatures: F.LT. F.L.T. O.C. A FLIGHT, No.65 SQUADRON; G.W.Laumbell F/LT Sqn Ldr O.C. No 65 Squadron]

List of Illustrations

1. Spitfires of 65 Squadron on their way to patrol over Dunkirk. (© The estate of Gordon Olive)
2. Supermarine Spitfire K9903, YT-A, of 65 Squadron, Gordon Olive's regular aircraft in the early days of the war. (© The estate of Gordon Olive)
3. Amid the swirling thick black smoke from oil fires at Dunkirk, Gordon Olive's painting depicts vivid memories of his desperate air battle of 28 May 1940. (© The estate of Gordon Olive)
4. Scramble at Manston, 12 August 1940. (© The estate of Gordon Olive)
5. Ideal RAF tactics of the Battle of Britain. Because of their higher performance, Spitfires (of 65 Squadron) climb to engage the escorting German fighters while Hurricanes attack the bombers. (© The estate of Gordon Olive)
6. Gordon Olive just prior to the fighting over Dunkirk. (Beryl Olive)
7. 'We nosed down one behind the other, the speed mounting rapidly ...' (© The estate of Gordon Olive)
8. Scramble at Manston, 12 August 1940. (© The estate of Gordon Olive)
9. 25 August 1940, Me 110s flying in defensive circles. (© The estate of Gordon Olive)
10. About to leave Australia on the P&O liner, Narkunda in January 1937. (Beryl Olive)
11. 25 August 1940. 'I noticed several smaller dots diving in – the Hurricanes and Spitfires from the squadrons closer to London ...' (© The estate of Gordon Olive)

31. A section of Spitfires preparing to dive onto a box of Heinkel He 111 bombers. (© The estate of Gordon Olive)

32. Cockpit of the Heinkel 111 bomber. (Courtesy of Jonathan Reeve, JRb540 59)

33. Escorting Me 109s make a head-on pass to disrupt the Spitfire attacking their bombers. (© The estate of Gordon Olive)

34. Messerschmitt Me 109E. (MAP)

35. Although the ideal situation was for Spitfires to hold off the escort fighters while Hurricanes attacked the enemy bombers. (© The estate of Gordon Olive)

36. Hurricanes peeling off to attack. (© The estate of Gordon Olive)

37. Spitfires diving in line astern to carry out a Number One Attack on the incoming bombers. (© The estate of Gordon Olive)

38. A bomber gunner's view of a pair of Spitfires closing in for the 'kill'. (Alf Pascoe via Betty King)

39 'The German ace of aces, Adolf Galland, writing about the Luftwaffe air offensive in 1940, claims that he took part in raids of more than a thousand aircraft at this time ...' (© The estate of Gordon Olive)

40. W/Cdr Gordon Olive DFC in a caricature by Dubois. (Maria Marchant)

41. An air fighting rule of 1940: 'Beware of the Hun in the sun.' (© The estate of Gordon Olive)

42. Pat Hughes in a quieter mood. (Bill Hughes)

43. Air fighting rule: 'The advantage of height is half the battle.' (© The estate of Gordon Olive)

44. Me 109E under attack. It is damaged and one wheel of its undercarriage has dropped down. (AWM)

45. Gloster Gauntlets at RAF Hornchurch at the Empire Air Day in May 1937. (Beryl Olive)

46. Cadets of the Point Cook class of 1936. (RAAF Museum Point Cook)

47. A line up of Heinkel He 113 fighters. (MAP)

48. An Australian student in Germany, Pete Bjelke-Petersen, walking through the streets of Berlin, the trappings of the Nazi movement evident everywhere. (Pete Bjelke-Petersen)

49. 'Stuart Walch from Tasmania was killed off Portland Bill ...' (Brenda Walch)

50. A line-up of 65 Squadron pilots. (John Wallen)

51. Gordon Olive at 'Readiness' at Tangmere in December 1940. (John Wallen)

52. No. 456 Squadron's last CO, S/Ldr Bob Cowper DFC and Bar. (Bob Cowper)

53. 'Another tragedy was the loss of Pat Hughes. (Bill Hughes)

54. Desmond Sheen considered himself one of the luckiest pilots in the Battle of Britain being shot down twice and surviving. (Desmond Sheen)

55. Robert Bungey, the CO of 452 RAAF Squadron in the second half of 1941. (Richard Bungey)

56. Dick Power from Gordon's 1936 Point Cook class also survived the war. (Dick Power)

57. 'The latest bomber, the Bristol Blenheim, was fifty miles an hour faster than the fastest fighter in service ...' (Reg Moore)

58. The first twin-engined fighter flown by Gordon Olive was the Westland Whirlwind, as his logbook shows. (IWM via Bryan Philpott)

59. Messerschmitt Me 110. (Courtesy of Jonathan Reeve, JRb539 043)

60. A portion of one of the Honour Boards of Presidents in Brisbane's United Service Club. (© The estate of Gordon Olive)

61. Wing Commander Gordon Olive DFC RAF, prior to him rejoining the RAAF. (Beryl Olive)

62. Gordon Olive inspecting a Battle of Britain display at Mudgeraba in Queensland. (© John Wallen)

63. A Bristol Beaufighter IIF powered by two Rolls Royce Merlin engines. No. 456 RAAF Squadron re-equipped with the type. (MAP)

64. Gordon Olive was a champion javelin thrower in service and inter-service athletics. (Beryl Olive)

65. Famous pre-war photograph of Spitfire Mk Is of 65 Squadron RAF in formation. (IWM via Bryan Philpott)

66. The twentieth anniversary of the Battle of Britain and the reunion of members of 'A' Flight, 65 Squadron RAF. (Beryl Olive)

67. Junkers Ju 88, the first German type to be shot down by 65 Squadron. (MAP)

68. Acknowledgement by letter of leaving the RAAF, March 1946. (© The estate of Gordon Olive)

69. Gordon Olive's Short Service Commission, 19 February 1937. (© The estate of Gordon Olive)